BOOKS OF DEFINITION IN ISLAMIC PHILOSOPHY

The language of early Islamic philosophy owes its origins to the blending of Greek philosophy with early Islamic theology. Its technical language consisted of words borrowed from Greek and Persian as well as common Arabic words adapted for technical use. This book studies how Islamic philosophers, beginning in the ninth century AD and including al-Kindi, al-Farabi, and Ibn Sina, developed an indigenous set of terms and concepts. These choices, as reflected in their books of definition, not only influenced the development of the Arabic language, but also laid the foundation for the terms of discourse in Islamic philosophy.

Books of Definition in Islamic Philosophy presents a framework for incorporating an Islamic and historically contextualized philosophy into a continuum of world philosophies. At the core of this framework is Ibn Sina's *Kitab al-hudud*, which the author has translated into English, and it is situated in its correct geopolitical framework. In establishing a historical and literary context for the writing and circulation of Ibn Sina's *Definitions*, this book breaks new ground in the integration of Islamic philosophy within a general history of philosophies.

This fascinating and comprehensive study will be of interest to scholars and postgraduate students of Islamic philosophy. By offering an English translation of *Kitab al-hudud*, Kennedy-Day also opens the door to a wider range of readers.

Kiki Kennedy-Day teaches at Eugene Lang College, New School University, New York. This is her first book.

BOOKS OF DEFINITION IN ISLAMIC PHILOSOPHY

The limits of words

Kiki Kennedy-Day

LONDON AND NEW YORK

First published in 2003
by RoutledgeCurzon
11 New Fetter Lane, London EC4P 4EE

Simultaneously published in the USA and Canada
by RoutledgeCurzon
29 West 35th Street, New York, NY 10001

RoutledgeCurzon is an imprint of the Taylor & Francis Group

© 2003 Kiki Kennedy-Day

Typeset in Times New Roman by LaserScript Ltd, Mitcham, Surrey

Printed and bound in Great Britain by
MPG Books Ltd, Bodmin

All rights reserved. No part of this book may be reprinted or reproduced or utilised in any form or by any electronic, mechanical, or other means, now known or hereafter invented, including photocopying and recording, or in any information storage or retrieval system, without permission in writing from the publishers.

The publisher makes no representation, express or implied, with regard to the accuracy of the information contained in this book and cannot accept any legal responsibility or liability for any errors or omissions that may be made.

British Library Cataloguing in Publication Data
A catalogue record of this book is available from the British Library

Library of Congress Cataloging in Publication Data
A catalog record for this book has been requested

ISBN 0-7007-1723-4

To Ross
From Kiki

CONTENTS

Acknowledgements	ix
List of abbreviations	xi
Map The Abbasid Caliphate	xiii

Introduction   1

PART 1
Definitions of the philosophers   7

1   What is a definition?   9
2   Al-Kindi: the first Arabic *Book of Definitions*   19
3   Al-Farabi: the emergence of Arabicized Greek logic   32
4   Ibn Sina: the second *Book of Definitions*   47
5   Comparison of vocabulary   61

PART 2
Ibn Sina's *Book of Definitions*   85

6   The socio-political milieu of Ibn Sina   87
7   Translation: *The Book of Definitions*   98
8   Commentary   115

Appendix	160
Notes	167
Bibliography	191
Index	198

ACKNOWLEDGEMENTS

Many people have helped in different ways in completing this project. Thanks to those who helped me write and complete the dissertation, especially Professor Charles E. Butterworth for his assistance above and beyond the call of duty, including a careful reading of the text and many invaluable suggestions. Thanks to Professor Shukri Abed for his patience in reading and remarking on draft versions, and his constant belief in me.

I owe a debt of gratitude to many Arabic teachers, including my tutor Omar Qaddoumi, and for additional translation advice, Haydar Elawad.

I would like to thank the readers for Curzon, particularly Oliver Leaman and Alparslan Açikgenç, for their remarks. Alparslan has been entirely gracious not only in encouraging Fatih University to bring me to Istanbul for a year's teaching, but in continuing to share his knowledge and give practical advice via email. Both Oliver and Alparslan gave me constant encouragement which has helped see the work through to publication. Majid Fakhry read and commented on an earlier version of the translation. While many people have offered suggestions for various aspects of the translation, in the last regard, any mistakes and shortcomings are my own responsibility.

Thanks also to the many librarians who gave help in the Asian and Middle Eastern Division of the Research Library of New York Public Library, particularly Gamil Youssef, Todd Thompson, and John Lundquist; and at the Special Collections Office, Wayne Furman and Eli Weitsman, who arranged use of the Wertheim Study. Much of Part 2 was written there. Thanks to the past and current reference librarians and Interlibrary Loan Librarians at New York University, especially Meryle Gaston, Marlayna Gates, and Dennis Massie.

Thanks for the support of the Islamic Philosophy community – they know who they are.

Thanks to the late Nicholas L. King, who gave me such unquestioning support; I only regret he was unable to see the project's completion. I wish to thank the following scholars and friends for their suggestions and advice: Gerard Ettlinger, Peg Fowler, Flora Kaplan, and John Richardson.

ACKNOWLEDGEMENTS

Special thanks to C. Gerald Fraser for editing assistance and encouragement, as well as bringing hard-to-find books from Egypt. Thanks to my colleagues at the Kevorkian, particularly Ubai Nooruddin, Phyllis Saretta, James Pavlin, Lawrence Gleicher, and Kristin Sands.

I particularly wish to thank my parents, John and Eleanor Kennedy, for their continuing support in my academic pursuits. Without their encouragement to go to law school, I doubt if I ever would have been driven to complete a doctorate.

Finally, thanks to Ross Day, who survived the stress not just of writing, but of rewriting, and read every word several times, giving me helpful criticism and encouragement. He kept me going every time I wanted to give up. And a little prayer for Sasha, my faithful friend for many lonely hours of writing, and Willow who continues the tradition. Another prayer that Shehrazad will learn to be such a pleasant companion.

LIST OF ABBREVIATIONS

Alfaz	Al-Farabi. *Al-Alfaz al-musta^cmala fi al mantiq*. ed. M. Mahdi.
Allard	al-Kindi. "L'Épître de Kindi sur les définitions et les descriptions." trans. Michel Allard.
Alpago	Ibn Sina. "Tractatus de diffinitionibus." trans. Andrea Alpago.
AR	al-Kindi. *Rasa'il al-Kindi al-falsafiyya*. ed. M. A. Abu Ridah.
BSOAS	Bulletin of the School of Oriental and African Studies
Burhan	al-Farabi. *Kitab al-burhan*.
Fihrist	Ibn al-Nadim. *Kitab al-fihrist*.
Frank	al-Kindi. "Al-Kindi's 'Book of Definitions'." trans. Tamara Zahava Frank.
Gimaret	al-Kindi. *Cinq épîtres*. ed. D. Gimaret.
Hudud	Ibn Sina. *Kitab al-hudud*.
Huruf	al-Farabi. *Kitab al-huruf*.
al-Ilahiyyat	Ibn Sina. *al-Shifa': al-Ilahiyyat*.
IJMES	International Journal of Middle Eastern Studies.
Jalinus	al-Farabi. *Fi al-radd ^cala Jalinus*.
JAOS	Journal of the American Oriental Society.
JNES	*Journal of Near Eastern Studies*
Mantiq Aristu	Aristotle. *Mantiq Aristu*.
Maqulat	al-Farabi. "Kitab al-maqulat." In *Mantiq ^cinda al-Farabi*, ed. Rafiq al-^cAjam, vol. 1.
Masa'il	al-Farabi. *Risala fi jawab masa'il su'ila ^canha*.
Najat	Ibn Sina. *Kitab al-najat*.
Siyasa	al-Farabi. *The Political Regime*. ed. Fauzi M. Najjar.
al-Tabi^ca	Aristotle. *Al-Tabi^ca*.
Tafsir ma ba^cd at-tabi^cat	Ibn Rushd. *Tafsir ma ba^cd at-tabi^cat*.
Ta'rikh	al-Qifti. *Ta'rikh al-hukama'*.

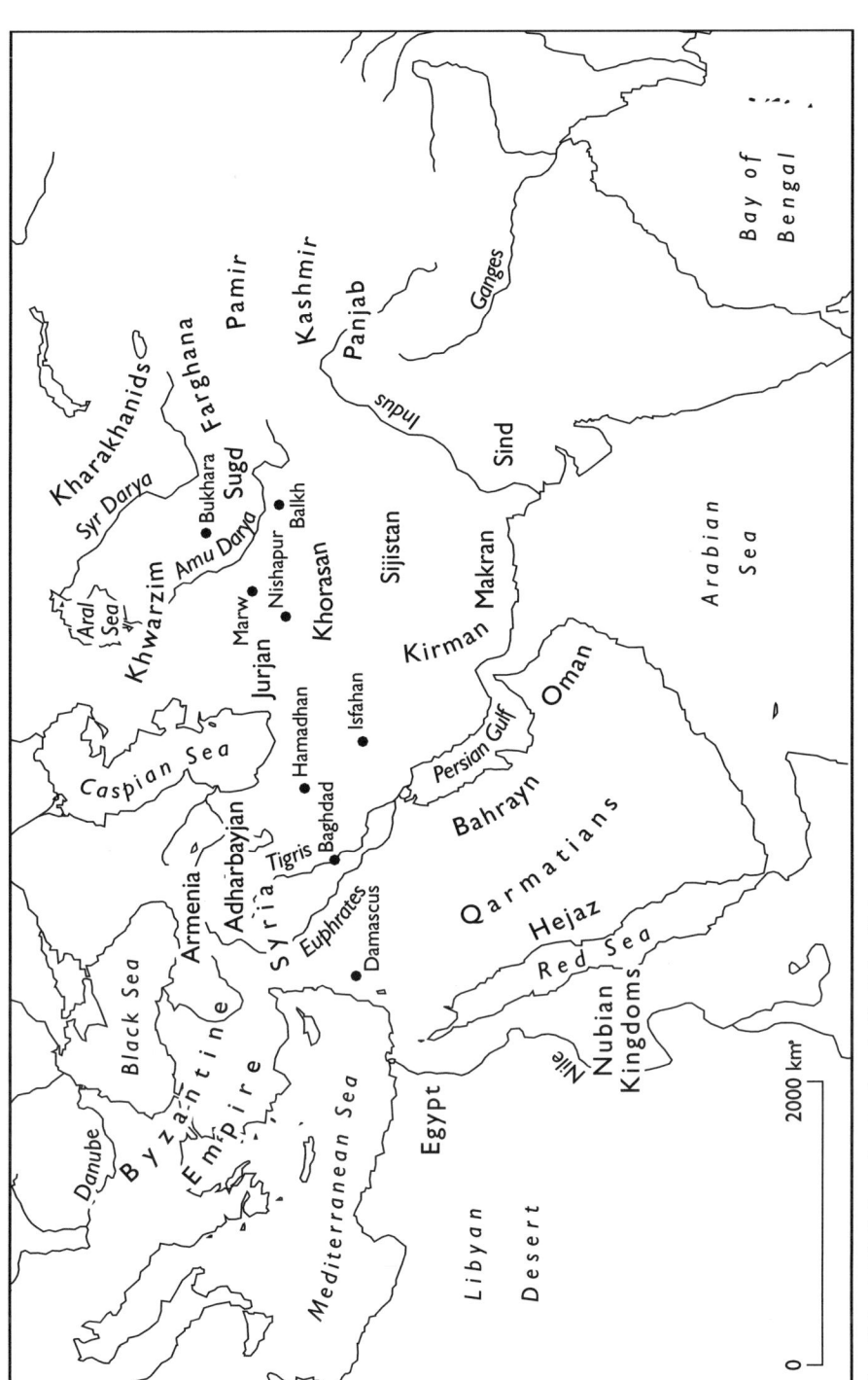

The Abbasid Caliphate in the first half of the 10th century

INTRODUCTION

This book is a study of an underexposed aspect of philosophy, definition. At first blush the question of definition may appear so self-evident as to be unnecessary, but little work has been done in the field recently. Definition is the key to understanding how the *falasifa* looked at their universe, as envisioned in Islamic philosophy. Due to the unusual origin of philosophy in the Islamic world, originally a hybrid of translated Greek philosophy and early Islamic *kalam* (theology), it was in particular need of a technical vocabulary. If rational thinking is the tool of thought, words are the medium for its expression. Contrary to the opinion expressed by the Red Queen to Alice, words must mean exactly what they say; for development in philosophy to occur meanings must not shift in the hands of each successive writer.

Part 1 of this book grew out of my dissertation, "Definition in the Philosophy of al-Kindi, al-Farabi and Ibn Sina." The translation of Ibn Sina's *Kitab al-hudud* that forms the core of Part 2 was a logical extension, since it was one of the primary texts used in Part 1. It is always hard to step back from a project that one has worked on so intensely and try to explain it to non-specialists, but that is indeed my hope. For me and for some of my colleagues, the story of Islamic philosophy that now needs to be told is as an integral part of the continuous history of world philosophy. Thus, although in spatio-temporal terms we stand outside the world of classical Islamic philosophy, it forms part of the tradition that has come down to us. The seduction of philosophy is that we the readers are tuning in on a conversation that has been continuing through the centuries. Ibn Sina picks up a dialogue with al-Kindi, although the latter had been dead for about a century and a half by the time of Ibn Sina's writing. However, because these treatises are written in philosophical Arabic, they tend to be fresh and adorned with a modern sleekness.

Through an investigation of the first three major philosophers, Part 1 of this work follows the development of definition theory in Islamic philosophy. I examine and compare the same terms in their historical development. Chapter 1 begins with a study of definition in its historical and analytic contexts prior to Islamic philosophy. There is an examination of the concept of definition in Aristotle's philosophy and the different kinds of definition. The next three chapters focus on the three philosophers in isolation. In Chapter 2 al-Kindi's definitions are discussed, using his book *On the Definitions and Descriptions of Things* (*Fi hudud al-ashya' wa rusumiha*). Chapter 3 reviews al-Farabi's definitions as found in his works, primarily his *Book of Letters* (*Kitab al-huruf*). Chapter 4 details Ibn Sina's definitions in his *Book of Definitions* (*Kitab al-hudud*). In Chapter 5, I compare their definitions, analysing the way each of the terms used by each philosopher works in comparison with the others. Primary comparison of terms will be found in this chapter, while secondary comparison of the philosophers' methods and techniques can be found in earlier chapters. The correlation of terms used in the definitions may be found in the Appendices in the Tables for each term.

The three chapters of Part 2 contain the translation of Ibn Sina's *Book of Definitions*, with a short introduction to Ibn Sina's time and a commentary on the work. In Chapter 6, I discuss the socio-political aspects of Ibn Sina's environment. Chapter 7 is the translation of *Kitab al-hudud*, and Chapter 8 is the commentary. Although many scholars have failed to appreciate the importance of *The Book of Definitions*, it is significant in the history of Islamic philosophy: for Ibn Sina's theory of definition as a philosophical tool, for what the definitions show us about his thought, and as a foundation for further understanding his philosophy. There are subtle hints in *The Book of Definitions* that are suggestive of important issues, such as his treatment of the word *jinn* and his discussion of al-Kindi's definition of ᶜ*ishq*. This work was translated into Latin by Alpago and into French by A.-M. Goichon. It is among many books by Ibn Sina that have not previously been translated into English. To undertake a reasonable study of classical Islamic philosophy there must be a general translation project, similar to al-Ma'mun's *bait al-hikma*, to enable students to read many of these treatises, not just a few acknowledged major ones. Furthermore, I intend the commentary which follows the translation to illuminate various aspects of Ibn Sina's thought, beyond the well-known and well-documented Aristotelian influence. This commentary was inspired by the question-and-response format of Thomas Aquinas's commentaries. While it is widely recognized that *Kitab al-Shifa'* is heavily Aristotelian, which Ibn Sina himself states, it is not necessarily indicative of his most personal thought. Some years ago I asked a friend if he thought Ibn Sina would be surprised that we were reading him. My friend, who is a male Muslim, replied, "Not me. But I think he might be surprised that you are reading him."

One long-standing problem for scholarship in Islamic philosophy has been that the same treatises – recognized as of "seminal importance" – have been translated into European languages again and again, while others molder away in the attics of history, pining for someone to look at them.

INTRODUCTION

Philosophers, like artists, produce sketches as well as finished paintings, and often the lines of the sketches may be suggestive of a philosopher's thinking in ways that a more formal treatise may not.

The reader will notice that the familiar topics of Islamic philosophy, such as Ibn Sina's metaphysics of the Necessary Existence (God) and possible existence (creatures), and al-Farabi's political philosophy, are mentioned only in passing. Instead the focus in this study is the attempt to analyze the growth and stabilization of a philosophical vocabulary in Arabic. In certain ways this study makes the working assumption that definition is the basis of philosophy, rather than its end result, an assumption necessitated by the project. It should not be considered proved, but rather part of the *modus operandi*; it is an investigation for the future. In view of the enormous expanse of the question, it was necessary to narrow it down.

Dates are given, wherever possible, in both Hejira and Christian years. By convention, the Hejira date is given first, followed by a slash, and then the Christian date. For example: Al-Kindi's death date is between 252–260 AH/AD 866–873.

I have used the *International Journal of Middle East Studies* transliteration, with modifications. No diacritical marks are used, except that the hamza is indicated by an apostrophe and the ʿayn with a superscript c (ᶜ). Other authors are quoted with their own transliterations as they appeared in the originals (but also without diacritical marks). The original Arabic for the definitions under discussion may be found in the Appendix; full references are also given to the Arabic texts used.

English is short on synonyms for some basic philosophical terms such as "element" and "matter." Contemporary words such as atom, particle, and subparticle are anachronistic in dealing with the eleventh-century views of the physical world. The aim of this translation is to put the words into English, not into transliterated Arabic or Greek, which is a comfortable solution only for readers of those languages. While matter$_1$ for *hayula* and matter$_2$ for *madda* may be awkward, they are meant to distinguish two words used in the Arabic text, without overtranslating into a greater precision than Ibn Sina used. I am trying to avoid the problems raised by translating *hayula* as "prime matter" as discussed by W. Charlton in his Appendix to *Aristotle's Physics*. An Aristotelian vocabulary would co-opt Ibn Sina prima facie before even considering his arguments. It robs Ibn Sina of the opportunity for any native contribution outside of the inexorable view of the history of philosophy as the history of Hellenistic philosophy.

In Part 2, the translation of *Kitab al-hudud*, the number at the beginning of each paragraph refers to Goichon's edition. Although I also consulted the 1881 Constantinople edition of *Kitab al-hudud*, published in the collection *Tis Rasa'il*, the numbering from Goichon's edition is retained for easier reference for readers who wish to consult the Arabic text.

INTRODUCTION

One famous Arabist said that all translation from Arabic into another language is interpretation. The halo effect is a primary reason for this – words have their main denotative meaning and perhaps some secondary meanings, but each word in a given language also has a unique constellation of references, usages by famous ancient poets and in sacred scriptures, whose existence may be understood on a subliminal level by its recitation. Because of these associations in the original language, which do not transfer to the receptor language, translations are impoverished. Furthermore, in the case of Arabic to English, the translation is from a Semitic language to an Indo-European language. Structurally, Semitic differs in having nominal sentences and specific pronouns and cases – not word order – to explain the meaning. If language is like the human body, then grammar is the skeleton and words are the flesh. Muslims say the Qur'an cannot be translated into any other language. But really no Arabic work can be translated into English – interpreted and rendered, yes, but not exactly translated.

The specific purpose of this translation is to make Ibn Sina accessible to all interested readers. Maybe it will even escape the academic bunker and enter the real world.[1] While it is scholarly, it is not meant to be overly technical. If eminent specialists feel that it is only 80 per cent accurate, that is 80 per cent more than was available to English-speakers before. Thus, to give an example, *al-kull* is translated as "the cosmos" for greater readability and understanding. The literal meaning of *al-kull* is "the whole," and one reader suggested "the whole universe" would be better. This seems wordy. However, in this definition Ibn Sina is discussing mind and soul as universal mind and universal soul. Consequently, it became too confusing to talk about the universal, while the cosmos conveys the idea sharply. This is not meant to be an academic translation in the sense that readers will be able to translate the English back to the original Arabic. The hope is to open up Ibn Sina's work for intelligent readers of Western philosophy. Therefore, this translation is not for someone who reads the English and sees the Arabic words, it is for someone who does not read Arabic.

Similarly, translation that immediately makes Ibn Sina sound like a Greek philosopher is avoided. The perfect translation exists only in the translator's mind.[2] The aim is to translate the most important words consistently, as technical terms. However what makes the translation most difficult is not the words, but trying to understand the thought processes of a member of a sophisticated civilization, far removed from the contemporary world in both time and place. In translating medieval Arabic, it is unfortunately always possible to understand the words and not the thought. Thus the endnotes of the translation and the commentary text are planned to answer many of the questions in the reader's mind. The definitions of physical terms are some of the most difficult to understand, because the eleventh-century view of the physical world in particular is so different from the twenty-first-century view.

INTRODUCTION

I hope in a small way that this book will open some minds to the discovery of Islamic philosophy, and encourage readers to seek out more. The bibliography lists works in English as well as Arabic, which readers may find interesting if they wish to continue reading in Islamic philosophy.

My ultimate aim is to make Islamic philosophy accessible and even enticing to readers who cannot read the original Arabic, and who might enjoy discovering the thoughts of philosophers from a millennium ago if the obstacle of language were removed.

New York City
December, 2001

Part 1

DEFINITIONS OF THE PHILOSOPHERS

1

WHAT IS A DEFINITION?

But the essence of the Plotinian system lies in the new meaning which the whole imposed on the parts; its true originality is not in the materials but in the design (as, indeed, I suspect is the case with every great philosophical system).

E. R. Dodds[1]

The role of definition in philosophy

Scholars of Islamic philosophy have tended to view the history of Islamic philosophy in terms of Greek philosophy. This is due, on its face, to the fact that early Islamic philosophy originated from Arabic translations of Greek philosophy, which formed the starting point for a native philosophy. Since the initial philosophical writings in the Arabic language were translations, someone had to fashion lists of philosophical vocabulary to express technical philosophical language in Arabic. This also led to books of definition, short lexicons of terms used to express foreign concepts. If philosophy was an imported science, books of definition were evidently indigenous, as they existed in many fields. The evolution of philosophical terms is a historical process that can be observed by investigating these books. While modern scholars of Islamic philosophy have sometimes gone so far as to assert that developments in Islamic philosophy merely reflected the changing status of translation techniques from Greek to Arabic, via Syriac, this is not the case. They have rarely concentrated on the Arabic in itself, as used over time by the Islamic philosophers.[2] In the period under consideration here, the ninth to eleventh centuries AD, scholars consider al-Farabi as having a more accurate acquaintance with Aristotle. By way of explanation they point to the purportedly improved quality of the translations from Greek to Syriac to Arabic between the ninth to tenth centuries AD.

Individual studies and translations have appeared of the books of definitions of al-Kindi and Ibn Sina. Among the published studies, Samuel Stern gives a critique and partial translation of al-Kindi's *Book of Definitions*, and A.-M. Goichon gives a French translation of Ibn Sina's *Book of Definitions* with references to many Aristotelian sources and similarities to Ibn Sina's definitions.

Here the development of a set of terms from the earliest Islamic philosopher, al-Kindi, who lived in the ninth century AD through al-Farabi, an interim figure who lived in the tenth century, to Ibn Sina, who died early in the eleventh century, is under consideration. The words are a selection of terms for substance, cause, and matter, chosen in part because the ideas behind these terms are basic for any philosopher's organization of a philosophical universe and because words to express these ideas had to be adapted from ordinary language Arabic.

The word for substance, *jawhar*, is adopted from the Persian language and originally means "jewel" or "gem." The word for cause, *ᶜilla*, means "illness" or "deficiency" in the ordinary language. For matter, the philosophers used either *madda* or *hayula*. *Hayula* is a transliteration of the Greek term, *hyle*, which Aristotle appropriated from the ordinary language and used to refer to the stuff of the universe. Although Arabic is a rich language, the philosophers had to re-imagine it to do the work they needed: to form abstract nouns, to find names for concepts without expression, and to indicate the process that happened to something. These terms are not only central to philosophical thought, but used by all the philosophers, which allows comparison.

The term *jawhar* (substance) is not only one of Aristotle's primary terms in the *Categories*, but of the ten categories, it is the single most important term. Substance represents the underlying entities of the universe to which things happen, in contrast to the nine remaining categories, which are accidents, in Aristotle's scheme. Substance is neither a particularly Arab idea, nor an ordinary language one in this usage. *ᶜIlla*, cause, is another alien idea and immediately calls up the debate on who is the agent of change. Is it human? Is it God? Who has responsibility? Thus *ᶜilla* (cause) represents a major debate from Islamic philosophy and theology. It leads to questions about the agent of creation, and what that might mean, particularly in terms of human responsibility and punishment. The justice of God is also at stake, since if God is the cause of all acts, how can God justly punish humans for those acts? Matter as expressed in the terms *madda* or *hayula* represents the basis for the physical nature of the universe. Matter's relation to form and cause also informs one of the ongoing dialogues of philosophy. These terms are also selected to demonstrate three different relationships of the terms: one term that reflects similar definitions across the *falasifa*'s work, one term that demonstrates differing definitions, and one term that is of interest for the use of terms in its definition. Ultimately the most critical aspect is that a basis of comparison exists.

All three terms appear prominently in both al-Kindi's and Ibn Sina's lists of definitions. They first appear in the Arabic translations of Aristotle's philosophy; thereafter the Islamic philosophers incorporate them in their original works. The focus is not only on large changes in meaning, but also on shifts in the way the same or similar ideas were expressed. Given the nature of Islamic philosophy and its roots in Greek philosophy, the reader should be satisfied to observe small shifts in the diachronic scheme rather than major shifts in meaning or contradictory forms.

A term's use in the Qur'an is one of the standard earmarks of early usage. The selected terms *jawhar* (substance), *ʿilla* (cause), and *madda* (matter) are not found in the Qur'an.[3] The Arabic language developed terms for philosophical ideas in the process of translating Hellenistic philosophy. Some documents suggest that the *falasifa* consulted with and amended the translators' word selections. The indication is that the translators also realized they were dealing with a technical terminology. This is apparent when a translator who was a contemporary of al-Kindi states that al-Kindi "corrected" (*aslaha*) the translations.[4] After the initial work of translation there remained the secondary task of interpreting and explaining the new vocabulary to the readers. Supposing that a new vocabulary developed organically as the translators worked, manuals or lexicons to explain this new technical vocabulary would be required. The early books of definition served this purpose, since the study of philosophy was new to the whole Arabic-speaking society, its audience as well as its practitioners. If one imagines a sophisticated, literate society whose primary expression is found in poetry, grammar, histories, and other similarly concrete endeavors here one sees guidebooks for philosophical works appearing. Since it had long been assumed that oral instructions and then written commentaries would be necessary to explicate philosophical texts, surely a word book to explain the concepts would help too? By the time of Ibn Sina's *Book of Definitions*, about 100 words were defined in a ready guide for students who wished to understand philosophical works. The popularity of these lists can also be seen in the similarity of terms from list to list, especially in the early words.[5]

In observing the usage of the *falasifa* each term will be examined as defined by the individual *failasuf*. This investigation focuses on the development of these terms in the period from al-Kindi to Ibn Sina, the third to the fifth centuries AH/ninth to eleventh centuries AD For al-Kindi and Ibn Sina their definitions are found in their respective books of definitions – *Fi hudud al-ashya'* and *Kitab al-hudud*. For al-Farabi they appear in *Kitab al-huruf* (*The Book of Letters*), his commentary on Aristotle's *Metaphysics*.[6] Thus, it will be demonstrated how definitions change over the two centuries of our study, both in regard to the references they make, and in the words selected in the definientia. As much as possible each of the terms will be followed from one philosopher to the next, except where a different term is used for the concept discussed. This development and the enduring effect of the *falasifa*'s definitions in Islamic philosophy as exemplified in these terms will form the focus of the study.

This work will deal with the development of terms for a technical philosophical vocabulary in the Arabic language, but a "source-hunt" will not serve that purpose.[7] While one cannot deny Greek influence, especially in the case of al-Farabi, to view the *falasifa* as copyists of Aristotle is an oversimplification. The focus is on how they expressed themselves in Arabic, rather than tracking such inspiration as they may have received from Greek philosophy. Neither is it an attempt to trace the Hellenistic origin of each idea, or of each phrase, or even of each atomistic part. One might expect that Islamic philosophical enquiry proceeded along a trajectory similar to that followed by the Greeks. Thinkers speculating about metaphysics will need words for the objects of metaphysics, such as substance, cause, element and so on.

The working point of view will be to consider the transparent meanings generally, eschewing esoteric interpretations. This is not a discussion of Greek vocabulary, but of Arabic terms needed to discuss these ideas. These terms may or may not be equivalents of the Greek counterparts. For purposes of this study language will be considered as the tool of philosophy, adopting the viewpoint of E. R. Dodds, that what is original about a philosophical system is the design of the complete and finished structure – the completed mosaic – rather than the origin of each tessera.

In the mid-ninth century when al-Kindi began his philosophical enquiries, no ready-made philosophical vocabulary existed in Arabic. Consequently, he was obliged to develop terms to discuss the ideas he encountered. When particular translations demonstrate direct influence of the available texts used by the individual *falasifa*, then related developments in translation technique will be covered. This is shown by their understanding of particular concepts, such as, *sabab* in the writings of al-Farabi, which is based on particular translations.[8] However, a detailed discussion of the role of the translators in developing this vocabulary is a separate issue and it is not the focus here.[9] Al-Kindi's *Fi hudud al-ashya'* served as the first Arabic lexicon of philosophical terms. It was a professional lexicon, giving a technical meaning of terms that needed to be explained in this new science, philosophy. It includes terms referring to physics, metaphysics, and psychology. He proceeds by explaining the terms in wording that uses an intuitive understanding of the words, even if the meaning thus evoked is not completely accurate in philosophical terms.

It is apparent and unsurprising that al-Kindi's choice of language will be shown to be more limited than that of his successors. This fact is attributable to his position as a trailblazer in philosophy. One noteworthy point is that al-Kindi deliberately chose terms to avoid religious connotations in some instances thereby isolating philosophy from theology and Qur'anic studies. It will become evident that such usage fades out in the work of his successors. However his instincts were good, in trying to segregate philosophy from theology, as al-Ghazali later executed a frontal attack on philosophy from a theological perspective.

Al-Farabi, writing in the tenth century, consciously attempted to form a language that would be more philosophical and technically specific. He used Arabic translations of Aristotle to acquire what he presented as a more accurate view of genuine Aristotelian philosophy. Traces of Aristotle that did not exist in al-Kindi's time appear in al-Farabi's work from new translations.[10] While al-Farabi internalized the translated Greek philosophy more thoroughly than al-Kindi had, al-Farabi also made greater use of Arabic words to express the ideas in an Arabic context.

In a sense the al-Farabi of this study is a synthetic model, looking at his metaphysical definitions, culled from his commentary on Aristotle's *Metaphysics*. Al-Farabi was the political philosopher par excellence in the Islamic world; other questions only hold his interest to the extent that he needs their concepts to build and defend a complete political system. Al-Farabi does not write treatises on metaphysics as such. Al-Farabi's insistence on hypertechnical usage sometimes gives his work an artificial and stilted quality. Al-Farabi marks the midpoint in the growth cycle of the philosophical vocabulary: it is more exact and rigorous than in al-Kindi's writing, but it does not yet flow as smoothly as it will in coming generations.

In the late tenth century and early eleventh century, the philosophical vocabulary reaches full maturation in the writing of Ibn Sina. He has soaked up the concepts and terms propounded by al-Kindi and al-Farabi, and given them back fully formed. The transliterated words have become accepted into Arabic and are in some cases used alternatively as synonyms for Arabic words. For example *hayula*, a transliteration of *hyle*, for matter is used nearly as a synonym for *madda*, the Arabic language word. The use of *tin* – al-Kindi's suggestion for matter – has nearly died out. *Tin* means "clay" and the etymology must be something like *hyle* originally, except it never caught on. Later philosophers use either *hayula* or *madda*. Ibn Sina is totally comfortable with the vocabulary and writes for a knowledgeable audience, certain that his terms will be understood. Although the pressure for political conformity also fell on Ibn Sina, he attempted to escape it by moving geographically ever westward and finding new patrons.

In the ninth century by contrast, probably due both to his own central location (Baghdad), and to the more centralized khalifal authority, al-Kindi was under greater religious pressure to conform to a state-sponsored official religion. This is apparent in the institution of the *mihna* (inquisition), which examined the religious orthodoxy of officials on the basis of test questions.[11] Contemporary Arabic accounts show that while the questioning was supposedly on religious beliefs, a quest for political control lay under the religious zeal of the khalif.

By the late tenth/early eleventh centuries, questions of religion were disassociated from political power – or exerted a much weaker pull. Discretion might still be advisable, but it was not a matter of a tribunal passing judgment. The *mihna* was dead. The greater maturation of a philosophical vocabulary can be seen to the extent that when Ibn Sina used a term in an unusual manner, it was obvious to all.

The next famous *failasuf* is Ibn Rushd (d. 595 AH/AD 1198), who is particularly renowned for his commentaries on the works of Aristotle. He wrote a huge body of works, many of which survive in Latin and Hebrew texts. Furthermore, the works of Ibn Rushd including those in Latin or Hebrew have not been completely studied in one body. R. Arnaldez said, "A complete and meticulous study on this point would be desirable, but it would be a long and difficult task."[12] While his influence on the scholastic philosophers of the Latin West, such as Thomas Aquinas, was great, it was less marked in the Islamic East, and here the focus is on the development of Islamic philosophical terms in the eastern Islamic world.[13] With Ibn Sina there exists an adapted, complete vocabulary for philosophy. For this reason, the study will end with Ibn Sina. A study of the influence of Islamic philosophy on the Latin West is a topic that remains to be studied and analyzed in detail.

Similarly, the Greek sources are used sparingly and only in Arabic translation. Other scholars have studied the Greek sources extensively, certainly in a more worthy manner than is possible here, and the field is best left to them. Therefore the focus is trained on the writings of the *falasifa*, and primarily on their books of definition where possible.

Types of definition

Definitions are fundamental to understanding the concepts employed in the study of philosophy. They may represent either the final result of philosophy or its foundation, depending on the particular method employed, but they are necessary. The importance of definitions in classical Islamic philosophy can be recognized by the fact that *falasifa* devoted not just chapters of their works, but entire treatises to the study of definitions. When a *failasuf* lays out definitions, he is drawing a detailed map for the reader to comprehend the construct of his system.

Philosophers list three kinds of definitions: essentialist, prescriptive, and linguistic.[14] Briefly, essentialist definitions attempt to discover a core meaning that all members of a class share; prescriptive definitions give rules and assign which members qualify in a class; and linguistic definitions merely report on current practice. All definitions are definitions of a class, not of an individual, thus a certain element of generalization is necessary. Both Plato's and Aristotle's definitions attempted to define essence, as mentioned above;

philosophers refer to such definitions as E-type definitions. They are sometimes also called "real definitions." Philosophers view prescriptive (P-type) or stipulative definitions as symbolic conventions. They consider prescriptive definitions to be semantic rules for linguistic operations. P-type definitions formally assign names to objects, but they do not seek an "essence" or look for the truth-value of a definition. P-type definitions come at the beginning of philosophical enquiry, to "settle significations" rather than communicate information gleaned from the realm of essences. In this way P-type definitions can "clear up ambiguities."[15] They do not delve into the world of essences. In geometry, definitions are P-type used at the beginning of investigations.

Linguistic (L-type) definitions are empirical reports on linguistic behavior. While such definitions communicate information, L-type definitions are not viewed as necessarily, absolutely true, the way E-type definitions are. This is because their value is only as a posteriori reports on how language is used. In fact definitions cannot be of simple things, only of the complex – a point expressed in a recent article by Hugh H. Benson. In the essay, "Misunderstanding the 'What is F-ness?' Question," Benson states that Socrates did not object to Hippias' first definition of fineness. In this definition Hippias says, "A fine maiden is fine."[16] Although this definition focuses on only one aspect of fineness (beauty in a woman) Socrates did not object, because this is a trait found in many women, and as such is not a concrete particular, meaning it is not applicable to only one woman. Therefore, in this sense it fulfills the requirement that definitions must be of the universal, not of a concrete particular. The fact that Meno defined particulars was where his definition went wrong, in Benson's opinion.[17] To give a concrete particular as an answer to "What is F-ness?" is a category mistake. Socrates' questioners failed to understand that his question can have only one universal as a correct answer, and that is why they supplied more than one universal in answering.[18]

In the following chapters, as the definitions of al-Kindi, al-Farabi, and Ibn Sina are discussed in detail, it will be apparent that the stated goal of the *falasifa* was to follow the Greek tradition, attempting to find essentialist definitions. Ibn Sina, for example, quoted Aristotle's definition of definition in his own *Kitab al-hudud*. He said:

> The definition of definition is what the Philosopher (Aristotle) mentions in the book, *Topics*: definition is a statement indicating the quiddity (*mahiyya*) of a thing, that is, definition is a statement in regard to the perfection of a thing's essential existence. The nature of something is what the thing acquires from the near genus and its differentia (*fasl*).[19]

Definitions in a historical context

A condensed and selective survey of the history of definitions in Greek philosophy may serve to put Islamic definitions in historical perspective. Definitions may either begin with a general concept and move to the particular cases or begin with particular cases and move to the general concept. Plato's search for definition embodied the first method, wherein Socrates asked a question which sought to find knowledge of definitions inductively. In Plato's dialogue *Euthyphro* Socrates asks about the nature of piety and impiety. When Euthyphro responds to Socrates' question, Socrates emphasizes that he is looking not for two or three examples, but a total definition of piety. He wants "the general idea which makes all pious things to be pious."[20] At the end of the dialogue he objects that Euthyphro has not shown him the "essence" of piety, offering only attributes instead.[21] In the *Euthyphro* Socrates gives these criteria for a definition: it must specify what is common to all (5d); it must give the nature of the quality, not only its distinguishing marks (6d and 11a); and it must provide criteria for determining borderline cases (6e).

In the *Meno* (72c) he also covers the first two requirements again.[22] In this dialogue Socrates asks: What is "excellence" (*arete*)? He objects that Meno finds "a swarm of excellence."[23] Socrates states his question:

> So if I said after this, "Then tell me about this itself, Meno; that in respect of which they do not differ but are all the same, what do you say this is?" I imagine you would have an answer to give me.[24]

He objects that he does not want a separate excellence for each man, woman, child, slave, and so on, but the common factor. At the end of this dialogue, having failed to find a definition of excellence, Socrates says that he not only does not know what this quality is, but has never met anyone else who knew what it was and could define it either. Some writers have discussed Socrates' view of definition as "the priority of the definition principle", which H. H. Benson summed up as, "If A fails to know what F-ness is, then A fails to know anything about F-ness."[25]

Another view of Socrates' method comes from C. C. W. Taylor, who states that a Socratic definition is not a definition of a term, or work, or concept, but should answer the question "'What is ... ?', where the blank is filled in by a word designating some quality or feature of agents, such as courage or excellence."[26] The logical problem appears to be that Socrates is asking the interlocutor to consider x (some quality) as an abstract entity stripped of its physical manifestation in a particular instance. However, the human mind is unable to grasp such a pure abstraction, much less define it, without reference to its existence in the substrate. Thus it rather appears that Socrates is asking for a definition of a form.

WHAT IS A DEFINITION?

Aristotle denied the existence of a class of ideal forms, but in his search for definitions he appeared to be looking for a definition of the general, moving from the particular as manifested in an individual. In the *Topics* (1. 5. 101b 36–102a 5) Aristotle gives this definition of definitions: "A 'definition' is a phrase signifying a thing's essence. It is rendered in the form either of a phrase in lieu of a term, or of a phrase in lieu of another phrase; for it is sometimes possible to define the meaning of a phrase as well."[27] Another recent translation, by H. G. Apostle and L. P. Gerson, changes the emphasis slightly: "A definition is an expression which signifies the essence of a thing. It is stated either as a phrase in place of a name, or as a phrase in place of a (shorter) phrase, for it is possible to define some things signified by parts of a phrase."[28] In this definition, one finds the origins of Aristotle's delineation of the essentialist position, with his statement that the work of definition is finding a thing's essence. He continues (*Topics* 1. 8. 103b 6–11):

> For every predicate of a subject must of necessity be either convertible with its subject or not; and if it is convertible, it would be its definition or property, for if it signifies the essence, it is the definition; if not it is a property – for this was what a property is, viz. what is predicated convertibly, but does not signify the essence.[29]

In the essentialist definition, of which this is an excellent example, the philosopher assumes that there is an underlying essence which can be studied and defined. Aristotle further states "the definition consists of genus and differentia" (103b 15).[30] While no one individual is entailed by a definition, the definition will be specific enough to give meaningful information about the individuals in a class. Thus Edward Booth says of *Metaphysics* 7. 7–9, "These chapters should be regarded as essays at a completely empiricised account of the process of coming to be, undertaken in the hope that it might bring together the individual with its definition."[31] Booth points out that Aristotle attempts to unite the individual with its definition, in considering the individual as a generated member of a class.[32]

Aristotle's discussion of definitions thus includes rules to formulate accurate definitions (*Topics* 1. 5. 102a ff). First a definition signifies a thing's essence. It must be a phrase, not merely a term. Accidents and properties are not sufficient for definitions; they must be of the essential nature of a thing. For instance, while a man may be capable of learning grammar, this is a property of man, rather than an essential difference – even though this property belongs to man alone (102a 20–21). Man's essential difference has been classically that he is rational. The capacity to learn grammar is a subset of rationality. An accident may or may not belong to the same thing at any particular time; for example, being seated (102b 7–8). An accident may be a temporary property or demonstrate a thing's relation to something else, but it is not an absolute. Synonyms are not definitions.

The ideas of Plato and Aristotle reached the *falasifa* through the translation movement. In a treatise *The Harmonization of the Opinions of Plato and Aristotle* al-Farabi combined the views of these two philosophers.[33] It was not unusual for the *falasifa* to view Plato and Aristotle as complementary. Al-Farabi's view of the two philosophers may be seen in this comment at the end of *The Attainment of Happiness*, "So let it be clear to you that, in what they presented, their purpose is the same, and that they intended to offer one and the same philosophy."[34] Translations were made from Greek texts either through Syriac and then into Arabic, or directly into Arabic. Translation of philosophical texts into Arabic also necessitated the development of a technical philosophical vocabulary to represent ideas such as substance, form, matter, cause, and so on. While the philosophical texts formed only a small part of the total translation effort, they strongly influenced the development of philosophy in the Islamic culture.

2

AL-KINDI: THE FIRST ARABIC *BOOK OF DEFINITIONS*

In philosophy, Abu Yusuf Ya'qub b. Ishaq al-Kindi (d. circa 260 AH/AD 873) is generally credited with writing the first surviving philosophical *Book of Definitions* in Arabic.[1] The earliest cited example of *hudud* (definition) literature in Arabic is *Kitab al-hudud*, written by the grammarian al-Farra' (d. 207 AH/AD 822), but it does not survive.[2] Al-Kindi's book, *Fi hudud al-ashya' wa rusumiha* (*On the Definitions and Descriptions of Things*), indicates the importance the *falasifa* placed on accurate philosophical terminology. Because al-Kindi was the first philosopher writing in Arabic, he faced problems concerning the expression of technical terms that were not faced by his successors.

When the Arabs began translating Greek texts in the third/ninth century there was not a pre-existing technical vocabulary in Arabic to express philosophical concepts. Rather scholars such as the early translators and *falasifa* had to develop a vocabulary to express philosophical concepts in Arabic. They did this in a variety of ways: by transliterating Greek words; by adopting foreign (Persian) words; and by dedicating ordinary language words to a technical philosophical use or concept. The *falasifa* needed terms for substance, matter, and cause, in specific meanings not previously found in their ordinary language. Similarly, early Greek philosophical writers had to develop a technical philosophical language. For example, the philosophers took the word *hyle*, originally meaning "forest, woodland", and later "timber", and designated it to mean only "matter" in the strict philosophical sense.[3] Aristotle used it to refer to "the *stuff* of which a thing is made, material."[4]

Another factor in the development of a technical philosophical vocabulary is the tension between theology and philosophy evident in early works. Both sciences attempted to delineate the terminology. As it might appear initially that theology and philosophy would cover the same ground, the *falasifa*'s vocabulary will be checked to observe if their terms are found in the Qur'an.

The first section will contain an examination of the style of al-Kindi's treatise *On the Definitions*. In the second section there is a discussion al-Kindi's definitions of *jawhar* (substance), *ᶜilla* (cause), and *hayula* (matter). In the third section early findings about al-Kindi's definitions will be summarized, however a full comparison of the three *falasifa* will appear in Chapter 5.

The style of al-Kindi's On the Definitions[5]

The treatise known as *On the Definitions* exists in three known manuscripts which are found in Istanbul, London, and Lisbon. When M. A. Abu Ridah published the first edition of this treatise in 1952, he relied solely on the Istanbul (Aya Sofiya 4832) manuscript. Indeed, he was convinced that this was the sole extant copy of the treatise. In addition to this treatise, the Istanbul manuscript contains 23 other treatises by al-Kindi, which Abu Ridah edited and published along with the treatise on definitions.[6] While the definition treatise was found with a set of al-Kindi's manuscripts, Abu Ridah remarks in his Introduction that the handwriting of the definition treatise differed from the other treatises, which may raise questions about its authenticity.[7] All the other Kindian treatises which Abu Ridah edited have an introductory dedication and comments (*dibaja*), but such introductory material is lacking in *On the Definitions*, which raises further questions whether the complete treatise has survived in its original state.[8]

In his "Notes on al-Kindi's Treatise on Definitions", Samuel M. Stern used the London British Museum manuscript to publish what he characterizes as a series of emendations to Abu Ridah's edition of the Istanbul manuscript.[9] Stern also published thirteen definitions not found in the Istanbul manuscript. He believes the additional thirteen definitions should properly be attributed to the anonymous author or authors known as Ikhwan al-Safa' (the Sincere Brethern), rather than attributing them to al-Kindi. Stern suggests that this British Museum manuscript (Add. 7473) written about 640 AH/AD 1242, may have been copied from the same source as the Istanbul manuscript, for they vary only slightly from one another.

Thirty years after the publication of the Istanbul manuscript, Felix Klein-Franke published the Lisbon Academy of Sciences manuscript. The colophon of this manuscript indicates that it was copied in AD 1305 at Alexandria.[10] It differs from the Istanbul manuscript in that it is often shorter in its individual definitions. Moreover, after the first 12 definitions, the order in which the definitions are listed varies from the Istanbul manuscript. Klein-Franke points to extra definitions being given for *kawn* (generation), *fasad* (corruption), and the first part of *al-kull* (universality).

In terms of modern translations, there are two English and two French translations: Atiyeh (1966) and Frank (1976) in English; Allard (1972) and Gimaret (1976) in French. George N. Atiyeh closely paraphrased or translated into English important sections of *On the Definitions* in his book *Al-Kindi:*

the Philosopher of the Arabs.[11] Michel Allard published a French translation of the treatise, using a revised edition of the Istanbul manuscript, which depended heavily on Stern's emendations. Allard worked from Abu Ridah's edition and, in addition, from a copy of the Aya Sofiya manuscript sent to him by R. J. McCarthy.[12] Tamar Zahara Frank translated the treatise into English in her 1976 dissertation.[13] Daniel Gimaret translated the definitions into French in a 1976 monograph, using the available published editions of Abu Ridah, S. Stern, and M. Allard.[14]

There are ninety-nine definitions in Abu Ridah's edition, 103 definitions in Allard's translation and 109 definitions in Klein-Franke's. Here the Abu Ridah edition forms the main text, with reference to the others as necessary.[15]

As a literary form, the style of al-Kindi's *On the Definitions* is comparable to many other books of definition, regardless of subject. For example, Ibn Furak's tenth- or eleventh-century *Kitab al-hudud fi al-usul* follows a similar format.[16] Ibn Furak's definitions cover those employed in both theological and juristic topics. The definitions are written in a similar manner to those of al-Kindi – short, terse, and using plain language, although the definitions are not philosophical, taking a theological bent. Ibn Furak's book covers 133 definitions, which is somewhat longer than the length of al-Kindi's (about 100). However, in the brevity of his definitions, Ibn Furak is comparable to al-Kindi.

In al-Kindi's *On the Definitions*, a definiendum is given, followed by its definiens, which may be as short as a few words, or as long as several lines. There is no copula pronoun in the Abu Ridah edition. Nothing serves to separate the definiendum from the definiens. Furthermore, in al-Kindi's definitions there are no examples of the things defined. For example, in his discussion of *jawhar* (substance) al-Kindi gives its attributes, but he does not name any substances; nor does he state that substances may be primary or secondary, a distinction made by Aristotle. Al-Kindi appears to use many ordinary language expressions to convey philosophical concepts to his audience. On this evidence one might assume that his audience does not have a working knowledge of philosophy, perhaps his readers are interested beginners in philosophy, perhaps members of the court. Many of the definitions are short enough to memorize, or to be substituted by a reader, who might not understand the philosophical use of these terms in a text.

Then there is the question of the basis for al-Kindi's organization in his list of definitions. The treatise begins with definitions for: the first cause, the intellect, nature, the soul, body, and creation. More specialized and complicated words come near the end of the treatise: the virtues, science of the stars, humanity, and angelicity. Unlike al-Farabi and Ibn Sina, al-Kindi does not give a definition of *hadd* (definition).[17] The *Fihrist* states: "These are the letters (i.e., the chapters of *Metaphysics*) which Ustath, who had information about them, translated for al-Kindi."[18]

Bearing in mind that Ustath translated Aristotle's *Metaphysics* for al-Kindi, it certainly appears that al-Kindi would have had access to the *Metaphysics*. Possibly al-Kindi had the order of Book *Dal* in mind when he composed his own *On the Definitions*. This is however, only a possibility, as it appears to follow Aristotle's arrangement too closely to be entirely coincidental. In comparing the order of Aristotle's definitions in the *Metaphysics* with that found in al-Kindi's *On the Definitions* the arrangement is shown below:

Aristotle[19]	**Al-Kindi**
the beginning (*al-ibtida'*)	first cause
cause	intellect
element (*ustuqas*)	nature
nature	soul
necessary	body
one/many	creation (*al-ibda^c*)
identity	matter (*hayula*)
substance	form
[lacuna][20]	element (*^cunsur*)
prior/posterior	act
choice	work
potentiality/actuality	substance
quantity	choice
quality	quantity

In looking at the raw data one finds both lists begin with a type of first start or origin. Aristotle's first term is *al-ibtida'* (the beginning). Al-Kindi's first term is *al-^cilla al-ula* (the first cause). Aristotle's second term is *al-^cilla*, (cause). The next term in Aristotle's list (the third) is *al-ustuqas* (element), while in al-Kindi it is *al-^caql* (intellect). Aristotle's fourth term is *al-tabi^ca* (nature), corresponding to al-Kindi's third term *al-tabi^ca*. Consequently one sees that *al-^cilla* (cause), *al-tabi^ca* (nature), and *al-jawhar* (substance) fall in the same relative order in both lists and in similar positions. Cause is second in Aristotle and first in al-Kindi. Nature is fourth in Aristotle and third in al-Kindi. Substance is eighth in Aristotle and twelfth in al-Kindi. *Al-ikhtiyar* (choice), *al-fa^cl* (act), and *al-kamiyya* (quantity) also fall in fairly close proximity: tenth, eleventh, and twelfth in Aristotle's list, and tenth, thirteenth, and fourteenth in al-Kindi's list. Therefore, while al-Kindi's arrangement of definitions does not demonstrate total correspondence with Aristotle's order, it is measurable and suggestive. One small point is that al-Kindi chooses '*unsur* for element, which is an Arabic word, he does not use *ustuqas* – a Greek loan word.

Al-Kindi's definitions

A few selected terms will be analyzed in depth. They are: *al-jawhar*, the term for substance, *al-ᶜilla al-ula* for the first cause, *al-ᶜilal al-tabiᶜyya* for the natural causes, and *al-hayula* for matter. These kinds of terms are among those necessary for any philosophical scheme. As such they are of basic importance to the *falasifa*.

Jawhar (substance)

Substance (*jawhar*) is (1) [the thing] subsisting in itself; (2) accidents can be predicated of it without changing its essential nature; (3) it is described, not describing. One says: (4) it is not receptive to generation or corruption, or of [those] things which increase for each one of the things, whichever, like generation and corruption in the particularity of a thing's substance. (5) These things, when they are known, accidental qualities in each one of the particular substance are also known, without their being intrinsic themselves to a particular substance.[21]

Comment The word *jawhar* itself is of Persian origin. It comes from *gawhar*, meaning gem or jewel.[22] It was adopted into Arabic and then used by the philosophers in a technical sense. *Jawhar*, like *hayula*, is useful because, as a foreign word, it does not have a lot of connotative baggage. Insofar as foreign loan words are blank slates in the receptor language, they exhibit a cleanness that indigenous used words do not have. Verbal purity may be one of the reasons for the success of adopting loan words, and maintaining them for a technical usage. Their very artificiality gives them a usefulness.

Al-Kindi makes five basic points in this definition. He begins with the statement that (1) substance is subsisting in itself, "*al-qa'im bi-nafsihi*." Substance in Aristotle covers a range of ideas, including a combination of form and matter.[23] Whatever substance is, it is self-subsistent. Next (2) al-Kindi states that accidents are predicated of substance without changing its essential nature.[24] Substance is usually considered to have an essence or quiddity and while it supports accidents – which are by their nature non-essential – it does not change the nature of a substance. Thus human beings may have different hair colors, without changing their essential nature. Red-haired or black-haired is an accident that may be predicated of a human. As understood by philosophers, hair color does not change the quiddity of a human. (3) Next, al-Kindi says it is described, not describing, which could also be translated as attributed, not an attribute. First the passive, then the active participle of the same verb root (*w-s-f*) are employed here, to bring out the idea that substance is an inert entity, not acting on other entities in the aspect al-Kindi is considering here. (4) Substance is not susceptible to generation or corruption, meaning it does not come into being or pass away. The next phrase is ambiguous, and it appears to mean nothing else subject to generation and corruption increases a substance, that is, nothing is added to it which has anything like generation or corruption.[25]

The second half of the definition is problematic to translate and understand. To examine the scope of the problem, first the translations published by other scholars are reviewed.

George Atiyeh's paraphrase of substance from *On the Definitions* is as follows:

> The most important characteristic of substance is self-subsistence; or to put it another way, a substance is not found in a subject, but itself is the subject which does not suffer in essence when predicates are asserted of it. Other characteristics of substance are that it cannot admit a contrary, it cannot be what it is and be something else at the same time; and that it cannot be more complete than what it is. It is also prior in definition; if one defines a substance one is also defining, at the same time, those accidental qualities which do not form a part of its essence, but enter in the formation of each particular substance.[26]

Michel Allard translated it into French as follows:

> La substance – C'est ce qui subsiste par soi, c'est ce qui supporte les accidents sans changement essentiel, c'est ce qui reçoit les qualifications et qui ne qualifie pas autre chose. On a dit aussi: c'est ce qui n'est en soi-même sujet ni à la génération ou à la corruption, ni à d'autres entités surajoutées, ni à toutes les entités semblables à la génération ou à la corruption; c'est encore ce dont la connaissance entraîne celle des entités qui surviennent accidentellement à chaque substance partielle sans être intérieur à la substance elle-même.[27]

Tamar Zahara Frank translated this passage into English:

> Substance: That which subsists by itself, an essentially unchanging substrate for accidents; it is a recipient, not a maker, of attributes. Others say, "It is neither generable nor corruptible nor receptive in its special substance to any additional thing similar to generation and corruption – things which, when known [the nature of the substrate], there are also known through the knowledge of their knowledge, the things which are accidental to each particular substance without their entering into the essence of its unique substance."[28]

Daniel Gimaret also translated this definition:

> La substance: c'est ce qui subsiste par soi et (ce) qui supporte les accidents; dont l'essence ne change pas; qui est qualifié et ne qualifie pas. On dit aussi: c'est ce qui ne saurait recevoir, dans le propre de sa substance, la génération et la corruption, ni les choses pareilles à la génération et à la corruption, qui s'ajoutent à chaque substance, et qui, une fois connues, permettent également de connaître les choses qui surviennent dans chaque substance particulière, mais sans qu'elles entrent dans sa substance propre(??).[29]

In his footnote Abu Ridah notes that the text is short, saying, "... despite the deficiency of the phrasing."[30] The full text of his footnote reads:

> It is thus in the original, and the definition – despite the deficiency of the phrasing – is clear: substance is subsisting in itself, it is not coming into being or passing away, or receptive to what is similar to coming into being and passing away of things which adhere to it as accidents, because in this case it is not a substance subsisting by itself. The basis of this, all of it, is that substance does not receive anything except accidental, changeable predicates, thus it does not receive anything else essential.[31]

Thus Abu Ridah interprets the passage to mean that whatever is substantial can only receive accidental qualities, it cannot receive substantial qualities, because they would alter its essence.

Many would agree with Abu Ridah that the text appears to be deficient in phrasing. First, as previously mentioned, in this definition al-Kindi does not distinguish between primary and secondary substances, which the reader might logically expect to find. Second, although the received text can be forced into a semblance of meaning, it is not very clear. Generally al-Kindi writes in a clear and usually elegant manner. Abu Ridah's interpretation is philosophically acceptable, but whether this is the way al-Kindi wrote the text might be questioned. As can be seen from the translations quoted above, others have interpreted this part of the definition in various ways, which also appears to indicate either a corrupt text, or an unusually opaque one. George Atiyeh interprets the text as meaning that at the same time one is defining substance one is defining accidental qualities which appear to have an intermediate existence. They do not form part of its essence, but enter into its formation. Perhaps Atiyeh is thinking of Aristotle's primary substances: that defining a concrete individual also entails knowing the attributes of the individual, and those attributes are called accidental qualities. These accidents are not intrinsic, that is, they are not essential, but they are still included in our knowledge of the substance. Thus in defining the substance, one has a complete definition of both the accidental qualities and the essential qualities of the substance. This is philosophically untenable. It is not logical that at the same time an accidental quality may not be an integral part of a substance and also enter into the substance's formation. This is a contradiction.

The same objections apply to Allard's translation. T. Z. Frank interprets the last part of the definition to mean that the accidental qualities of a substance are known with the knowledge of the substance. This seems as improbable as Atiyeh's assertion that one is defining accidents with the substance. How can one know accidental qualities as the concomitants of substance if they do not form part of that substance's essence? Gimaret follows a similar line: that one will know the particulars of a substance, but they are not in the substance itself. However, Gimaret appears to have expressed his uncertainty with the passage by adding double question marks after his translation. He also adds that the text is obscure and notes that it is found in only one of the three manuscripts. It seems that Abu Ridah is more convincing in this controversy and that it is more plausible to take the text to be deficient than trying to complete the author's deficient sentence by interpreting it anew. It is notable in passing that the second part of this definition also resembles Aristotle's description of the First Mover: "... there is a substance which is eternal and unmovable and separate from sensible things. It has been shown also that this substance cannot have any magnitude, but it is without parts and indivisible."[32]

Al-Kindi's definition is constructed on opposites. First *al-jawhar* is opposed to *al-ᶜarad* (accident). *Al-jawhar* is also equated with what is *dhatiyya*, referring to its essential nature. Next there is a contrast between the active and the passive participles of *wasafa* – a contrast between what describes and what is described. *Al-jawhar* does not receive either generation or corruption, another pair of contraries. After examining the other two philosophers' definitions, a comparison of al-Kindi's word use will be found in Chapter 5.

The definitions that define cause

First definition – *al-ᶜilla al-ula* for the first cause:

> The first cause – creating, doing, completing everything, not moving.[33]

Second definition – *al-ᶜilal al-tabiᶜyya* for the natural causes:

> The natural causes are four: what a thing comes into being from, that is, its element; the form of a thing, by which it is what it is; the principle of motion of a thing, which is its cause; and that, for the sake of which the agent does whatever is done.[34]

Comment In these two definitions, one sees two different approaches to the idea of cause. In the first definition, the first word al-Kindi uses in his definition of "first cause" is *mubdi͑a* meaning "creating" (from the root *b-d-͑*) and a word used in the Qur'an in relation to Allah's creating the heavens and the earth.[35] Another word used for creation in the Qur'an is *khalaq*.[36] In an Islamic context, with regard to any word for creating, the question becomes, Is it creation from nothing or a shaping of existing matter? In his sixth definition, al-Kindi states that *al-ibda͑*, that is "creation", is *͑an laysa* "from nothing."[37] In the Lisbon ms., Klein-Franke reads *͑an shay'*, "from something."[38] He does not comment on this manuscript variation from the other two printed editions (Allard and Abu Ridah) both of which read *͑an laysa* (from nothing). However, this is a startling variation and if Klein-Franke regards it as correct, one would expect him to comment on such an important point. This passage may increase the evidence for viewing the Lisbon manuscript as less authoritative than the Istanbul one.

The two obvious choices for the concept of cause in Arabic are *sabab* (pl. *asbab*) and *͑illa* (pl. *͑ilal*). In the second definition (2.b.), al-Kindi employs the word *al-͑ilal*, rather than *al-asbab* for causes. In the known Arabic edition of Aristotle's *Physics*, the translator Ishaq b. Hunayn, who lived after al-Kindi, used *al-asbab* for causes, not *al-͑ilal*.[39] Al-Kindi appears to prefer *al-͑ilal* which is the term many later *falasifa* used. He may also have been distancing himself from theology, by indicating a technical vocabulary for philosophy. He may have hoped to protect himself from religious controversies by expressing his ideas in non-religious language.[40] In this definition, the word *͑unsur*, element, refers to what is usually called the material cause in Aristotle's scheme. It is interesting that al-Kindi uses *͑unsur* for the material cause, rather than a word derived from *madda* or *hayula*, the more common words for matter. Furthermore, Ibn Sina continues to use *͑unsur* in the same way, for the material cause.

Some of al-Kindi's definitions, like this one, are formed of these components that one might call mini-definitions. The mini-definitions lend themselves for substitution as short components in longer definitions where clarification of unfamiliar terms is necessary. For example, he gives this definition of form (*sura*): "Form – the thing by which a thing is what it is."[41] While *sura* is a common Arabic word, this is a specific, technical usage as a philosophical term. This is a very short and immediately intuitable definition of the concept form. For a reader unfamiliar with the concept it would be easy to snap the whole phrase into another sentence where the term *sura* appears, just like a mathematical formula, where a number is substituted for x in the equation. One may consider the definition as the formula for the term "form." In the definiens of the four causes al-Kindi has parenthetically repeated his definition of *al-sura* after the word. The only cause he explicates with a repeated definition is *al-sura*, leading one to speculate that it may have been the least known to his readers. This use of mini-definitions allows readers to use al-Kindi's definitions as components in a new thought system.

The natural causes are also mentioned in another treatise, *Fi al-ibana ᶜan al-ᶜilla al-faᶜila al-qariba li-l-kawn wa al-fasad* (*On the Explanation of the Proximate Active Cause for Coming to be and Passing Away*).⁴² In the metaphysical treatise *Fi al-falsafa al-ula* (*On First Philosophy*) al-Kindi says: "Because every cause will be either element or form or agent – meaning what is from it is the beginning of motion – or final, meaning that for the sake of which a thing is."⁴³

In all three of these treatises al-Kindi uses *al-ᶜilla* for cause. In the Qur'an this word for cause does not appear. In the Arabic translation of Aristotle's *Physics* the word for cause is *al-sabab*, although the translation still extant was written by a man who lived after al-Kindi. The evidence tends to show that al-Kindi was employing a word deliberately that did not have too much baggage (that is, it was not Qur'anic), and for which he could give a specific, limited definition.

Next under consideration is al-Kindi's definition of a word for matter, *hayula*.⁴⁴

Hayula (matter)

Matter – a potentiality, put down for bearing the forms, it is acted upon.⁴⁵

Comment This term is a Greek loan word: *hayula* is from ὕλη (*hyle*), meaning matter. Employing the formulaic method mentioned under the term *sura*, where form is "the thing by which a thing is what it is", this definition can be rewritten as: "Matter is a potentiality put down for bearing the thing by which a thing is what it is." In this definition of *hayula* the aspect of matter that is emphasized is its potential, rather than its concrete nature. In al-Kindi's definition of *jawhar* (substance) he remarks that substance bears accidents. Inasmuch as matter has accidents, it is a substance. Thus two related aspects of matter are being defined, matter as bearing forms and as bearing accidents. In the previous definition al-Kindi does not use *al-hayula* for the elemental, or physical cause, but rather *al-ᶜunsur*.

Al-hayula, as a Greek loan word, indicated matter, and in the philosophically useful sense became a non-specific term, not calling to mind a particular sort of material. Other words al-Kindi might have used for matter in Arabic include *madda*, *tina*, and sometimes *ᶜunsur*. It is true, a more specific stuff – wood – was originally indicated by *hyle*, but Aristotle succeeded in adopting it as a technical term for matter in philosophy.⁴⁶ It then had a long history of acceptance as a philosophical term for *matter* in general. Here we see an example of abstraction (in the sense of non-exactness) in definition working better than precision. Philosophically, matter denotes physical stuff, but without specific properties. As with *jawhar*, another word of foreign origin, *hayula* is a blank slate on which to inscribe concepts.

In an essay "Vagueness and the Desiderata for Definition", Roy Sorenson points out that while "vague" can mean underspecific, which is a negative trait, there is also a useful sense of vagueness which allows one to include borderline cases. Vagueness here refers to inclusion of less easily identified cases, rather than ambiguity. Sorenson's point is that terms may exclude possible cases. This also draws a distinction between vague and ambiguous. He states that his main thesis is that "definitions must preserve borderline cases to the same extent as clear cases."[47] Which term should be used for "matter" seems here to be one of those cases where a certain amount of vagueness is an advantage; the point of matter is as stuff which can bear forms; in this aspect it is not important whether the matter is wood, metal, clay, or something else. In his definition, al-Kindi is looking for what all these different kinds of matter have in common. In contrast, *al-tin* or *al-tina* is an Arabic word, used in the Qur'an for the matter of creation and frequently translated as clay. One use of *al-tin* in the Qur'an is, "With a sign from your Lord, is that I make for you out of clay (*al-tin*), as it were, the figure of a bird, and breathe into it, and it becomes a bird." (S. 3.49)[48] In al-Kindi's definition of ʿ*unsur* he says it is "*tina kull tina*," that is, "the element – matter of all matter." Literally, it means clay of all clay. Here he uses *tina* as the definition.[49] Al-Kindi appears to be using a familiar, even ordinary, word (*al-tina*) to explain a technical philosophical usage of *al-*ʿ*unsur*. In these definitions al-Kindi uses the pedagogical technique of building up a reader's knowledge, beginning from what a reader knows to what she does not know, until the reader gradually becomes acquainted with the philosophical way of thinking.

Conclusions

Al-Kindi's contribution to Islamic philosophy appears to be either the invention or collection of a suitable terminology for the discussion of philosophical problems. Of the three terms examined in al-Kindi – *al-jawhar*, *al-*ʿ*illa*, and *al-hayula* – none is found in the Qur'an.[50] *Al-jawhar* is a Persian loan word and *al-hayula* is from the Greek. In a strict sense the need to import a word for "substance" may have been more unavoidable than importing a new word for "matter", as the concept of substance may not have been found in Arabic before the *falasifa* investigated the nature of the world. There is no word in Arabic with a set of meanings equivalent to *al-jawhar*. As mentioned above, there were local terms for matter and al-Farabi uses the native Arabic word *al-madda* for matter. Ibn Sina even used *tin* on rare occasions. The Arabic language already possessed two words for cause – ʿ*illa* and *sabab* – and both were used philosophically.

Whatever the influence of Greek philosophy it is an influence, not a complete transplant. Al-Kindi wrote commentaries on Aristotle's *Prior Analytics*, *On Sophistical Refutations*, and an abridgement of the *Poetics*. He also wrote a commentary of the *Theology of Aristotle* (as Plotinus's *Enneads* were known). Al-Kindi may also have had translations of the *Rhetoric, Physics, On the Heavens, On Generation and Corruption, On the Soul*, the *Book of Animals*, and at least some of the *Metaphysics*.[51] Al-Kindi wrote commentaries or abridgements to Aristotle's *On Interpretation, Categories*, and *Posterior Analytics*.[52] According to his bibliographer al-Kindi may also have had access to Plato's *Republic*, under the title of *al-Siyasa*, which was explained in a commentary by Hunayn b. Ishaq (d. 260 AH/AD 873); as well as to the *Laws*, translated as *Kitab al-nawamis* by Hunayn ibn Ishaq.[53]

For al-Kindi, philosophy was one of the foreign sciences received with the Islamic conquests and transformed into an acceptable science. The Arabic-speaking society was an Islamic society in which the culture as well as the religion of Islam permeated the matrix of society. As has been frequently noted Islamic society practiced a monotheistic religion and perceived God as an agent in Muslims' lives. This contrasts strongly with the Hellenistic society which emphasized the humans' role and left the gods on Mount Olympus. The Arabs had a rich literary tradition of poetry and tales, an awareness of their cultural identity as Arabic-speakers. Also, there is a major difference between the Arabic language, by virtue of its Semitic structure, and the Indo-European structure of Greek. The use of *mawjud* and other words serve as a substitute for the copula, which exists in Greek but does not exist in Arabic.[54] Such grammatical differences lead one to expect other differences, if only because it is so difficult to make exactly the same statement in Arabic that one can make in an Indo-European language. Furthermore, the Arabs had a revealed book in their language; the Greeks did not. This undoubtedly changed their perspective and influenced the way they received the Greek tradition. The Greeks were not interested in creation from nothing. The idea of creation from nothing was prevalent in Islamic culture and religion, thus the *falasifa* were nearly forced to discuss it.

Geography was destiny. While some information came from the West (the old Greek lands), the centers of civilization (Baghdad, Damascus) of the Islamic empire received a steady infusion of Easterners from Central Asia, including such notables as Ibn Sina, who originated in the extreme Eastern edge of the old Persian empire. These intellectuals brought their own Eastern backgrounds with them, adding a new dimension to their perception of Hellenistic thought.

Al-Kindi's enduring influence can be seen in the ethical writings of the tenth/eleventh century philosopher Miskawayh. Miskawayh must have read al-Kindi's treatise *Fi al-hila li-daf^c al-ahzan* (*On the Art of Averting Sorrows*), because he quotes it extensively in his own ethical treatise *Tahdhib* *al-akhlaq.*[55] Miskawayh refers to his forerunner by name, Abu Yusuf ibn Ishaq al-Kindi. Al-Kindi influenced Ibn Sina in the definitional word order of *Kitab al-hudud* (*The Book of Definitions*). It follows the order of al-Kindi's *On the Definitions* written a century and a half earlier in such a way as to indicate Ibn Sina's familiarity with his predecessor's work. Likewise Ibn Sina quotes al-Kindi's definition of *al-ᶜishq* (passionate love), which is further evidence of his knowledge of the earlier *failasuf's* work. However Ibn Sina does not refer to al-Kindi by name.

In the next chapter al-Farabi's contribution to terminology in philosophy will be observed. By concentrating more closely on the translations of Aristotle and other sources, al-Farabi was able to refine the philosophical language. Already in the tenth century philosophy had acquired a well-established foundation, thus al-Farabi had a strong basis to develop his ideas about philosophy, language, and grammar. In the next chapter, the definitions of al-Farabi will be appraised, using those found in his *Kitab al-huruf* (*The Book of Letters*).

3

AL-FARABI: THE EMERGENCE OF ARABICIZED GREEK LOGIC

Abu Nasr al-Farabi (d. 339 AH/AD 950–951), the second *failasuf*, was particularly gifted in the field of logic. The great cataloger of Islamic humanities, Ibn al-Nadim, considered him as ranking with the foremost of the logicians.[1] Al-Farabi's other field was political philosophy – analyzing the relations of citizens in the state. In his book *Kitab al-huruf* (*The Book of Letters*), al-Farabi gives what is a philosophy of language approach to philosophy. He considered that people of other nations using all languages pursued logic and philosophy, in their own languages.[2] Al-Farabi argues that expressions in Arabic such as *al-mawjud* had their logical equivalents in other languages including Sogdian, Greek, and Persian. In Persian the expression is "*yaft*" and in Sogdian "*viyrd*."[3] In the same vein, he says that these words appear in Greek, Syriac, and other languages as well, although he does not give examples taken from any other languages.

Nevertheless, at the same time al-Farabi tried to domesticate the foreign science of philosophy by using indigenous Arabic words, and Persian words already used in the Arabic lands, rather than Greek loan words. While a word like *jawhar* (substance) comes from Persian, the widespread borrowing between Persian and Arabic meant it was not as foreign to Arabic speakers as a Greek word would be. Altogether the effect of al-Farabi's efforts is to Arabicize the vocabulary of Islamic philosophy. In this chapter, al-Farabi's usage of technical terms is scrutinized to distinguish it from al-Kindi's usage and to see what light this throws on the development of Islamic philosophy. The net effect is an attempt on al-Farabi's part to Arabicize philosophy.[4] The fame of his political philosophy is demonstrated by his most renowned work, *Kitab mabadi' ara' ahl al-madina al-fadila* (*The Book of the Principles of the Opinions of the People of the Virtuous City*), a Utopian view of the city, which focuses on the political organization of society.[5] Michael Marmura, in a review of Muhsin Mahdi's translation of *Alfarabi's Philosophy of Plato and Aristotle*, gives this summation of al-Farabi's attitude to metaphysics: "Indeed, throughout this treatise Alfarabi seems to deliberately avoid metaphysics. ... This is not to say that metaphysical discussion is totally absent, or that the argument does not operate within a metaphysical framework."[6] For example, in *The Virtuous City* he presents a metaphysical structure in order to legitimize political systems. Al-Farabi's views on metaphysics and natural philosophy emerge as an ancillary interest in books that deal overwhelmingly with logic or political philosophy. Therefore, to discuss metaphysical questions from al-Farabi the reader should be aware that these are not his primary interests, but only metaphysical tidbits collected and categorized from wherever they are available.

This chapter proceeds as follows: first a discussion of the relative merits of early and later translations from Greek into Arabic inasmuch as they affected al-Farabi; next stylistic points of al-Farabi's *Book of Letters*; then al-Farabi's definition of definition; followed by his definitions; and finally some conclusions about his views on definition.

The state of Greek translation in the tenth century

The translations from the Greek literature are specifically interesting for observing al-Farabi's use of particular translations. If these are translations which were not available to al-Kindi (because their date is known to be later than al-Kindi) then evidence exists that only al-Farabi could have used them. However whether or not al-Farabi had better translated texts to work with is a hotly debated issue. The traditional view is that translation technique improved drastically in the ninth century, when Hunayn ibn Ishaq and Ishaq ibn Hunayn created a more technical method of translating. This idea is expressed by H. Hugonnard-Roche as follows:

> Aux yeux de l'historien moderne, les conditions d'exécution des traductions d'oeuvres logiques et philosophiques paraissent changer radicalement vers le milieu de IXe siècle, grâce aux travaux de Hunayn ibn Ishaq et son fils Ishaq ibn Hunayn. Parmi les facteurs décisifs ayant entraîné ce changement se trouvent certainement la création par Hunayn et Ishaq d'une langue technique arabe apte à refléter de près la structure du grec (ou du grec par l'intermédiaire du syriaque), leur connaissance du grec bien supérieure à celle de leurs devanciers (et aussi leur bonne connaissance de l'arabe), leur attention portée aux problèmes de critique textuelle, et leur effort lexicographique.[7]

In most cases a quantitative comparison is difficult. Usually two versions of translated work (early and late) have not survived. A modern researcher is forced into the position of trusting hearsay evidence from early sources. When authors talk about "old translations" they may not still exist and consequently there is no basis to judge them objectively. J. N. Mattock did a comparative study of one text that survived in two versions, and concluded that the early translation might not be as accurate as the later, but neither was the early translation done in the unsophisticated word-for-word manner as is sometimes asserted.[8] A myth has arisen that early translators used a word-by-word technique, and later translators worked sentence-by-sentence, making sure they conveyed the sense. According to this school of thought, the early translations resulted in an inferior text.

Sebastian Brock divides the hellenization process, which includes the translation enterprise from Greek into Syriac into three phases. In the initial phase of the first period, according to Brock, Syriac Christians were hostile to what they viewed as pagan, Hellenic culture. The fourth-century Syriac writer Ephrem may serve to demonstrate the anti-Hellenic attitude with his remark, "Happy is the man who has not tasted of the venom of the Greeks."[9] This attitude shifted to admiration and imitation in the second phase, as Syriac Christians incorporated many Hellenic ideas into their own culture in the fifth and sixth centuries. Even devout Christians recognized the importance of rearing children "'in the wisdom of the Greeks.'"[10] The Hellenic slant became so pronounced that it was occasionally impossible to decide about a particular work if it was by a Syriac author working in Syriac as an original work, or a Syriac translation of a Greek work. In the third period, from the mid-eighth century to the mid-ninth century interest waned. Beyond Brock's timetable, a new cycle of revitalized interest began when the Caliph Ma'mun showed renewed interest in the translation of Greek works. Brock states that as translation technique developed concern shifted from the receptor language to representing the nuances of the original Greek text. According to Brock's theory, the early translations showed a concern for the receptor language and "the cultural background of the reader," adding to the text whatever information might increase the reader's understanding.[11] Brock makes his point with examples from the Church Doctors: "it can equally be seen in the translations of the Greek Fathers: whereas the fifth-century translation of Basil's works, for example, is exceedingly free and expands the material by up to fifty percent, the subsequent retranslation of the sixth or seventh century follows the Greek text very closely."[12] The third phase included the following elements: the consistent translation of technical terms, the transliteration of some Greek terms, and a recognition of the importance of word order. Brock describes this as the "transition from free to an exceedingly literal technique of translation."[13] Brock explains that the relative prestige of the two languages is very important. By the time of the ninth-century translations into Arabic, the prestige of Arabic was much greater than that of Greek. At this time, a sentence-by-sentence translation was the approved method, to ensure conveying the sense, rather than the literal word-by-word translation, which risked being incomprehensible without either a knowledge of Greek or teachers to explain the meanings.[14]

In addition to Aristotle's *Prior Analytics*, his *On Sophistical Refutations, Poetics, Rhetoric, Physics, On the Heavens, On Generation and Corruption, On the Soul, Book of Animals*, part of the *Metaphysics, On Interpretation, Categories*, and *Posterior Analytics* were all available in the ninth century. *Topics, Nicomachean Ethics*, and the rest of the *Metaphysics* were also translated. Plotinus's *Enneads* circulated under the title *The Theology of Aristotle*. As mentioned previously Plato's *Republic*, under the title of *al-Siyasah*, and the *Book of Laws*, translated as *Kitab al-nawamis*, were also current. From this list one can see that most of the same works were available to both al-Kindi and al-Farabi, although al-Farabi may have used different translations. Perhaps the most famous translator Ishaq ibn Hunayn (d. 289 AH/AD 910–1) – himself the son of the earlier translator Hunayn – translated the books of Aristotle's *Metaphysics* from small *Alif* to Book *Mu*.[15]

The style of *Kitab al-huruf*

In the Arabic-speaking world, Aristotle's *Metaphysics* was known as *Kitab al-huruf* (*The Book of Letters*), taking its title from the letters which formed chapter headings. This is attested by Ibn al-Nadim.[16] Book *Delta* (known as *Dal* in Arabic) is often considered Aristotle's philosophical lexicon, because in it he discusses philosophical terms. Al-Farabi's *Book of Letters* was meant as a commentary on the earlier work.[17] However, the Table of Contents of *The Book of Letters* indicates that the author of this work did not limit himself to the plan of the *Metaphysics*. Rather al-Farabi talks about ideas dealt with in both Aristotle's *Categories* and *Metaphysics*, as Muhsin Mahdi states in his introduction to *The Book of Letters*.[18] Ibn al-Nadim states that al-Farabi "explained" (*fassara*) the *Categories*.[19] In Part 1 of *The Book of Letters*, al-Farabi discusses "The Particles and the Categories,"[20] including particles (*huruf*) such as *anna* (that), *mata* (when), then the names of the Categories, followed by *nisba* (relation), and so on through a series of terms. The philosophical terms al-Farabi chooses are not given in the same order as in Aristotle's *Metaphysics*, Book *Delta*, nor are they the same terms. Al-Farabi's terms frequently verge on the grammatical, as for example, the section "Morphology and Inflection of Words" (*Ashkal al-alfaz wa-tasrifuha*).[21] Among al-Farabi's definitions is a long discussion of *jawhar* (substance), which will serve as an example of his treatment of a long definition.[22] First he begins his definition with the usage of *jawhar* found among the common people.[23] He then moves on to discuss the philosophical usage of the term *jawhar*.[24] This is contrary to the practice of al-Kindi who did not give popular usages of philosophical terms but only the strict philosophical usage. Al-Farabi gives both.

Part 2 of *The Book of Letters* is "The Origin of Words, Philosophy, and Religion." Here al-Farabi discusses language in terms of the relationships between nations and languages. In Part 3 he discusses "Interrogative Particles."

The definition of definition

There are two definitions of definition in Aristotle that are frequently cited, one descriptive and the other prescriptive. Both demonstrate the theoretical framework on which they stand. In the Arabic translation of *Topics* Aristotle says: *"fa al-hadd huwa al-qawl al-dall ᶜala mahiyya al-shay'."*[25] "Definition is a statement signifying the quiddity (*mahiyya*) of a thing." Aristotle's second definition is a more prescriptive form of definition: *"al-hadd ma'khadh min jins wa-fusul."*[26] That is, "Definition is taken from genus and differentiae." In Aristotle's *Topics* the definition is the what-it-is of a thing (*ma huwa*).[27] Aristotle has already asserted that there are four elements in a dialectical argument: definition, property, genus, and accident.[28] Thus the importance of definition as the primary element in argument is established.

Al-Farabi was the first to write extensively on definition, including both formal aspects and contextual (meaning) aspects. However no specific book or chapter on definitions by al-Farabi has survived. The philosophical query, "What is a definition?" indicates a search for epistemology: "How do we know what we know?" As mentioned in Chapter 1, essentialist definitions are so named because they define the essences of things, and therefore what is knowable about them. It is this type of definition in which al-Farabi takes an interest. He specifically discusses definition in these treatises: *Fi al-radd ᶜala Jalinus* (*The Refutation of Galen*), *al-Alfaz al-mustaᶜmala fi al-mantiq* (*The Utterances Employed in Logic*), and *Kitab al-burhan* (his paraphrase of Aristotle's *Posterior Analytics*).[29]

In his treatise *The Refutation of Galen* al-Farabi says that while studying the four causes one will learn the essence of a thing and thus its definition.[30] Here knowledge of the causes – formal, material, efficient, and final – is equated with definition. Through the philosopher's study of the world, he is able to grasp a world view of the framework that underlies it.

> And that which the natural art teaches about every natural body is knowledge of its substance. It is what its definition signifies about it; definition makes known its matter, its form, and its agent which generated it ... and the final [cause] for the sake of which it came to be.[31]

Thus al-Farabi states that definition reveals the matter, form, efficient cause, and final end of thing; in theory, knowledge of these factors forms the basis of our knowledge about something.

Al-Farabi's discussion of the theory of definition in *al-Alfaz* is a further amplification of his thinking. He says:

> When a complete definition is of a thing itself, and that definition makes it possible that one may respond with it in answering the question, what kind of thing is it? and that one may use the definition in signifying how to distinguish a thing from whatever is other than it. Definition makes known two aspects with respect to a thing: one is that it makes known the essence (*dhat*) and substance (*jawhar*) of a thing; and the second is that it makes known what distinguishes it from whatever is other than it.[32]

Al-Farabi uses one of his common expressions for definitions he considers to be correct here: *al-hadd al-kamil*, indicating a complete or perfect definition. The complete definition enables the reader to do two things: (1) to give positive answers to questions regarding what kind of a thing something is, that is, what its nature is, and (2) to distinguish the thing being defined from everything else; in other words to identify what it is not. In a sense this refers to positive and negative aspects of definition: what a thing is and what it is not.

Correct definitions indicate objects for al-Farabi. "Moreover the definition of a thing is used to replace a thing; it may be considered that there is no difference between a thing and its definition."[33] This statement indicates that a definition must convey knowledge of a real thing. Here al-Farabi is not interested in distinguishing between real existents and concepts, a distinction which will rather be discussed at a later stage in *Kitab al-burhan*. The point of the argument here is that definitions must be very closely correlated with the essence of things defined. They are not nominal definitions.

Chapter 3 in *al-Burhan* is entitled "A discussion of definitions and their types."[34] In this chapter al-Farabi uses the term *hadd* (definition) in different ways. First though, it may be remarked that *al-Burhan* appears to indicate a subtle Kindian influence. The phrase which translates as, "let us now speak about definitions and the things defined," comes near the opening of Chapter 3 of *al-Burhan*.[35] This echoes the title of al-Kindi's treatise which translated literally is "*On the Definitions of Things and Their Descriptions.*"[36] The different emphasis in al-Farabi's phrase may indicate his interest in the connection between language and reality, as found in this chapter of al-Farabi's *al-Burhan*. Al-Farabi talks about *al-hadd al-kamil* (a perfect definition)[37] or *ajza' al-hadd al-tamma* (the parts of the complete definition)[38] – two phrases commonly used for complete essential definitions. In *al-Burhan* he adds an additional dimension to completing (*ʿala al-tamam*) the definition in reality which is "... to everything which is necessary for definition in reality."[39] Also in this chapter al-Farabi uses the term *al-hadd al-awsat*[40] which is the technical term for the middle term of a syllogism. The word *hadd*, frequently used as a term for "definition," in this case, is used for "term" in this phrase, signifying the middle term. It is also a standard philosophical usage. In *al-Burhan* al-Farabi also discusses *al-hudud al-yaqiniyya* (certain or positive definitions),[41] a phrase which indicates the importance of the truth-value of definitions, rather than their completeness. He does not always talk about "certain definitions," for example, in *The Book of Letters* he does not discuss the certainty or surety of definitions.

In this study, the major interest is in what al-Farabi says about definitions and how he defines terms, rather than the truth-values of these definitions. In the treatise *The Refutation of Galen* the level of discourse is basic. It is a straightforward discussion of definition as a means of knowledge. In *The Utterances Employed in Logic*, a more sophisticated work, al-Farabi discusses the terms used in logic, not specifically affirming statements or the existence of the concepts described by the terms. In *The Book of Letters* the level of discourse is theoretical, with rather little discussion of the relationship of these terms to physical reality.

al-Farabi's definitions

As with al-Kindi, the terms to be investigated are those which al-Farabi used for substance, cause, and matter. They are *jawhar* (substance), *sabab* (pl. *asbab*, cause), and *al-madda* (matter). Already two of the terms – *sabab* and *madda* – are different from those used by al-Kindi. The baseline text will be *The Book of Letters*, a mature philosophical work, where definitions by al-Farabi can be found. No book entitled *Kitab al-hudud* (*The Book of Definitions*) is extant for al-Farabi. According to scholarly speculation it is believed that *The Book of Letters* is one of his mature works. The work is a commentary on the *Metaphysics*, and since metaphysics is studied after logic, natural science, and mathematics, according to the formal curriculum, one may assume al-Farabi would have written the commentary on *Metaphysics* after books on these other topics. Furthermore, in terms of internal evidence, al-Farabi refers to some of his books in *The Book of Letters*, such as *Kitab beri ermaynas* (commentary on *Peri Hermenias, On Interpretation*) and *Kitab al-qiyas* (commentary on *Prior Analytics*). Al-Farabi does not refer to the political books, such as *al-Madina al-fadila, al-Siyasa al-madaniyya*, or *Kitab al-milla* (respectively, *The Virtuous City, The Political Regime,* and *The Book of Religion*). From this evidence Muhsin Mahdi deduces that these works were probably composed after *The Book of Letters*. Thus, *The Book of Letters* appears to fall at least midway in al-Farabi's career, and as such one may view it as a mature work.[42] Consequently *The Book of Letters* will be the primary source for al-Farabi's definitions. First here is his definition of *jawhar* (substance).

Jawhar (substance)

It is customary to call this [thing which is] pointed to "the perceptible" by which nothing at all can be characterized, except accidentally and not in a natural way. Whatever is defining what this pointed to [thing] is, is substance in the absolute sense; just as they call it "essence" (*dhat*) in the absolute sense. Because the meaning of the substance of a thing is the essence of the thing, its quiddity, and part of its quiddity, therefore what is an essence in itself and is not an essence of a thing at all is a substance in the absolute sense, just as it is an essence in the absolute sense, without being related to a thing or restricted by a thing. It is the substance of this pointed to thing that makes known what this pointed to thing is.[43]

Comment In this definition of *jawhar*, al-Farabi says that substance is only characterized by attributes "not in a natural way." To understand this meaning of natural the reader should bear in mind that the contrary of natural here is metaphysical, that is, beyond the natural world. This indicates that al-Farabi intends to speak in a metaphysical sense. The word translated here as natural (*al-tabi'yy*) is the nisba adjective of the word used for physics, in the sense of the natural world. This is the Arabic translation of the term which Aristotle used philosophically to denote the perceptible world. What is beyond the physical world is the metaphysical world, hence al-Farabi's reference to the metaphysical as "not the natural." Al-Farabi says substance (*jawhar*) is the essence (*dhat*) and quiddity (*mahiyya*) of a thing. In this definition the words for "essence" (*dhat*) and "quiddity" (*mahiyya*) become near synonyms for "substance" (*jawhar*). The essence of a thing is found in its substance. The real-world existence (as opposed to the conceptual-level existence) of the substance of a thing is not directly discussed here; it is implied, however, by the phrase *hadha al-mashar ilyhi*, "this [thing] pointed to," which appears to indicate a specific, physical thing, existing in the natural world, and capable of being pointed to or referred to. Whatever is an essence per se, without qualification, and in the absolute sense, is what he means by *jawhar*. To find the *jawhar*, one must strip away the additives. When one describes, or makes known, the "what-it-is" (*ma huwa*) of a physical thing, one makes known its substance.

In this definition al-Farabi defines substance as unqualified, unconditional, the entity in itself, not in relation to anything else. In his discussion of *jawhar* (in *The Book of Letters*) there is no mention of substance as the "bearer" of anything. However al-Farabi does say that *jawhar* may have accidents, while al-Kindi described *jawhar* as having accidents in his *On the Definitions*.[44] Al-Farabi says nothing at all is attributed (*yusafu*) to *jawhar*, except in an accidental mode. Al-Kindi said substance carried accidents, using *hamil*. As mentioned before, al-Kindi also uses the verb root *w-s-f* in his definition.[45] But to say it is an essence "in the absolute sense" can be interpreted as another way of saying it is the underlying subject, or the subject without properties. Al-Farabi's point here is not to deny the existence of attributes or characteristics, but to isolate the substance of a thing from them.

In contrast to al-Kindi, an ordinary language definition of *jawhar* immediately precedes and contrasts with this technical definition in al-Farabi's *Book of Letters*. Al-Farabi says that for the common people the meaning refers to something mined out of the ground; to precious gems, such as sapphires and pearls; and to what is valuable and rare.[46] This was the original meaning in Persian.

The *Book of Categories* (*Kitab al-maqulat*)[47] is another commentary, or paraphrase, that al-Farabi wrote on Aristotle's *Categories*.[48] In comparison with *The Book of Letters*, in *The Book of Categories* al-Farabi discusses the term *jawhar* (substance) in more obviously Aristotelian terms. In comparing the text of al-Farabi's statement with Aristotle's this becomes self-evident. Al-Farabi says: "Then there is no requirement for its subsistence in a subject at all, because substance (*jawhar*) is not in a subject, nor [is it said] of any subject."[49] In comparison, in the *Categories* Aristotle says in his chapter on *jawhar*: "It is a general feature of every substance that it is not in a subject, so primary substance is not said of any subject, nor is it in a subject."[50] Al-Farabi's statement is a very close repetition of Aristotle's statement: substance neither exists in a subject nor is said of a subject. Such passages indicate why al-Farabi is considered to be a very Aristotelian thinker.

In *The Book of Categories* al-Farabi states that *jawhar* is composed of form and matter, specifically stating that it has an embodied or corporeal aspect.[51] Al-Farabi gives examples of *jawhar* which indicate this: the heavens, the stars, the earth, water, and stone.[52] Individuals are the first substances and universals secondary substances.[53] Al-Farabi asserts that if a person imagines individuals who do not exist, this is a *mukhtaricʿan kadhiban* (false invention).[54] As mentioned above, he did not discuss the real-world existence of substances in *The Book of Letters* passage. Sometimes al-Farabi does not repeat Aristotle's teachings in the same words, but he may repeat the ideas or use examples found in Aristotle. This is shown in al-Farabi's definition of cause, *sabab*, which appears next.

Sabab/asbab (causes)

There appear to be three kinds of particles by which reasons (*asbab*) and causes (*ʿilal*) for the existence of a thing are sought: "Why?" does it exist, "by what?" does it exist, and "from what?" does it exist.[55]

Comment Al-Kindi used *ʿilla* for cause. Al-Farabi substituted *sabab* for *ʿilla* to signify cause. His use of *sabab* (cause, reason) is a primary example of an ordinary-language Arabic word being used in a specialized philosophical way. This use of specialized language frequently occurs in discussions of causation. Indeed, M. E. Marmura echoes this in his discussion of al-Ghazali, saying, "Al-Ghazali's use of causal language as ordinarily used in Arabic and in the way it is used by the Islamic philosophers is not a phenomenon that one meets only in the *Ihya'* and subsequent works."[56] Like ʿilla, sabab means cause. While either word can be and is used for cause, the link between cause and effect is weaker and more specialized than the ordinary language version. Al-Farabi may have been influenced by Ishaq b. Hunayn, translator of Aristotle's *Physics*, who frequently used asbab.[57]

With this definition al-Farabi indicates his understanding of Aristotle's causes as relating to the means, reasons, or principles of a thing. Al-Farabi uses sabab extensively for "cause" unlike al-Kindi who uses ʿilla. Such shift in emphasis as seen in al-Farabi is due to his interpretation of Aristotle in connection with his own interests, namely grammar and logic. Initially he remarks that he will deal with the kind of particles used to discuss the reasons and causes of a thing. Here, al-Farabi moves in a linguistic, as opposed to biological direction. This inclination also follows Aristotle's direction, in the sense that scholars have observed grammatical, as well as philosophical perspectives in the *Categories*. As many of the terms in the text of the *Categories* are ambiguous, the primary focus can be argued either way. The linguistic interpretation may account for al-Farabi's restatement of Aristotle's four causes in terms of the grammatical particles used to elicit them.

Al-Farabi has considered the questions involved in the four causes and has recast them in three groups. His three questions are why? (*lima*), by what means? (*bi-madha*), and from what? (*ʿan madha*). The question asked by *lima* (Why?), like the particle *li-ajl*, indicates what Aristotle called the final cause, or purpose and end.[58] The second, *bi-madha*, includes the preposition *bi*, indicating "by means of what?" The expression of a search for the agent indicates the efficient cause of a thing. The third phrase *ʿan madha* indicates the material cause and formal cause, inasmuch as the particle *ʿan* means the same as *min* "from." The particle *ʿan* combines the two intrinsic causes.[59] This is consistent with al-Farabi's other writings, as he uniformly denies the separate existence of form and matter.[60] These questions and even the form he puts them in, reflect al-Farabi's reinterpretation of Aristotle. He does not just list the causes as Aristotle does, he reinterprets them as questions. This shows he is thinking through the implications of the causes, not just parroting them. Aristotle's discussion in the *Physics* (*al-Tabiʿa*) also collapses three of the causes together into one.[61] As mentioned previously, the ideas about definition grew out of the question, what is it (*ma huwa*)? The questions al-Farabi now asks radiate from the central "what is it?" question. When he can answer "what is it?" then al-Farabi will ask, "why is it?" (or, "what is its final cause?"), "from what is it?" (and this can be asked about the material and formal causes), and "by what means is it?" The question "what is it?" is a logical one. Therefore, according to this analysis, in his logical mode al-Farabi does not really discuss metaphysical questions. Cause is reviewed only in terms of the effects generated on the sublunar world, not as an active, divine entity.

"The terms *ᶜilla* and *sabab* are frequently used synonymously to mean 'cause,' except that in some cases *sabab* is used in a less precise sense referring to motives and apparent causes."[62] As mentioned above, al-Farabi rarely uses the word *ᶜilla*. Al-Kindi, on the other hand, uses *ᶜilla* for "cause" in at least two senses. He uses it as the First Cause, for the creator – this is in the sense of an agent, an actively involved sense, and, he uses the plural, *ᶜilal*, when he discusses the four causes – formal, final, efficient and material. However the word Ibn Ishaq frequently uses for "causes" in his translation of *al-Tabiᶜa* (*Physics*) is *al-asbab*.[63] These are impersonal and Aristotelian, and refer to cause and effect as natural laws in the scientific sense, rather than the volition of a being as an active or agential force. In another treatise al-Farabi separates out the second sense and uses *mabadi'* as the word for "causes" or "principles" referring to this set of four causes mentioned by Aristotle.[64]

Next is al-Farabi's discussion of matter, using *al-madda*.[65]

al-Madda (matter)

It is clear that the perfect quiddity of the thing is only by means of a thing's form when it is in matter, adapted, supporting in actuality, generating it. Thus matter inevitably enters into its quiddity. Thus by a thing's form its quiddity is in its matter which was only generated for the sake of its form that is generated for a certain end. When it is thus, there is the disposition which is what people mean by their term "substance"; which is only the quiddity of a human being, and it is that by which a human is a human in actuality. Thus they mean only by substance the quiddity of a human, it is thus that Zayd is a substance, or his ancestors, or his kind. Also thus it is they think that his fathers and his mothers and his kind – from antiquity – are material components from which they are generated. They think when the material components of a thing are good, the thing is good, like the components of a wall or the components of a bed. They think that when the wood is good, the bed is good, because the goodness of the wood is the cause of the goodness of the bed; and if the stones, unburnt bricks, baked bricks, and clay are good, the wall built of them will be good also, because the goodness of these is the cause of the goodness of the wall. It is according to this example that they reason concerning the fathers, the mothers, and the ancestors, the *qabila*,[66] the community, and the people of the country of human beings; for many people imagine that these are the material components from whom or by means of whom the human being comes to be. The material components of a thing are either its quiddity or the parts of its quiddity. Therefore they mean by substance here only its quiddity or what [is] a quiddity by means of it.[67]

Comment While this thing's quiddity is perfected by its form, matter is also intrinsically part of the quiddity, that is, the essence of a thing. Matter supports and adapts the form in the actual world. In this section al-Farabi argues for the impossibility of either matter or form existing independently of the other. This ties in with the notion of substance being a combination of form and matter.

Al-Farabi states that when a thing's quiddity exists it does so by its form and in matter, once again emphasizing the interconnection of the two. Matter exists only through form. Then he moves into a discussion of general opinions on matter. He states that people think that when the matter composing a thing is good, the thing itself will be good. It is interesting that his first example is of the material components of human beings. If they are good, the humans will be good. What are the material components of humans? He then describes how human beings are good. According to al-Farabi, the material aspects of a human being are his or her parents and ancestors. As al-Farabi says, "... his fathers and his mothers and his kind – from antiquity – are material components from which they are generated."[68] By the analogy of a wall or a bed, with other material elements, these components are their ancestors, going back in time, as well as their parents and their stock. In all of these cases, when the materials are good, the resulting things are good. This raises the indirect issue of predestination or predetermination of acts in genetic terms. If humans are good because their material components are good, they will do good acts. They are predisposed to good acts, by their good material components. If good wood is used to make a bed, the product will be good.

Al-Farabi uses chiefly *madda* (pl. *mawadd*) for matter, and rarely the transliterated Greek loan word, *hayula*. One of his rare uses of *hayula* does occur in *Masa'il*: "Matter is the last of the identities, and the lowest of them. Were it not to receive the form, it would actually be non-existent, [indeed] it was non-existent in potentiality then it received the form, so it became a substance. ..."[69] *Madda* is an Arabic word, but not a Qur'anic word. In observing the Farabian use of *madda*, this may be interpreted as a desire to Arabicize the vocabulary, rather than to use the Greek loan word *hayula*. It also compartmentalizes philosophy keeping it separate from the Qur'an by not using a word found in the Qur'an. The word preferred in the Qur'an for the matter of creation is *tin* (literally, clay).[70] The ideas al-Farabi expresses here are compatible with the Aristotelian concept of form and matter as co-existent. In *The Book of Letters* he rarely speaks about matter at all. He uses words derived from *jism* (body), not *madda*, in his discussion of the material aspect of *jawhar* in *al-Maqulat*.[71]

In comparison, he gives this treatment of the concept matter in *The Political Regime*, also using *al-madda*:

> Form is the corporeal substance in a body, like the shape of a bed is in the bed, while matter is like the wood of the bed. Thus form is that through which an embodied substance becomes a substance in actuality, while matter (*madda*) is that through which it is a substance in potentiality.... Matter only exists for the sake of forms.... Thus when there are no forms, the existence of matter is false.... Thus it is not possible for prime matter[72] to exist deprived of a form.[73]

As this quote demonstrates, when al-Farabi has occasion to discuss "prime matter" he uses the expression *al-madda al-ula*.[74] He does not use *al-hayula*. This leads the reader to wonder if he may consider *al-madda* and *al-hayula* to be interchangeable terms. Al-Farabi denies that there is a prime matter without form.[75] He also denies matter can exist without form.[76]

Conclusions

Another aspect of al-Farabi's thought was his interest in combining the views of Plato and Aristotle, as seen in his treatise *The Harmonization of the Opinions of Plato and Aristotle*.[77] He is known for emphasizing Aristotle's teachings in his philosophy. While neo-Platonic elements, such as emanation, can be found in al-Farabi's philosophy, the scholarly debate rages over whether he actually believed in emanation. Some scholars think that al-Farabi mentioned it merely to make philosophy more palatable to general readers of his popular works.[78] Al-Farabi was tremendously concerned with putting items in order[79] and giving them a rank. His idea to harmonize the thought of Plato and Aristotle is apparent throughout his work. Al-Farabi is Platonic in appearing to believe in the world of the Forms, since a thing must exist in potentiality before it can become "real." He is Aristotelian in paraphrasing many of Aristotle's ideas – those found in the *Categories*, and Aristotle's description of the sphere, for example. While it is the current academic trend in the twentieth century to focus on the intellectual conflicts between Plato and Aristotle, it can be just as valid to focus on their similarities.

Scholars are still debating the exact contribution of al-Farabi, but whatever the case, he was not merely a blind follower of Aristotle. Zimmermann says:

> This is not, however, to say that al-Farabi's theory of language and thought must have had a precise model in the Greek tradition. Such fragments of Greek tradition lost to us as he may have been able to draw upon are not likely to have been much more explicit than those surveyed above; and in reconstructing ancient theory he no doubt

produced some new ideas. But the preceding excursus has shown that his synthesis was broadly based indeed; and because his writings, while rarely specifying their sources, purport to reproduce the teaching of "the ancients" it is hard to tell where tradition ends and his own contribution begins.[80]

Al-Farabi's writings leave the impression of being more strongly influenced by the Greeks than al-Kindi's were. This impression is the case even when specific texts cannot be identified, both because his remarks frequently sound similar to Greek philosophy – particularly Aristotle – and because al-Farabi often states he is repeating the teachings of the Ancients. The first factor is exemplified by his description of substance as not being in a subject.[81] This is an example taken from Aristotle.[82] Even when not repeating Aristotle's words, he writes in a similar manner or with similar ideas, such as in his discussion of the four causes mentioned above. Al-Farabi reiterates these ideas in a different, but recognizable form. Richard Walzer is convinced that al-Farabi merely repeats Greek texts, possibly lost, but ones that he read.

The quest for the identity of the Greek authorities whom al-Farabi used in the *Ara'* and similar writings does not yield absolutely certain results. This cannot be otherwise, since only a fraction of the Greek philosophical literature which became accessible to Syrians and Arabs from the fifth and eighth centuries respectively eventually reached the Western Latin tradition and thus became known to Western scholars.[83]

Similarly Walzer believes al-Farabi's commentary on Aristotle's *Peri Hermeneias* depended on a lost commentary by Porphyry.[84] The second factor, namely al-Farabi's comment that he is repeating the teachings of the Ancients, may be attributed to the value placed on tradition in Islamic society. Consequently it was not unknown for authors to cloak their own ideas in the names from the past; it is not a statement to be taken at face value.

Al-Farabi mentions the Necessary of Existence (*wajib al-wujud*) and the possible of existence (*mumkin al-wujud*).[85] Both of these concepts refer to cause: a thing with no cause is Necessary of Existence; those with causes are possible of existence. While this sense of causation is touched on only briefly in the Farabian world view, it will be expanded in the following century in the philosophy of Ibn Sina. Nevertheless, these germinative terms first appeared in the works of Ibn Sina's predecessor.

In the next chapter the definitions of Ibn Sina, as found in his *Book of Definitions* (*Kitab al-hudud*), will be investigated. In Ibn Sina there is a combination of al-Farabi's re-Aristotelianized concepts with a Kindian influence and other factors, resulting in a style that is distinctly Ibn Sina's.

Although Kindian influence on Ibn Sina, both in form and content, has not been much remarked, there are quantifiable traces. In Chapter 4 the focus is primarily on Ibn Sina in isolation. In Chapter 5, the comparative chapter, his relationship with his predecessors will be more closely examined.

4

IBN SINA: THE SECOND *BOOK OF DEFINITIONS*

First there was the pioneering Philosopher of the Arabs, al-Kindi; next the *failasuf* al-Farabi who melded Greek thought with a more Arabic and Islamic frame of mind; and third came Ibn Sina, a philosopher who absorbed influences from many intellectual trends and synthesized them into a new world view. Ibn Sina had the fortune to be born in Bukhara during "interesting times" which led to his fleeing ever westward in a search for political security and royal patronage.

Ibn Sina's writings owe a substantial debt to the content and style of al-Kindi's *On the Definitions* – even though al-Kindi did not discuss definition per se – as will become apparent. As is typical in Islamic manuscripts, Ibn Sina did not formally acknowledge a debt to al-Kindi's work, even when quoting him directly. Ibn Sina was also influenced by al-Farabi, especially in his views on what constitutes a definition.

Abu ᶜAli al-Husayn Ibn Sina (d. 428 AH/AD 1037) wrote a treatise on definitions, known as *Kitab al-hudud (Book of Definitions);* it is only the second major philosophical work on definitions in that genre that survives.[1] Like al-Kindi's *On the Definitions* a large number of terms are defined briefly. It contrasts with al-Farabi's *Book of Letters*, which resembles more clearly the technique of Aristotle's Book Delta (the *Metaphysics*) stylistically, giving longer and more thorough definitions for a smaller number of terms.

The first section of this chapter will cover the style of Ibn Sina's *Book of Definitions*. Style here is meant to include the content of his work, its organization and such characteristics as may serve to differentiate it from his predecessors. In considering Ibn Sina's *Book of Definitions* the order of his definitions will be compared with that of al-Kindi's treatise, *On the Definitions*. In the second section there is an analysis of Ibn Sina's definition of definition. In the third section his definitions of the three concepts under investigation are examined. This section will lay the groundwork for a detailed comparative analysis of his definitions with those of al-Kindi and al-Farabi in Chapter 5. The fourth section serves to summarize the ideas of this chapter.

The style of Ibn Sina's Book of Definitions

Although it is longer than al-Kindi's treatise, *The Book of Definitions* is still a very short work. Unlike al-Kindi's book, Ibn Sina's begins with a formal introduction (*dibaja*).[2] Ibn Sina opens by saying:

> Friends asked me to dictate the definitions of things to them; they requested me to define specific things.[3]

The order of Ibn Sina's definitions is compared to that of al-Kindi in the following chart.[4] The order of words defined in Ibn Sina is: definition, description, and the Creator (*al-bari*) followed by the rest of the definitions. Between the definition of description and that of the Creator he inserts the word *fasl* (chapter), perhaps to indicate a break before the main body of definitions. Structurally the Introduction leads into a discussion of definition, followed by the definition of definition. For purposes of charting definition (*hadd*) and description (*rasm*) are ignored, and the list begins with "the Creator," since these terms come before the main definitions and since al-Kindi did not define these terms. The purpose of these charts is to discover whether or not there is a congruence of word order in the two books. As the text contains the word *fasl* (chapter) immediately before Ibn Sina's definition of the Creator (*al-bari*) it appears to be a signpost indicating a new section. Apart from this adjustment, the chart shows the order of the two lists as they occur.

Al-Kindi	**Ibn Sina**
first cause	the Creator (*al-bari*)
intellect	intellect
nature	soul
soul	form
body	matter (*al-hayula*)
creation (*al-ibda^c*)	the subject
matter (*hayula*)	matter (*al-madda*)
form	element (*^cunsur*)
element (*^cunsur*)	element (*ustuqas*)
act	building block (*rukn*)
work	nature (*tabiy^ca*)
substance	disposition (*tabi^c*)
choice	body (*jism*)
quantity	substance (*jawhar*)

Al-Kindi[5]	Ibn Sina
first cause	the Creator (*al-bari*)
intellect	intellect
...	...
soul	soul
matter (*hayula*)	form
form	matter (*al-hayula*)
element (*'unsur*)	element (*'unsur*)
{nature}	nature (*tabiy{c}a*)
substance	substance

The first chart represents the raw order of the two philosophers' lists. The second chart represents a modified scheme, demonstrating the correlation of word order between al-Kindi and Ibn Sina. Both lists begin with a term referring to God, called the First Cause in al-Kindi and the Creator in Ibn Sina. After the definition of God the following terms also fall in the same relative order: intellect (*al-{c}aql*), soul (*al-nafs*), form (*al-sura*), element (*al-{c}unsur*), and substance (*al-jawhar*). In al-Kindi's list nature (*al-tabiy{c}a*) occupies the third place, while it is eleventh in Ibn Sina's. Both have gaps before defining substance (*al-jawhar*) – in the twelfth position in al-Kindi and the fourteenth in Ibn Sina. One of the words for matter, *al-hayula*, falls within one line of the same position.

This group of eight terms is too congruent to be accidental. Based on this side-by-side comparison it appears that Ibn Sina followed a modified version of al-Kindi's order. Furthermore in their respective definitions of nature, soul, matter (*al-hayula*), and substance there is a similarity of definitions. Ibn Sina repeats some part of al-Kindi's definitions in these terms. The definitions of God are dissimilar – Ibn Sina gives a definition similar to that of the Mu{c}tazilis in the sense that it lists negative qualities.[6] The definitions of intellect, form, and element (*al-{c}unsur*) are also dissimilar.[7] However, the similarities demonstrate a Kindian influence on Ibn Sina, both in definitional order and content. We will discuss the nature of this influence in greater detail in Chapter 5.

In Ibn Sina's *Book of Definitions* the body of definitions follows the introduction. They may be as brief as a line or a sentence. The longer definitions are laid out in dictionary style; he gives several meanings, assigning ordinal numbers to each, and then directs the reader's attention to the appropriate meaning by using examples. The definitions are concise, and many of them are laid out in a formulaic manner. In most of the definitions the definiens follows the definiendum immediately, without the addition of a copula (i.e., pronoun).[8] Likewise, the word *hadd* (definition) sometimes appears before the term under consideration, sometimes not.⁹ The basic structure is: "x: y with a and b" or "x: y which is a and/or b." Many of Ibn Sina's definitions begin with the formula: "x is a common term (*ism mushtarak*) with several/a number of meanings."¹⁰ They may prove to have several different senses, listed one after the other, and separated by the conjunction "and" *wa*, indicating a break in thought. After these different senses, the following paragraph indicates which sense (of the term) refers to a particular notion. In the definition of substance, for example, he says that whiteness, heat, and motion are examples of *jawhar* (substance) in the first sense, while *hayula* (matter) is a substance in the fourth and fifth senses; *hayula* is not a substance in the second and third.¹¹ Al-Kindi's definitions are short to aid in memorization, while Ibn Sina's definitions are mostly too long to memorize. After the last definition Ibn Sina ends the book with a short statement that it is finished.

Ibn Sina on definition of *"hadd"*

Ibn Sina, in contrast to al-Kindi who did not define *hadd* (definition), begins his book of definitions with the definition of *hadd*. In the introductory matter of the treatise before the technical definitions, Ibn Sina discusses definition in a discursive manner, somewhat reminiscent of al-Farabi's discussion of definition in *The Book of Letters*. Ibn Sina says that in true definitions logic guides in demonstrating the quiddity of a thing, the perfection of its essential existence, with no separation of the essential predicates of a thing from it, unless they are included either in actuality or in potentiality. Such a definition is in reality equal to the thing defined.¹²

In comparing Ibn Sina on definition with al-Farabi on definition, there are some remarkable similarities. While al-Farabi writes about *al-hudud al-yaqiniyya* (certain definitions), Ibn Sina discusses *al-hudud al-haqiqiyya* (real definitions).¹³ For Ibn Sina definition is: "a signification (*dalla*) of the essence of the thing."¹⁴ For al-Farabi definition is used: "in signifying (*dalala*) how to distinguish the thing."¹⁵ Thus, for both philosophers, the purpose of definitions is to signify, or indicate something. For Ibn Sina it signifies the essence of something; for al-Farabi it signifies the distinction of something from something else. They both use the same root, *dalla*, meaning "to signify, indicate," although in different forms. At this point, Ibn Sina says that a definition is complete (*kamal*) under certain circumstances. Al-Farabi has begun this section referring to a complete (*kamal*) definition. Furthermore, as mentioned in Chapter 3, al-Farabi says that while studying the four causes one will learn the essence of a thing and thus its definition. While not specifically relating definition to four causes, Ibn Sina still emphasizes that form and matter combine to generate the essence of a thing which is defined – so at least two of the causes (formal and material) are worked into his theory of definition. Al-Farabi says of definition, "... it is considered that there is no difference between a thing and its definition."[16] Ibn Sina says, "When a definition is thus it is equal to the defined thing in reality."[17] Consequently it is clear that Ibn Sina has relied on al-Farabi for his ideas about essential definitions.

Ibn Sina explicitly indicates his debt to Aristotle in the *Topics* in his technical definition of *hadd*.

> The definition of definition is what the wise man (Aristotle) mentions in the book, *Topics*: it is *a statement indicating (pointing to) the quiddity (mahiyya) of a thing*, that is, regarding the perfection of its essential existence. It (definition) is what is obtained from its proximate genus and its differentia (*fasl*).[18]

The italicized portion of the definition is quoted from Aristotle's definition in *Topics*. The second part is paraphrased from Porphyry's *Eisagoge*.[19] The definition of *rasm*, usually translated as "description," follows the definition of definition (*hadd*).[20]

In *al-Ilahiyyat*, Ibn Sina discusses definitions and what exactly they signify in detail. After stating that both matter and form are found in definition he says:[21]

> ... [R]ather it is a combination of form and matter (*madda*), for this is what the composite is; and quiddity is this composition. So form is the one to which composition is added, and quiddity is this self-same composition that combines form and matter. The unity arising from the two of them is through this one.

In this definition Ibn Sina states one of the basic philosophical problems, the relationship of form and matter. Here he states that both form and matter unite to compose the quiddity or essence of a thing, and this essence must be defined in a definition. If definitions define both form and matter, then true definitions yield knowledge of real things.

Ibn Furak (d. 1015), who wrote definitions of Islamic theology and law, gave this definition of definition: "It is a statement distinguishing between the thing defined and what has nothing to do with it in any way."[22] This demonstrates the strong contrast between Ibn Sina's philosophical definition, which particularly indicates the use of definitions to search for the essence of things and the point of view of a jurisprudent who initially takes an ordinary language approach. This comparison is interesting because Ibn Furak is a close contemporary of Ibn Sina, but Ibn Furak's definition reflects his professional bias, rather than his era.

Ibn Sina's definitions

For the term substance Ibn Sina also uses *al-jawhar*, like both his predecessors. For cause there are brief definitions for both *al-ᶜilla* (cause) and *al-maᶜlul* (the caused). For matter Ibn Sina defines two terms in his *Book of Definitions*: the Greek loan word *al-hayula* and the Arabic word *al-madda*. While a thorough comparison of Ibn Sina with al-Kindi and al-Farabi will be found in Chapter 5, a few points will be noted here.

Jawhar (substance)

The definition of substance (*jawhar*). It is a common term. Substance is said of the essence of every existent, such as a human being or whiteness. Substance is also said of every thing existing in itself, because its essence does not need another essence associated with it for it to be subsisting in actuality. This is the meaning of their phrase "substance is self-subsisting."

Substance is also said of whatever has this attribute and is such as to receive opposites in succession. Substance is also said to belong to every essence whose existence is not in a substratum. Substance is said to belong to every essence whose existence is not in a subject. Ancient philosophers since the time Aristotle have adopted the usage of the expression "substance." We have already differentiated previously between subject and substratum. The meaning of their phrase "an existent not in a subject" is: the existent is not associated[23] with the existence of the substratum; it is self-subsistent in actuality; self-establishing in itself; it does not matter that it is in a substratum, although the substratum does not subsist without it in actuality, for even though it were in a substratum, it would not be in a subject.

Every existent, whether it is whiteness or heat or motion, is a substance in the first sense. The first principle is substance, in regard to the second, fourth, and fifth meanings; it is not substance in the third sense. Matter is substance in the fourth and fifth senses. It is not substance in the second and third senses. Form is substance in the fifth sense, but it is not substance in the second, third, and fourth senses. It is not necessary to squabble over the terms.[24]

Comment This definition has five shades of meaning. *Jawhar* is, briefly: (1) the essence or quiddity (*dhat*) of everything; (2) subsisting in itself; (3) having the ability to receive opposing qualities; (4) not in a place; and (5) not in a subject.

Initially *jawhar* is defined as: *dhat kull shay'*. This sense functions as a synonymous term, rather than a definition. *Dhat* is a problematic word, translatable as "essence," but not providing much information to the uninitiated. One meaning of the word *dhat* is to indicate a thing-in-itself; the philosophical usage focuses this reference in a technical way indicating the essence of a thing-in-itself.[25] In this phrase *dhat* signifies "the *x*-ness" of everything, which is its essence. The word *jawhar* also signifies the essence or quiddity of a thing. Ibn Sina initially gives two examples of this meaning: a human being and whiteness.

The idea of subsisting in itself reiterates al-Kindi's comments. We may note that Ibn Sina's phrase "subsisting in its essence" is similar to al-Kindi's phrase "subsisting in itself," in his *On The Definitions*, in both words and meaning.[26] Ibn Sina's phrase may be translated either as "which is self-subsisting" or, like al-Kindi's phrase, "subsisting in itself." Ibn Sina also adds that it is subsisting in actuality. This emphasizes substance as present in reality, in actuality, over "in potentiality." The dichotomy between actuality and potentiality is one of the primary Sinawiyyan distinctions.[27]

Ibn Sina's third sense is being able to receive contrary qualities. It may imply substance as a bearer of accidents. Contrary qualities must be qualities which are non-essential in nature. When substance receives them these qualities do not change a substance's nature in an essential way. Viewed in this light substance resembles al-Kindi's phrasing, that it is the "bearer of accidents," although Ibn Sina does not explicitly state this.

Substance is neither in a place, nor in a subject. *Jawhar* is not the object of physics, an additional point that is borne out by Ibn Sina's statement in *al-Ilahiyyat*.[28]

Although these five discrete senses may not be apparent initially, the fact that Ibn Sina spells out in the following paragraph which sense is used in particular ways along with examples and a numerical reference to the sense, indicates that he does intend this. He gives examples for *jawhar*'s five meanings. Matter (*hayula*) is a substance in the fourth and fifth senses. Matter is not something that has quiddity in itself (first sense). It must exist with form (second sense). Therefore matter is not a substance *in itself*. Secondly, it does not exist by itself. On the other hand, it is a substance in the last two senses. Matter is not in a place (fourth sense), and it belongs to every substance whose existence is not in a subject (fifth). Ibn Sina did not give a specific example of his third sense. One must conclude that he believed it was self-evident and obvious.

The idea that substance is not receptive to generation and corruption may be implied in the emphasis given to its independence, i.e., it does not owe its existence to another. Ibn Sina does not state this directly, however. As for existing in the particular – another Kindian idea –, Ibn Sina says every existent (*kull mawjud*) is a substance. Ibn Sina's terminology differs from that of al-Kindi, referring to the particulars by the term "every existent." His examples here are rather general (whiteness, heat, motion).

al-ʿIlla (cause)

Cause. Every being which exists has existence from another essence in actuality. This being has existence in actuality and existence of this being in actuality is not from the existence of that one in actuality.[29]

al-Maʿlul (the caused)

The caused is every being (*dhat*)[30] whose existence in actuality comes from the existence of another being, but the existence of that other being is not from its existence. The meaning of our phrase "from its existence" is not the same as the meaning of our phrase "with its existence." Indeed, the meaning of our phrase "from its existence" is that a being is, in consideration of itself, a possible existent, and its existence only becomes necessary in actuality, not from itself; but rather because another actually existing being makes the existence of the second being necessary on its account. A being has possibility in itself. Thus it has in itself possibility without condition; and it has existence in itself by condition of the necessary cause. A being has existence in itself on condition that there is no cause to prevent it.

The difference between our phrase "without condition" and the phrase "with a condition of not" is like the difference between our phrase "there is no white stick" and "a stick is not white." As for the meaning of our phrase "with its existence," it means that if one of the two beings is presumed existent, it follows logically that one knows the other is existent. If one is supposed removed, it follows that the other is removed. The cause and the caused come together in the meaning of these two concomitants. Aspects of the concomitants are different; because one of the two, which is the caused, if one supposes it existent, it follows logically that the other was already itself in existence, therefore this being existed. As for the other, which is the cause, if one supposes it existent, it follows logically that its existence will be followed by the existence of the caused. If the caused is removed it follows logically that the cause had been removed first; it is sound that this one could be removed, but not that the removal of the caused necessitated the removal of the cause. As for the cause, if we abstract it, the caused will be abstracted by necessity of the abstraction of the cause, which abstracts it.[31]

Comment Cause is what brings entities into actual existence. The first definition does not mention possibility or potentiality. Existent *x* had *no* cause itself. It is subsistent in and of itself alone. However, it was only able to bring *a*, *b*, *c*, *d*, *e*, and so on into existence because they contained a kernel of potential existence. There is one cause *x*, which is the only existent without a cause.

That it is this potentiality or possibility of existence which Ibn Sina is referring to becomes clear when we look at the following definition "the caused" or "the effect."

The term *bi-al-fi^{c}l* reverberates with the idea of the efficient cause.[32] This cause is outside the entity in question in every case. The cause itself does not have an external cause in actuality. Ibn Sina does not accept the idea of an infinite regress. The definition of *ma^{c}lul* may imply one cause behind all other entities, which is not from those others, and which brings out the potentiality in the substance/substrate of every thing.

In this definition the caused must have a possibility, which gives it potentiality to be brought into existence by the cause. This core of potentiality is that which allows a thing to become actual – like a metaphysical kernel within a substance. In these definitions, Ibn Sina is not discussing the four causes, nor do they appear in *The Book of Definitions*. He is discussing the immediate cause. "Cause" refers to an actuality; the cause is an essence in actuality, it gives existence to other essences.

In his *Metaphysics* Ibn Sina discusses the four causes in a more Aristotelian manner. He says: "The causes are, as you have heard, form, element, efficient, and final."[33] In this case Ibn Sina uses *^{c}unsur*, the term for "element" to indicate what is usually known as the "material" cause. This follows al-Kindi's usage in his work *On First Philosophy* (*Fi al-falsafa al-ula*).[34] This is an interesting confluence of terms, particularly as Ibn Sina does not use either *madda* or *hayula* here to represent the material cause. In his definition of "element" (*al-^{c}unsur*) in *The Book of Definitions* Ibn Sina states that it is "material" (*al-hayula*).[35]

Ibn Sina makes a distinction between "from (*min*) its existence" and "with (*ma^c*) its existence." "From (*min*) its existence" means "from" in the sense of "out of" (partitively) – therefore entities partake of the existence of another thing. Possible existents are only necessary in the sense that they become actualized from another existent, and this existent makes them necessary. "With its existence" incorporates the notion that a cause exists with the caused; the caused did not generate itself. Likewise, if the cause exists, the caused must flow from it.

The distinction between "without condition" and "with a condition [of] no" is the distinction (shown in his example) between completely negating the existence of something, and denying a certain characteristic of a substance. In the examples given, the first denies the existence of any white stick, and the second denies that a stick is white. Thus one phrase denies a substance, and the other denies an attribute. If the substance is denied, all of its attributes are also denied, by default. The text is slightly confusing because Ibn Sina has reversed the order of the examples which illustrate his two classes.[36]

In *The Book of Definitions* Ibn Sina prefers ᶜilla, the word for cause used by al-Kindi, over the word *sabab* used by al-Farabi. Ibn Sina did not define *sabab*. Evidence that he prefers ᶜilla to *sabab* includes: (a) ᶜIlla is the word he uses for cause in *The Book of Definitions* and in *al-Ilahiyyat* for the four causes.[37] (b) In the first section of *al-Ilahiyyat* Ibn Sina mentions the existence of *al-ᶜilal* and *al-asbab* in a parallel construction, indicating their similarity. Arabophone authors frequently repeat two words with nearly identical meanings for emphasis, as a stylistic device.

> This in reality is based on establishing the causes, and determining the existence of causes (*al-ᶜilal*) and causes (*al-asbab*).[38]

Ibn Sina's preference for ᶜilla (pl. ᶜilal) may indicate a reversal from al-Farabi's usage of *sabab* and return to al-Kindi's usage.

The next terms are Ibn Sina's terms for matter. First a brief description of the translators' usage of terms for matter – *hayula* and *madda*, and also a specialized use of ᶜ*unsur* – in their rendering of Aristotle's books. The three examples show the use of *al-hayula*:

1 "It is called the nature of prime matter, and this is said in two ways ..."[39] (Ustath)
2 "... the substance of things which have the origin of movement in them is at their essence; matter is said of nature because it receives this ..."[40] (Ustath)
3 "Prime matter of them is conserved. Of this kind they say that the elements are the nature of natural things. Some of them say that they are water ..."[41] (Ustath)
4 The following two examples show the use of *madda*:
   a) "Thus changes exist in the contrary only when it is in each one, and it is necessary that matter has the capacity to change only when it has the possibility to be all of them previously."[42] (Abu Bishr Matta)
   b) "Thus there are changes in individual contrarieties, and for matter (*al-ᶜunsur*) to have the capacity to change it is necessary that it has the potential for two states."[43]
5 "All things which change have matter except that it is different; thus what are eternal things, all of which are non-generable, but are moveable in position, have matter ..."[44] (Abu Bishr Matta)
6 In the following quote (and 4b above) ᶜ*unsur* is the word that indicates an aspect of matter:
   "In regard to elemental (ᶜ*unsuri*) substance it is appropriate that it not go out from us about it, that it is, if all of it were one thing, nevertheless there is to each one something peculiar to it, such as phlegm or the bitter."[45] (Ustath)

These quotations demonstrate that the translators used both *madda* and *hayula* for matter; they even used *ᶜunsur* for matter considered in its elemental aspect. *Hayula* frequently refers to the aspect of matter which is an ability to receive something: in number 2 above it receives the origin of movement. However in number 4, *madda* also indicates a potentiality, here the potentiality to receive contrary qualities. Again in number 5 the quality of having matter is linked to having the capacity for change. In number 6 the translator here uses *ᶜunsur* as an adjective describing *jawhar*, and meaning "elemental substance" or "material substance." Both al-Kindi and Ibn Sina use *ᶜunsur* with cause, in the sense of "elemental" or "material cause." *ᶜUnsur* indicates a third aspect of matter, its elemental quality – that is, as a building block of nature. It shows matter in relation to cause or substance.

William Charlton has analyzed Aristotle's use of terms for matter and prime matter.[46] Through an analysis of passages in which various terms which might mean prime matter appear, Charlton concludes that Aristotle did not believe in prime matter. Charlton indicates that prime matter, as he understands it, would be "an ultimate indeterminate matter, to be discovered by conceptual analysis."[47] However, Aristotle's metaphysical scheme needed something like prime matter implicitly, according to Charlton's analysis, although Aristotle did not state this explicitly. In Charlton's opinion our ideas about "prime matter" are a conflation of ideas from both Plato and Aristotle.[48] These two facts – the varied uses of *madda* and *hayula* in the Arabic translations as noted above, and Charlton's analysis of "prime matter" – appear to indicate that there was not a firm distinction between *madda* and *hayula* in the writings of the *falasifa*.[49] Particularly in Ibn Sina we will see there is very little distinction.

Now the two words for matter which Ibn Sina defined in *The Book of Definitions*, namely *al-hayula* and *al-madda*, will be discussed together.

al-Hayula (matter$_1$)

The definition of matter$_1$.[50] Absolute matter$_1$ is a substance which exists in actuality only when it receives a corporeal form from the potentiality of matter$_1$ to receive forms. Absolute matter$_1$ does not have in itself any form particularizing it, except in the sense of potentiality. The meaning of my statement, "There is a substance belonging to matter$_1$" is that the existence which comes to matter$_1$ in actuality belongs to it in itself. One also says that matter$_1$ belongs to everything from the point of view[51] that it receives a certain perfection or something which it did not have. Therefore it will be matter$_1$, in relation to what is not in it and it is a subject in relation to what is in it.[52]

al-Madda (matter₂)

About matter₂. Matter₂ may be said to be a term, which is synonymous with matter₁. Matter₂ is also said of every subject which receives perfection by its being joined to another subject, and accruing to the subject little by little, the way sperm and blood accrue to the form of an animal. Sometimes what it joins with is of its kind, and sometimes it is not of its kind.[53]

Comment In the first place both terms, *hayula* and *madda* are translated by matter, with the subscript ₁ or ₂ to distinguish the original Arabic word.[54] The theory here is to avoid overtranslating and not to prejudice the findings before investigating the evidence, particularly since Ibn Sina himself says the two terms are synonymous. His apparent strategy is to take *hayula*, the translated Greek loan word, which presumably means matter in the ultimate sense and define it first. Then, using this definition as a benchmark, he defines *madda*, the Arabic term and explains it is a synonym for the first term. Thus Ibn Sina gives his stamp of approval to an Arabic word, making it acceptable for technical use in philosophy.

In light of the Aristotelian texts quoted above it appears that the translators did not make a rigid distinction between *hayula* and *madda*. Ibn al-Nadim states in *al-Fihrist* that named translators worked on certain passages. He states that both Ishaq and Ustath translated the *Metaphysics*; the former up to Book *Mu*, and the latter for al-Kindi.[55] Parallel translations have survived in only a few examples, making it difficult to assign any given passage to a particular translator.[56] However, by Ibn Sina's time all these translations were in circulation, so he may have been influenced by any of them. Our interest here is in the range of uses found in the translations. Furthermore any distinction in translating *hayula* and *madda* appears artificial in light of the *failasuf*'s opening statement in his definition of *madda* that they are synonymous.

While Ibn Sina perhaps intends two aspects of matter, this particular distinction is not always maintained in the terms as he actually uses them. In his definition of *hayula* (in *The Book of Definitions*), he mentions that it has the potentiality to receive forms and only comes into actual existence when it receives form. Of *madda* he says that it receives perfection, that is completion, by the assembling of matter little by little.[57] The material elements (blood and sperm are mentioned) accrue to a thing little by little and result in the form of an animal. He does not mention the *potentiality* of *madda* to receive perfection in this text. In *Kitab al-najat* he also mentions matter (*madda*) as existing in actuality with forms and not separable from them.[58]

In the second part of the definition of *madda* here, it is not a simple substance, because additional elements come together to form a composite.

Ibn Sina mentions no components of *hayula* in the first definition. But in both definitions Ibn Sina states that matter has the ability to receive form. For comparison purposes we can see how Ibn Sina defines *hayula* and *madda* in *Kitab al-najat*.[59]

1. Thus when a place is dispensable in its establishment of the thing that occupies it, then we may only call it a subject with reference to it; and if it were indispensable for it, we would not call it a subject, rather we may call it matter (*hayula*).[60]
2. When it is a place in itself and there is no composition in it, then we call it absolute matter (al-*hayula al-mutlaqa*).[61]
3. We say that this matter (*madda*) also cannot possibly be separated from bodily form, and it subsists as an existent in actuality.[62]

These comments on matter in the *Najat* reflect some of the basic Sinawiyyan concerns about matter, which are also found in *The Book of Definitions*. In the first quote Ibn Sina distinguishes matter from a subject. In the second he states that uncomposed matter is absolute or undetermined matter. In the third he reiterates the necessary coexistence of matter and form in an actual existent.

Conclusions

In this chapter Ibn Sina's views on the definition of substance (*jawhar*), cause (*cilla*), and matter (*hayula/madda*) have been held up for examination. In the first place, there is an apparent connection between the order of al-Kindi's *On the Definitions* and Ibn Sina's *Book of Definitions*, particularly in the first eight terms. Further similarities in the content of their definitions will be revisited in the next chapter. Like al-Farabi, Ibn Sina discussed the definition of definition (*hadd*), repeating Aristotle's definition and expanding it. In *al-Ilahiyyat* Ibn Sina states that a definition must discover the quiddity of a thing by defining it in form and matter.

The term for substance, *al-jawhar*, is defined similarly by all three philosophers. It is also interesting to note that the same word is used for substance in each *failasuf*. *Al-jawhar* is the only term in this study used unanimously and with the same technical meaning by al-Kindi, al-Farabi, and Ibn Sina. This may have been necessary because all these philosophical systems needed a word for substance (*jawhar*) or a similar concept as the foundation of the natural scheme, an idea to be considered in the next chapter. In certain philosophical usages *dhat* (essence) is close to functioning as a synonym for *jawhar*. As a word of Persian derivation *jawhar* is useful for its freedom from excess connotative baggage. In the second concept examined, cause (*cilla*), Ibn Sina mentions that there is only one actual existent which is not from any other. This is consistent with his description of the Necessary Existent, who is the only one without a cause. This single cause then brings all other beings into existence. The caused, as shown in the subsequent definition, has as its one qualification that it is "possible of existence." In his definition of the four causes, Ibn Sina emphasizes that the material cause (ᶜunsur) contains potentiality within itself; by being potential, by being possible, it can come into existence. In this statement we see that potentiality, far from being an accident, is an essential part of a thing, thus the essence of each thing contains the potential for its existence – "Thus there is in its essence the potentiality of its existence which is not by accident."[63]

The third concept, matter and the words used for it, brings up the question of how to translate *hayula* and *madda*. It is difficult to be certain whether or not Ibn Sina intends for the two terms for matter – *al-hayula* and *al-madda* – to be interchangeable. Sometimes he draws a specific distinction between *hayula* as the potential in matter to receive forms, and *madda* as actually existing forms in matter, but not always. He also says both form and matter exist together, which suggests this distinction is made on the level of mentally existing concepts, rather than the physically existing world in this aspect. Ibn Sina may have viewed the terms as synonymous in the sense that *madda* was the Arabic name for the concept originally expressed by *hayula* in Greek. Rather than drawing a false distinction and jumping to false conclusions, here the reader may observe that in at least one concept, the Arabic name achieved parity with the Greek original. On the other hand, *al-tina*, a word with Qur'anic overtones, which al-Kindi used in his explanation of the basic matter, is absent. Goichon notes one use of *tin* in Ibn Sina's *Shifa'* where it is paired with *madda* and used in contrast to "form."[64] Whatever the reason *tin* or *tina* fell out of use, while *madda* achieved success.[65]

Ibn Sina's definitions of physical entities (*madda, hayula*, and so on) are direct and concise. His definition of cause (ᶜ*illa*) is also brief. The definition of substance (*jawhar*) is more circuitous, perhaps indicating a continuing complexity to the view of this term. Now that the philosophers' definitions of this set of words have been individually examined, it is time to compare the similarities and differences of their respective approaches. Thus in the next chapter these terms are placed side by side for a more comprehensive comparison.

5

COMPARISON OF VOCABULARY

Hadd, the word used in Arabic for "definition" means edge, boundary, limit, border. Thus in terms of definitions it gives the limits or boundaries of the meanings of words. It gives a limit or edge to words in the sense that a definition shows how far the meaning of a word extends and where it ends. Philosophically speaking, the *falasifa* were able to delineate or limit the meaning of a term. This was a useful activity to clarify and limit the technical usage of philosophical terms. Philosophers are very concerned about language and conveying a specific concept.

This chapter will focus on the diachronic development of the vocabulary items which were previously analyzed in isolation, by a comparative examination of the three major terms. Of the terms, one will represent a similar usage by the *falasifa*; a second will represent a dissimilar usage; and the third will demonstrate an interesting variation in their treatment. All three *falasifa* used *jawhar* to express the notion of substance; this will serve as the example of similar usage. The second concept to be examined comparatively is cause, which is expressed by ʿ*illa* in the works of al-Kindi and Ibn Sina. The word more often used in *The Book of Letters* of al-Farabi is *sabab*. These terms for "cause" will serve as an example of dissimilar usage. The third concept for comparison is *madda*, matter, and its synonym, *hayula*, which will illustrate many of the interesting facets of their usage.

Each definition will be compared in two aspects. First, in regard to the issue of the repetition of words, the coincidence or dissonance of words in the definiens in these three cases will give some indications of the exact similarity or dissonance of meaning and will speak to the issue of influence. Second, the concepts which the *falasifa* are defining may be similar, even if the terms to express them differ and this possibility must be investigated by the meaning of the definition, not just the words. In the comparative review of the definitions, the views of the *falasifa* on definitions should become clearer.

The *falasifa* have very different styles. Al-Kindi and Ibn Sina each wrote a *Book of Definitions*; and these share some stylistic and organizational conventions. In this literary genre a large number of terms – over seventy –

receive a fairly abbreviated treatment. Al-Farabi did not write a book of definitions per se. His *Book of Letters* more closely resembles the structure of Book 5 (Delta) of Aristotle's *Metaphysics*, which defines some of Aristotle's terms, giving longer definitions of fewer terms.

Al-Kindi's *On the Definitions* served as a dictionary for those readers unfamiliar with philosophical terms; this may be explained by his historical placement at the beginning of the philosophical movement in the Islamic world. Those innocent of philosophical terms were able to use al-Kindi's definitions as components to decode the new thought system. His abbreviated style readily forms components that might be called mini-definitions. His pedagogical technique is to build on what a student may be presumed to know from ordinary language Arabic, until he gradually acquaints the novice with a complete scheme.

This is possible through al-Kindi's use of a simple Arabic language and clear, obvious grammar, which invite an intuitive understanding. Even if the intuited understanding was not entirely faithful to the new concept al-Kindi was trying to convey, it would be close enough for an initial understanding which could then be refined later. Thus, although a reader might understand only 85 percent of the meaning of a term, this represents 85 percent more than when he started. Al-Kindi did not offer the popular usage of his terms. For example in *The Book of Definitions* al-Kindi never states that he is giving the popular, common meaning of a term, be it "cause," "intellect" or "soul."[1]

Al-Farabi begins by defining the popular, common meaning of a term, then expounds on how that differs from the philosophical meaning. As an example, in his long discussion of the term *mawjud* in *The Book of Letters*, he begins with an exposition of what the term meant in the general language of the Arabs.[2] He additionally describes how a verb with the same signification is used in Persian (*yaft*), Soghdian (*viyrd*) and in Greek (verb not given).[3] In contrast to al-Kindi, al-Farabi tries to develop technical, rather than intuitable points. We see in al-Farabi a development beyond the point where al-Kindi had taken his audience through al-Farabi's concerted attempt to be technically accurate. He writes on a cerebral level, philologically aware and including many ideas he has absorbed from the Hellenistic tradition. He is more self-consciously Aristotelian in attitude, shown by a love of order for its own sake which will be discussed below.

Ibn Sina departs from both of his predecessors. There is a more advanced approach to definitions in *The Book of Definitions* than in al-Kindi's *On the Definitions*, demonstrated by his ease with both the concepts and the vocabulary. From his writings it would appear that he, like al-Farabi, assumed his audience had a familiarity with his material. These concepts had now been a part of Islamic high culture for the 150 or 200 years since al-Kindi's lifetime. While not a slavish imitator of Aristotle or his predecessors, Ibn Sina has incorporated many of their ideas in his philosophy, where they may remain implicit. Due to his greater comfort with Aristotelian concepts, Ibn Sina also more freely manipulated them for his own ends. Sometimes he quotes Aristotle directly,[4] sometimes he refers to Aristotle's ideas more obliquely.

The methodology in this chapter will be to review the definitions of each term of the *falasifa*, looking closely at each definition phrase by phrase and comparing it with the others. The study will proceed chronologically, exhausting first al-Kindi's definition of a term, then al-Farabi's and then Ibn Sina's. In this way some changes may be uncovered in the way the *falasifa* defined terms and reveal their attitudes toward definitions, and what students might need to know about them in each age.

al-Jawhar (substance)

Jawhar is the term frequently used by the translators to render the Greek word *ousia*.[5] This term is generally translated as "substance" in philosophical writings.[6] As we look at the treatment of *jawhar* we will see that it is used in very similar ways by al-Kindi, al-Farabi, and Ibn Sina. In the case of *jawhar* not just the ideas but many of the same words and phrases are passed down from one *failasuf* to the next.

THE TRANSLATED TEXT[7]

Al-Kindi

Substance (*jawhar*) is (1) [the thing] subsisting in itself, (2) accidents can be predicated of it without changing its essential nature; (3) it is described, not describing. One says: (4) it is not receptive to generation or corruption, or of [those] things which increase for each one of the things, whichever, like generation and corruption in the particularity of a thing's substance. (5) These things, when they are known, accidental qualities in each one of the particular substance are also known, without their being intrinsic themselves to a particular substance.[8]

Al-Farabi

It is customary to call this [thing which is] pointed to "the perceptible" by which nothing at all can be characterized, except accidentally and not in a natural way. Whatever is defining what this pointed to [thing] is, is substance in the absolute sense; just as they call it "essence" (*dhat*) in the absolute sense. Because the meaning of the substance of a thing is the essence of the thing, its quiddity, and part of its quiddity, therefore what is an essence in itself and is not an essence of a thing at all is a substance in the absolute sense, just as it is an essence in the absolute sense, without being related to a thing or restricted by a thing. It is the substance of this pointed to thing that makes known what this pointed to thing is.[9]

Ibn Sina

The definition of substance (*jawhar*). It is a common term. Substance is said of the essence of every existent, such as a human being or whiteness. Substance is also said of every thing existing in itself, because its essence does not need another essence associated with it for it to be subsisting in actuality. This is the meaning of their phrase "substance is self-subsisting."

Substance is also said of whatever has this attribute and is such as to receive opposites in succession. Substance is also said to belong to every essence whose existence is not in a substratum. Substance is said to belong to every essence whose existence is not in a subject. Ancient philosophers since the time Aristotle have adopted the usage of the expression "substance." We have already differentiated previously between subject and substratum. The meaning of their phrase "an existent not in a subject" is: the existent is not associated with the existence of the substratum; it is self-subsistent in actuality; self-establishing in itself; it does not matter that it is in a substratum, although the substratum does not subsist without it in actuality, for even though it were in a substratum, it would not be in a subject.[10]

In the present definition, al-Kindi discusses four main ideas about *jawhar*: its self-subsistence; it is a bearer of accidents; its not being receptive to generation or corruption; and its existing in the particular.

The first expression in al-Kindi, which may also be considered a mini-definition, is the participial phrase *al-qa'im bi-nafsihi* (subsisting in itself). The phrase is absent in al-Farabi. Variants appear in Ibn Sina, such as the verbal form *yaqum* instead of the participle *qa'im*; however he retains much of the same meaning, as both forms are from the same root, *q-w-m*. Ibn Sina, perhaps reflecting the vocabulary used by al-Kindi, then Ibn Sina states that *jawhar* is both *qa'im bi-nafsihi* and *qa'im bi-dhatihi* (self-subsisting) as well as *hata yaqum bi-al-fi^{c}l* (to be subsisting in actuality). Thus, Ibn Sina has repeated the vocabulary and the idea expressed by subsisting in, *qa'im bi*, seen in al-Kindi, even adding variants. Al-Kindi, however, emphasizes *bi-nafsihi* (by itself), meaning that the entity is independent. Ibn Sina emphasizes *bi-dhatihi* (in its essence) and especially *bi-al-fi^{c}l* (in actuality).

Second, al-Kindi says that *jawhar* is a carrier of accidents which do not change its essence. Al-Farabi discusses *jawhar* fully in *The Book of Letters*[11] but he does not mention that *jawhar* is a bearer of accidents. If this Kindian idea is interpreted to mean that substance is the essence, rather than whatever concomitant accidents may occur to an essence, al-Farabi comes close to this idea. Al-Farabi states that substance is the thing in itself, and substance does not have anything characterizing it. Things added to or stipulated of a thing may be interpreted as being accidents, which are predicated of a substance in the Kindian universe, in the common usage of the term accident. However, al-Farabi's vocabulary for the term *jawhar* is entirely different here from al-Kindi's. (See Table 1.)

Ibn Sina says that *jawhar* is able to receive contrary or opposite qualities. This appears to be his way of saying that substance is the entity which receives accidents. In this view if a quality and its opposite can both conceivably be predicated of the same substance, the quality signified must be accidental. Yet if the quality received were essential, the receiving of its opposite would change the substance. This is compatible with Aristotle's idea that a specific entity, which is an example of a substance – in his example a human being (*insan*) – can have different things predicated – black and white, for instance.[12]

The third major idea al-Kindi states is that substance is not receptive to generation and corruption. This being the case, its state must be permanent and eternal since it neither comes to be nor passes away. At this point in the definitions there appears to be a slight shift in emphasis among the three *falasifa*. Al-Farabi does not use this language, conveying instead a similar idea with his phrase that essence is without condition or qualifications. Al-Kindi also says that substance is not similar to things which increase, while al-Farabi says that substance is not added to or stipulated of a thing. This means that for both al-Kindi and al-Farabi substance is a kind of absolute entity. Ibn Sina does not discuss this issue in this definition.

The fourth idea al-Kindi discusses is that substance is existing in the particular; when the particulars are known the substance is known. The final sentence of al-Kindi's definition is confusing, and the reader may recall that not even Gimaret was able to make sense of it.[13]

Table 1 Word usage: *jawhar* – substance

Word or phrase	al-Kindi	al-Farabi	Ibn Sina
al-qa'im bi-nafsihi	x	–	x
dhat al-shay'	–	x	x
hamil lil-aᶜarad	x	–	–
yaqbal al-addad	–	–	x
ghayr qabil lil-takwin wa al-fasad	x	–	–
huwa dhat ᶜala al-itlaq	–	x	–
yaqum bi-l-fiᶜl	–	–	x

In considering this definition as a whole, there are two structural features typical of Kindian definitions. (a) It contains a number of short definitions of *jawhar* in the same way a dictionary gives different shades of meaning. While the definitions-within-a-definition are not numbered, they are set off from each other either with the conjunction *wa* (and), which often serves as a break – much as a period or a semi-colon would be used today – or they are set off with the expression "and he says." (b) Mini-definitions are often found in al-Kindi's longer definitions. Here, for instance, in considering the first phrase "substance is the thing subsisting in itself," we can interpret this as a full, albeit short, definition. The definition of *jawhar* brings out the salient point, its self-subsistence. His use of mini-definitions and their application will be discussed below.

Al-Farabi discusses the original common meaning of *jawhar* (in the Persian) as one relating to precious gems, especially their rarity and costliness in his definition.[14] We will not find either of the other two *falasifa* discussing this meaning of *jawhar*.

Al-Farabi says *jawhar* is *dhat al-shay'* (the essence of a thing) and also the *mahiyya* (essence) of something. The two words for essence *dhat* and *mahiyya* are nearly synonymous. *Mahiyya* is the literal translation of "what-it-is-ness." In other usages *dhat* is used for being or entity. As mentioned above, al-Farabi defined substance as having absolute existence. He also said it is not added to or stipulated of a thing. His final idea in this section is that "It is the substance of this referred to thing that makes known what this referred to thing is." For al-Farabi knowledge of a thing must be equal to and refer to the substance of a thing, in logical terms. For this reason, definition indicates knowledge of a thing. It is another indication of al-Farabi's linguistic and logical interests. Both al-Kindi's and Ibn Sina's definitions omit this point.

Ibn Sina, following closely the Farabian vocabulary, says *jawhar* belongs to the essence of everything (*li-dhat kull shay'*) giving the examples of "human being or whiteness."[15] While philosophers generally consider an individual human being to be a substance – Socrates and Zayd are frequent examples – the quality of being white is usually considered an accident rather than a substance. In Porphyry, for instance, black is given as one of the primary examples of accident; color is an accident affecting a class of entities. Crows are black and the Zenji (people) are black.[16] However, in contrast, Ibn Sina considers the whole, independent quality of "whiteness" as a substance, not a white thing.

Ibn Sina relates a number of slightly different definitions under the single heading *jawhar*, to an even greater degree than al-Kindi. In this instance *jawhar* is to be understood not in the sense of "substance," but in its sense as "every entity, or existent" (*kull mawjud*). Then the first part of the definition can be reinterpreted as referring to aspects or states of an existent. Of the first part of his definition, Ibn Sina says in the next paragraph: "Every existent whether it is whiteness or heat or motion, is a substance (*jawhar*) in the first sense."[17] Perhaps Ibn Sina hints that part of this definition is controversial with his final comment, "It is not necessary to squabble over the terms."[18]

It appears Ibn Sina does not mean substance only in the usual Aristotelian sense, as it is not possible that Ibn Sina was confused about the Aristotelian meaning of *jawhar*. He must be adding to or differentiating the original sense of the term. This is also borne out by the statement that opens many of his definitions, "*x* is a common term," thereby indicating to his readers it has different uses. And, in fact, the structure of the remaining portion of this definition further bears out the term's different uses.

Second, Ibn Sina emphasizes the existence of substance in actuality (*bi-al-fi'l*); third, the ability to receive contraries; fourth, he adds that substance is not in a subject or, fifth, not in a substratum. All these phrases refer to the unchanging nature of substance, except the third.[19] This definition also shows the Aristotelian influence on ideas about *jawhar*.[20] Ibn Sina has given a range of philosophical definitions of *jawhar* including the information that: every existent, such as heat and motion, is an entity (*jawhar*) in the first meaning; the first principle is a substance in the second, fourth and fifth senses; and matter (*hayula*) is a substance in the fourth and fifth senses, but not in the second and third, and so on.[21] After listing the five sub-definitions, Ibn Sina then states that the term *jawhar* goes back at least to Aristotle's time. He finishes this section by emphasizing that substance is an independent entity.

In summation, in their definitions of substance these three *falasifa* make some very similar points although they show a variety of strategies to do so. They all emphasize the self-subsistent and thus independent nature of substance. In slightly varying ways they indicate that substance is eternal and unchanging: al-Kindi by saying that it receives accidents which can be predicated of it, and that it is neither generated nor corrupted; al-Farabi emphasizes the absolute terms of its nature and that nothing could be added to it; Ibn Sina says that it has the capacity to receive opposites and that it exists in actuality. While Ibn Sina does not really describe its state as permanent per se, he states that it has existence in itself, subsisting in itself, and that substance does not owe its existence to any other substance. Knowledge of substance is through particulars for both al-Kindi and al-Farabi. Ibn Sina is silent on this aspect in his *Book of Definitions*.

Overall the first set of definitions discussed shows much similarity in ideas, although there is not much correspondence in word choice. (See Table 1.) There is a certain amount of variation in terminology and emphasis. For example, Ibn Sina emphasizes *bi-al-fi'l* (in actuality), rather than *bi-al-quwwa* (in potentiality). In other works he writes about both actual and potential states.

That the *falasifa* similarly conceptualized their terms for substance was probably dictated by the demands of their physical/metaphysical schemes. The schemes necessitated the logical explanation of the way beings of one class could maintain certain essential characteristics (essence) and undergo various changes (accidents); or how different members of one class could exhibit a widely varying array of non-essential characteristics (accidents), yet still be recognized as members of the same group. This meant there had to be something that did *not* change in material forms. This something was what they defined as *jawhar* (substance). While other details or parts of their schemes may have varied, they all perceived this part in the same way, with only minor variations. Consequently similar definitions were necessary.

al-ᶜIlla (cause)

The second set of definitions to be compared shows much more diversity, not only in the concepts but in the words used to express the concept defined. While the *falasifa* recognized what is generally called "cause" as an event to be explained, the link between "cause" and "effect" is not intrinsically necessary in philosophical terms. This is particularly true in the Islamic environment, as God is viewed as the cause of human's actions. Humans only acquire their actions, they do not create the actions. This already sets up a more precarious relationship between cause, effect and responsibility.[22] Ibn Sina's cosmology included the idea that all possible existents were from one ultimate existent, the Necessary of Existence. So although there are "natural causes," as al-Kindi mentions, found in the natural world, they are not the same as the ultimate first cause. They are on a different level. In al-Kindi there is even a definition of "first cause," thus there are definitions for two types of cause in al-Kindi, although the distinction is rather subtle. Consequently more latitude is left for conceptual interpretation in the term cause.

ᶜIlla is a term frequently translating *aition* in Aristotle, and often used to express cause in Islamic philosophy.[23] Although it is most commonly rendered as "cause" in English, the original meaning in Greek also indicates it means to be responsible for, to be accused.[24] Thus while we may expect it (*ᶜilla*) to refer to a connection between two ideas, it may not indicate "cause" in a simple sense. Indeed the fact that causes are often discussed in multiples indicates shared responsibility, or explanations:

Al-Kindi *al-ᶜIlla al-ula*

The first cause – creating, doing, completing everything, not moving.[25]

COMPARISON OF VOCABULARY

Al-Kindi *al-ᶜIlal al-tabiᶜyya* (The natural causes)

The natural causes are four: what a thing comes into being from, that is, its element; the form of a thing, by which it is what it is; the principle of motion of a thing, which is its cause; and that, for the sake of which the agent does whatever is done.[26]

Al-Farabi

There appear to be three kinds of particles by which reasons (*asbab*) and causes (*ᶜilal*) for the existence of a thing are sought: "Why?" does it exist, "by what?" does it exist, and "from what?" does it exist.[27]

Ibn Sina *al-ᶜilla* (cause)

Cause. Every being which exists has existence from another essence in actuality. This being has existence in actuality and existence of this being in actuality is not from the existence of that one in actuality.[28]

Ibn Sina *al-maᶜlul* (the caused)

The caused is every being (*dhat*) whose existence in actuality comes from the existence of another being, but the existence of that other being is not from its existence. The meaning of our phrase "from its existence" is not the same as the meaning of our phrase "with its existence." Indeed, the meaning of our phrase "from its existence" is that a being is, in consideration of itself, a possible existent, and its existence only becomes necessary in actuality, not from itself; but rather because another actually existing being makes the existence of the second being necessary on its account. A being has possibility in itself. Thus it has in itself possibility without condition; and it has existence in itself by condition of the necessary cause. A being has existence in itself on condition that there is no cause to prevent it.

The difference between our phrase "without condition" and the phrase "with a condition of not" is like the difference between our phrase "there is no white stick" and "a stick is not white." As for the meaning of our phrase "with its existence," it means that if one of the two beings is presumed existent, it follows logically that one knows the other is existent. If one is supposed removed, it follows that the other is removed. The cause and the caused come together in the meaning of these two concomitants. Aspects of the concomitants are different; because one of the two, which is the caused, if one supposes it existent, it follows logically that the other was already itself in existence, therefore this being existed. As for the other, which is the cause, if one supposes it existent, it follows logically that its existence will be followed by the existence of the caused. If the caused is removed it follows logically that the cause had been removed first; it is sound that this one could be removed, but not that the removal of the caused necessitated the removal of the cause. As for the cause, if we abstract it, the caused will be abstracted by necessity of the abstraction of the cause, which abstracts it.[29]

First, it is noteworthy that there is scarcely any word-correspondence in these definitions. (See Table 2.) In light of this, how are their ideas of causation to be understood? Al-Kindi and Ibn Sina both use ᶜilla but al-Farabi more often uses *sabab* for cause.[30]

When deconstructing al-Kindi's definition, it can be broken down into five ideas. The cause defined here is not a cause, but the First Cause. Initially, it appears likely that he is referring to God. Second, he describes the cause as creating (*mubdiᶜa*), which is a distinguishing characteristic for God: God is the Creator. Third, the Cause is *faᶜila*, which may be translated as active, acting, or an agent. Fourth, the Cause is the completion or perfection of everything. Fifth, it is not moved. This definition also demonstrates al-Kindi's

Table 2 Word usage: ᶜilla – cause

Word or phrase	al-Kindi	al-Farabi	Ibn Sina
ᶜilla	x	x[1]	x
sabab	–	x	–
mabdiᶜa	x	–	–
al-ula	x	–	–
fa ᶜila / bi-l-fiᶜl	x	–	x
ᶜunsur	x	–	–
mabda' haraka	x	–	–
min ajl	x	–	–
lima	–	x	–
bi-madha / bi-ha	x	x	–
ᶜan madha / minhu	x	x	–
mutammimat al-kull	x	–	–
ghayr mutaharraka	x	–	–
wujud al shay' / wujud dhat	–	x	x
mumkana al-wujud	–	–	x
al-ᶜilla al-wujud	–	–	x

Note
1 plural only in al-Farabi (ᶜilal)

awareness of the problem of infinite regress and his wish to avoid it. By naming his definition of cause "First Cause," he indicates he cannot accept an infinite regress. Since it is not moved, it is the basis; this is another way of saying it is without a cause itself. This definition could be interpreted as including the four causes of Aristotle. They can be interpreted as the efficient (*fa‛ila*), material and formal (*mutammimat al-kull*)[31] and final (*al-ula*) causes, especially if overlap is considered acceptable.[32] While these words may be interpreted as references to the Aristotelian causes, another interpretation is possible.

Alternatively al-Kindi may be describing the First Cause as the supernatural Creator. Numerous scholars have pointed out that the idea of a Creator was grafted onto the Hellenistic ideas sometime between the implementation of Greek philosophy and the rise of monotheistic religions. *Mubdi‛a* is occasionally used in theological references to God.[33] Cause was debated in many sectors of medieval Islamic society. The Mutakallimun (theologians) also wanted to explain cause, although they had an agenda which was different from the *falasifa*'s: to demonstrate that God is the absolute cause of all creation and the agent of continual creation in time.

Although *fa‛ila* can be interpreted narrowly as referring to the Aristotelian efficient cause and is used as a technical term with that meaning in later philosophical texts, it may not be used in such a limited, technical sense here. There are two possible interpretations. (a) This term is not, in fact, used technically. This is argued in considering *fa‛ila* in relation to *mubdi‛a*, a word from theology, meaning "creating," and implicitly indicating a Creator who is performing this action – which is decidedly not an Aristotelian notion. If the contiguous terminology is not technical, there is no reason to suppose the word in question is technical. In contrast, al-Kindi's second definition – the four causes – is specifically Aristotelian, as is al-Farabi's statement, which is much more self-consciously Aristotelian in reference. The vocabulary becomes much more formal in al-Farabi.

(b) Alternatively al-Kindi has embedded a mini-definition of cause in this definition, and the efficient cause and the final cause are conflated. That is "*fa‛ila mutammimat al-kull*" (doing, completing everything) may be a combination of these two causes. In addition to suggesting "efficient" cause, he mentions "completing everything." In this interpretation causes are the explanations for things. Furthermore, as will be seen in the discussion of al-Farabi, it was common to compress several causes into one reference, something which Aristotle himself did.

The curious aspect of this definition is that while the definiendum is an almost religious term the definiens is not, with the single exception of the word *mubdi‛a*. In interpreting this word to be an example of natural language, relying on intuitive understanding to explicate new philosophical concepts, it gives the reader a different slant: one can see al-Kindi using this term to explain a foreign concept, the idea of efficiency as originating from an agent. One understands him to be using *mubdiᶜa* not as a synonym for, but as an analogy to the Creator, a concept easily accessible in his culture.

The second Kindian definition repeats the Aristotelian four causes and in language which would become commonly used: *ᶜunsur* for material causes, *sura* for formal cause, and *min ajlihi* for final cause. His use of *mabda' haraka al-shay'* (the principle of motion of a thing) for efficient cause has proved less common. Prepositions are important factors in his explanation. In his mini-definition of *ᶜunsur* he says *ma minhu* (what it is of); and for *sura* he says *allati bihi* (by which). In al-Farabi's definition, he defines the four causes using the prepositions *bi, li*, and *ᶜan*. For the material cause, al-Kindi uses *min*; al-Farabi uses *ᶜan*. These two prepositions are similar, used in conveying "from" (what) or "of" (what), in the partitive sense. Al-Kindi and al-Farabi both use *bi* – al-Kindi uses it for the formal cause, al-Farabi apparently for the efficient cause. While al-Farabi's prepositional terminology may not be obviously derivative from al-Kindi, this example suggests al-Farabi may have been familiar with al-Kindi's definitions. *Mabda'* is a word al-Farabi frequently uses in the sense of principles which are causes, which may spring from al-Kindi's use of *mabda'*.[34]

Moving to al-Farabi, there is little evident congruence with al-Kindi's first definition. He states that he is investigating reasons (*asbab*) and causes (*ᶜilal*) for the existence of a thing. In contrast to al-Kindi, his investigation is stated to be a logical and philological exercise, because he is also investigating the kinds of particles used to ask about the causes of existence of a thing. The three questions he asks are: Why (*li*) does it have existence? In what way or by what means (*bi*) does it have existence? And from (*ᶜan*) what agent or material does it have existence?[35] Previously it was mentioned that Shukri Abed believes the particle *li* should be equated with the questions about the final cause, because it asks "for what end" does a thing exist. Abed decodes the particle *bi* as referring to questions about the efficient cause. The particle *ᶜan* inquires about efficient cause and material cause.[36] Since al-Farabi considers form and matter to be closely connected, one could argue that *ᶜan* also includes the formal cause.

One finds a precedent for subsuming the other causes under *lima* in the Arabic translation of Aristotle's *Physics*.[37] Al-Kindi may have read the *Physics* in an early translation, but evidently he did not write a commentary on it, as Ibn al-Nadim does not mention such a title in his extensive list of al-Kindi's philosophical and logical titles.[38] A translation was written by Ishaq b. Hunayn, who died about 298–9 AH/AD 910–11.[39] These dates made the translation available to al-Farabi, but not to al-Kindi. It seems likely that al-Farabi would have read this section, digested, and internalized it, and then had it in mind when he wrote his own remarks on the four causes. Evidence for such internalization is borne out by the fact that al-Farabi wrote a commentary on the *Physics* called, "An Explanation of Aristotle's Book The Physics, in regard to commentary."⁴⁰

These definitions also demonstrate an essential difference between al-Kindi and al-Farabi. Al-Kindi falls primarily under the *tabiʿyun*, or natural philosophers, writing about physics and metaphysics. Al-Farabi, a *mantiqi*, is interested in logic and political science. Al-Farabi's desire to give laws has been noted by Muhsin Mahdi,⁴¹ and it is palpably obvious to anyone reading al-Farabi that order and laws are of the utmost importance to him. For al-Farabi, causes are to be fitted into these basic categories. No mention is made of a First Cause, or a Creator.

While al-Farabi mentions ʿilal in the definition quoted, he rarely uses this term. He appears to be equating it with *asbab*, as it is in a parallel grammatical construction: *asbab wujud al-shay' wa ʿilalihi* (reasons of a thing's existence and its causes). One may notice, however, that al-Farabi is using the plural of reasons and causes with reference to a single existing thing. He then lists three particles which can be used to ask questions about a thing, indicating that he is not looking at cause in terms of a single principle. Although the four causes are not listed by their usual names in this passage, they appear in other Farabian analyses.⁴² From the use of the singular masculine pronominal suffix here, it is grammatically obvious that al-Farabi asks all three questions in regard to a single thing.

In reviewing the texts of Ibn Sina it becomes obvious that there is a different approach to this term. In his definition from *The Book of Definitions* Ibn Sina is interested in one cause, or aspect of cause: what might be called the cause in actuality. This is because he is describing the idea that each being has an actually existing cause, an efficient cause. Ibn Sina frequently uses the term ʿilla for cause. In this definition the beings or existents that Ibn Sina is signifying are indicated by *dhat*, used neutrally as a signifier of the essence of an existent. This definition is interesting for what it does not mention. There is no reference to what material *dhat* is created from; whether it is in fact created, or how it otherwise comes into existence; nor does the reader encounter any discussion of creation from nothing in either al-Farabi or Ibn Sina. Ibn Sina, however, makes a distinction between Necessary and Possible Existence. There is only one Necessary Existent; everything else is possible.⁴³

In the present definition his emphasis is on *bi-al-fiʿl*. However, Ibn Sina is not contrasting it with *bi-al-quwwa*, which is the common Sinawiyyan dichotomy. Even in this rather cryptic definition there appears also to be a wish to prevent an infinite regress. He is saying existence of *a* is from *x*, and there is an *x* which does not have another cause.

Thus al-Kindi and Ibn Sina both indicate an awareness of the problem of infinite regress. Al-Kindi solves the problem by naming the cause that he discusses the First Cause. In this respect, this part of the definition can be considered stipulative. Ibn Sina, on the other hand, structures his definition to show a primary interest in one aspect of causation – what we might call the cause in actuality.

The idea of action recurs, but differently. Now the reader will see the results of action, of a cause, a presence *bi-al-fi'l*, actually. Therefore, unlike the first term, *jawhar*, which had much consistent usage from one philosopher to the next, the second term, *'illa*, will show very little consistent usage from one to the next. Al-Kindi has put causation back to God, or the First Cause; al-Farabi reworks the Aristotelian causes; and Ibn Sina has affirmed indeterminate causation. The Necessary Existent is the cause in the Sinawiyyan universe, but it is impersonal in relation to the universe.

Additionally, while some translated Greek texts were available to al-Kindi, today only the text of *The Physics* which was available to al-Farabi survives. The four causes are one of the most notable aspects of Aristotle's philosophy, so one might expect a philosopher who prided himself on his Aristotelianism to refer to them, and al-Farabi does.

Thus one sees the development of technical terms in the vocabulary via the example of *'illa*. In al-Kindi, the tone of the definition is a medium level of abstraction, pegged to suggested religious ideas, rendering the definition intuitively understandable. In reading al-Farabi, who represents the second stage in term development, one finds that the definition has advanced to another level, more cerebral and more abstract, with fewer ties to quotidian language, and with a possible unacknowledged debt to al-Kindi's use of prepositions to refer to causes. Al-Farabi's self-conscious technicality of language is apparent in his interest in language, expressed in the titles of his books, such as *al-Alfaz al-musta'mala fi al-mantiq* (*The Utterances Employed in Logic*). This is a definition which al-Kindi in fact could not have written, because he did not have available Ishaq's translation of the Aristotelian text which al-Farabi would employ.

In the century following al-Farabi, Ibn Sina was free to adapt Aristotle as he pleased, and his comfort with Aristotelian concepts is apparent. Where al-Farabi makes an effort to follow Aristotle's text faithfully, the reader of Ibn Sina's writing becomes aware that Aristotle has become a familiar part of the philosophical landscape.

al-Hayula and *al-Madda*

Different terms are used for matter, as may be apparent from the previous discussions. To understand the background issues of this notion, first one aspect of the problem related to matter as a substratum from Aristotle will be recapitulated. In an essay entitled "Did Aristotle Believe in Prime Matter?" W. Charlton states that Aristotle does not explicitly propound the concept of prime matter. Charlton concludes that the idea of prime matter is a conflation of Plato and Aristotle. Nevertheless Aristotle relied upon a concept like prime matter, in Charlton's opinion. "It [the traditional view] derives, however, some support from a feeling, more widely held than admitted, that Aristotle does in fact need something like prime matter, that the positing of a universal substratum is in fact a conceptual necessity."[44]

Keeping Charlton's view in mind, here are the definitions of the *falasifa*. To avoid prejudicing the issue of prime matter, both *al-hayula* and *al-madda* are translated as matter.[45]

Al-Kindi *al-Hayula*

Matter – a potentiality, put down for bearing the forms, it is acted upon.[46]

Al-Farabi *al-Madda*

It is clear that the perfect quiddity of the thing is only by means of its form when it is in matter, adapted, supporting in actuality, generating it. Thus matter inevitably enters into its quiddity. Thus by its form its quiddity is in its matter which was only generated for the sake of its form that is generated for a certain end. When it is thus, there is the disposition which is what people mean by their term "substance"; which is only the quiddity of a human being, and it is that by which a human is a human in actuality. Thus they mean only by substance the quiddity of a human, it is thus that Zayd is a substance, or his ancestors, or his kind. Also thus it is they think that his fathers and his mothers and his kind – from antiquity – are material components from which they are generated. They think when the material components of a thing are good, the thing is good, like the components of a wall or the components of a bed. They think that when the wood is good, the bed is good, because the goodness of the wood is the cause of the goodness of the bed; and if the stones, unburnt bricks, baked bricks, and clay are good, the wall built of them will be good also, because the goodness of these is the cause of the goodness of the wall. It is according to this example that they reason concerning the fathers, the mothers, and the ancestors, the *qabila*, the community, and the people of the country of human beings; for many people imagine that these are the material components from whom or by means of whom the human being comes to be. The material components of a thing are either its quiddity or the parts of its quiddity. Therefore they mean by substance here only its quiddity or what [is] a quiddity by means of it.[47]

Form is the corporeal substance in a body, like the shape of a bed is in the bed, while matter is like the wood of the bed. Thus form is that through which an embodied substance becomes a substance in actuality, while matter is that through which it is a substance in potentiality. ... Matter only exists for the sake of forms. ... Thus when there are no forms, the existence of matter is false. ... Thus it is not possible for prime matter to exist deprived of a form.[48]

Ibn Sina *al-Hayula*

The definition of $matter_1$. Absolute $matter_1$ is a substance which exists in actuality only when it receives a corporeal form from the potentiality of $matter_1$ to receive forms. Absolute $matter_1$ does not have in itself any form particularizing it, except in the sense of potentiality. The meaning of my statement, "There is a substance belonging to $matter_1$," is that the existence which comes to $matter_1$ in actuality belongs to it in itself. One also says that $matter_1$ belongs to everything from the point of view that it receives a certain perfection or something which it did not have. Therefore it will be $matter_1$, in relation to what is not in it and it is a subject in relation to what is in it.[49]

Ibn Sina *al-Madda* (matter)

About $matter_2$. $Matter_2$ may be said to be a term, which is synonymous with $matter_1$. $Matter_2$ is also said of every subject which receives perfection by its being joined to another subject, and accruing to the subject little by little, the way sperm and blood accrue to the form of an animal. Sometimes what it joins with is of its kind, and sometimes it is not of its kind.[50]

The three approaches to defining matter have very little in common from a vocabulary standpoint and express the differences each *failasuf* takes in approaching the issue of definition. (See Table 3 for word correspondence and its absence in these definitions.) A theory of matter is necessary for a philosophical system in both a physical and a metaphysical sense. In *Masa'il* al-Farabi gives a simplified definition of *hayula*;[51] in *The Book of Letters* and *al-Siyasa* he offers definitions of *madda*. Ibn Sina gives definitions for both *hayula* and *madda* in his *Book of Definitions*.

First under consideration is al-Kindi's definition. *Al-hayula* is not the only word he uses for matter. He also uses *tina* (clay, matter), *ᶜunsur* (element), and *ustuqas* (element).[52] In contrast to these terms, he does not seem to have used *madda* as frequently. In *The Definitions* al-Kindi used *tina* to explain *ᶜunsur*; he may have considered *tina* a parallel term. Aristotle had previously transformed *hyle* from its common-language use, into an abstract technical

COMPARISON OF VOCABULARY

Table 3 Word usage: *madda / hayula* – matter

Word or phrase	al-Kindi	al-Farabi	Ibn Sina
tina	x	x[1]	–
madda	–	x	x
hayula	x	x	x
quwwa	x	x	x
mawdu^c /mawdu^{c}a	x	–	x
li-haml	x	–	–
al-suwar	x	x	x
munfa^{c}ala	x	–	–
jusmaniyy	–	x	x[2]
kashab	–	x	–
al-minan wa al-dam	–	–	x
bi-l-fi^{c}l	–	x	x
ma^{c}duman	–	x	–
wujuduha li-ajl al-suwar	–	x	–
mahiyya	–	x	–
madkhal	–	x	–
al-insan	–	x	–
mawadduhu	–	x	–
juda	–	x	–
shakl	–	x	–
al-madda al-ula	–	x	–
al-kamal bi-ijtima^{c}ihi	–	–	x
nu^c	–	–	x
al-mutlaqa	–	–	x
jawhar	–	x	x
qubuluhu	–	x	x
takhassuhu	–	–	x
li-dhatiha	–	–	x

Notes
1 variant, *tin*.
2 variant, *jismiyya*.

term.[53] In Arabic *tina* never achieved acceptance as a technical term the way *hyle* did in Greek, although al-Kindi appears to have favored words of Arabic origin, such as *tina* and ^{c}*unsur*, more often than *hayula*. Frequency of use is an interesting question to keep in mind, as there is no complete consistency in preference for loan words over retrofitted Arabic words. Al-Farabi, on the other hand, almost always uses *ustuqas* for element, rather than ^{c}*unsur*. Ibn Sina uses *tina* occasionally, but only for concrete physical matter. Ibn Sina frequently uses ^{c}*unsur*, while al-Farabi uses it much less frequently. Al-Farabi prefers *ustuqas* and *madda* rather than *hayula*. Ibn Sina uses both *madda* and *hayula*.

Al-Kindi is not totally comfortable with his sources; he is walking a fine line between sounding too much like the theologians and using the Quranic vocabulary on the one hand, and not being understood because he has distanced himself from everyday language. He will have no audience if he wantonly uses transliterated Greek words, because his readers will not understand him. There is an attempt to use mini-definitions or to allow readers to use his mini-definitions to decode foreign words in his definition of the loan word *ustuqas*. When he says that element (*ᶜunsur*)[54] is, literally, "the clay of all clay," meaning "the matter of all matter," he is trying to edge his readers toward an understanding not only of the meaning of the words (they can figure them out and the construction is elegantly simple), but of the philosophical concept of a basic matter, a raw stuff, which underlies the world as they perceive it. *Tina* is rarely used by later *falasifa*. A reader was confronted in al-Kindi's work, perhaps for the first time, with the idea of a basic universe, an underlying universe. *Ustuqas* is usually considered to mean "element." In part al-Kindi's definition of *ustuqas* reads: "It is the element (or matter) of the body; it is the smallest of things of the assemblage of the body."[55] This definition is very simple, both in its grammar and the use of well-known Arabic words.

And since the definition includes *ᶜunsur*, another crucial word itself also defined in his book, those who would have had trouble understanding his meaning could substitute his definition of *ᶜunsur* for the word "*ᶜunsur*" in this definition. Using this model we can rewrite the definition thus: "It is the matter of all matter of the body; it is the smallest of things of the assemblage of the body." He has used simple phrases previously defined to enlighten readers about the meaning of a foreign word. Clearly al-Kindi is helping his reader conceptualize philosophical terms, particularly those with foreign origins.

Al-Kindi's definition of *sura* (in *The Definitions*), commented on previously, is another mini-definition.[56] Al-Kindi says: "The form is the thing by which it is what it is."[57] In *al-Tabiᶜyyat* Ibn Sina says: "Its form is the essence by which it is what it is."[58] Thus Ibn Sina reiterates al-Kindi's definition of *sura*, quoting from al-Kindi's *On the Definitions* without acknowledgment, and incorporating it into his own definitions. That *sura* is a foreign concept can be seen by the care al-Kindi takes to add a very simple definition, using a totally indigenous, Arabic vocabulary. We can use the same strategy on al-Kindi's definition of *hayula*: "Matter – a potentiality put down for bearing the forms, it is acted upon."[59] If *sura* is pluralized and inserted into the definition, that definition becomes: "*al-hayula*: a potentiality, put down for bearing the things by which they are what they are, it is acted upon." The resulting definition is beautifully simple and crystal clear. The same can be seen in his definition of another Greek word, *ustuqas*. In al-Kindi the definition of *jawhar*, a foreign idea, has come down to us in a somewhat confused text, suffering from a "deficiency of phrasing,"[60] which may be further evidence of its foreignness. The ideas propounded in this definition were so strange to the copyists that they copied it incorrectly, perhaps thinking they were improving on the sense.

This definition of *hayula* can be broken into basic elements. Al-Kindi says that matter is a potentiality; it is a substrate; it bears the forms; and it is passive. In contrast to substance, which bears accidents, matter (*hayula*) bears forms in this definition. The idea of bearing, or carrying, the forms, which is also described as a potentiality, is a simple one to grasp. Al-Farabi also states that matter is receptive to form: it does not exist without the form. In al-Kindi it can be logically deduced that matter is coexistent with form. Thus the secondary idea of matter receiving (*yaqbal*) the forms is implied.

Moving next to al-Farabi's definitions of matter, the two quotations from his work considered here demonstrate that he makes remarks both similar to and different from al-Kindi. Unlike al-Kindi, al-Farabi uses the term *madda* extensively, rarely *hayula*. In his passage from *Masa'il*,[61] where he uses *hayula*, he says it is "the last of the identities," and he reinforces his meaning with the additional remark that it is "the lowest of them." This demonstrates the Farabian trait of ranking things and making lists. Matter, as the absolute physical aspect of things, is at the bottom of the scale; God, at the top. Al-Farabi states matter must receive forms to exist; otherwise it will be a privation in actuality, that is, it will not exist. Although it was potentially (in the sense of possibly) lacking in existence, when matter receives form, it becomes substance. Therefore matter includes the potentiality to receive form.

In the discussion of matter (*madda*) found in al-Farabi's *Book of Letters*, (p. 75 quoted above), he states that a thing can exist only when its quiddity is supported by form and matter. Therefore, matter, as much as form, is an intrinsic part of its quiddity. This composite existent is a substance. Substance here may refer either to a specific individual or an unspecified human being. It is notable that while "Zayd's substance" is defined, "Zayd" is not. Definitions are of a species, not of an individual; thus "Zayd" is defined only in what he has in common with the rest of humanity. Al-Farabi then compares Zayd as a substance with the substance of a wall or a bed. He discusses what is meant by "good matter" in a human, and compares it to good matter in a physical object. In a human, when the forefathers and people of a community are good, this indicates "good matter." They are matter in the same way the wood of which a bed is fashioned is matter; and if it is good, what is made of it will also be good. The material elements thus form part of a thing's quiddity.

The second of al-Farabi's definitions quoted here emphasizes the relationship of *madda* and *sura*. The first element of the definition of *madda* is that matter is the material of a thing, like wood for a bed. Al-Farabi's use of the root *j-s-m* in the active participle of the Fifth Form *mutajassim*, the form that means making into a body, graphically illustrates his definition. It becomes substance-in-actuality, a real existent, only when it receives the form. When he states, "Thus it is not possible for prime matter (*al-madda al-ula*) to exist deprived of a form," he denies the existence of prime matter, as mentioned earlier. If prime matter exists only in an "*en*formed" state, how does it differ from ordinary matter? Furthermore al-Farabi uses *al-madda* for his denial of prime matter, not *al-hayula*. This is part of al-Farabi's effort to Arabicize the vocabulary of philosophy by substituting *madda* for *hayula*. Matter with form is no longer simple, but compound. This definition heavily emphasizes the actual existence of matter versus its potential existence.

The next definitions of matter to be considered are those of Ibn Sina. Unlike al-Kindi, Ibn Sina does not write short-phrase modular definitions which can serve as substitutes for technical terms. The first of his terms for matter that is to be examined is *hayula*. Ibn Sina says *hayula* is unconditioned (*mutlaqa*). Here Ibn Sina combines a Greek loan word with an Arabic word, showing how thoroughly *hayula* has become integrated into the Arabic language. Ibn Sina "Arabicizes" *hayula* by its association with the indigenous Arabic term *mutlaqa*, here used philosophically. In comparison with the previous definition of *hayula* found in al-Farabi's *Masa'il*, Ibn Sina's definition assumes a deeper general knowledge on the part of the reader. After beginning at an abstract level by saying that *hayula* is unconditioned matter, Ibn Sina continues in the same vein, speaking of matter (*hayula*) in terms such as: actuality, receiving forms, and receiving perfection. Physicality, an aspect suggested in the Farabian definition, is notably missing from this definition. The only vocabulary item that relates to physicality is *al-jismiyya*, the nisbah of *jism*, meaning "of the body, corporeal, physical" and used as an adjective with *al-sura* to indicate "bodily form" or "embodied form." Ibn Sina's refusal to use words connected with physicality suggests that he is considering the metaphysical rather than the physical aspect of matter.

Ibn Sina says that *hayula* has a substance (*jawhar*). He states that substance comes to it in actuality, to its essence. Whether *jawhar* is translated as substance or essence here, it nevertheless refers to the place where a thing exists, which will be brought into existence when the form attaches to matter. The idea resembles al-Kindi's statement that matter bears form, although the vocabulary does not. This also reiterates al-Farabi's idea that form and matter exist only in conjunction with each other. Ibn Sina says explicitly that *madda* receives perfection (*kamal*) which brings it into existence, thus matter becomes a substance-in-actuality at that time. Ibn Sina says that *hayula* receives both form (*sura*) and perfection (*kamal*): specifically, Ibn Sina says *qabila lil-suwar* (receiving forms) and *yaqbal kamal ma* (receiving a certain perfection). He equates form with perfection when he says matter receives a perfection or completion.

Overall in this first Sinawiyyan definition for matter we find many of the same ideas found in al-Kindi. Ibn Sina repeats both the idea of matter as a potentiality and the idea that matter is actualized when it receives a form. According to Ibn Sina, matter is a passive, underlying thing, just as al-Kindi stated matter is passive (acted upon). Al-Farabi implies that it is passive.

The second term Ibn Sina uses for matter, which will be examined here, is *madda*.[62] Since Ibn Sina states bluntly at the beginning of this definition that "matter may be said to be a term, which is synonymous with *hayula*," it seems a false distinction to state that Ibn Sina believes *madda* indicates something substantially different from *hayula*. In al-Farabi's definition of *madda*, although he does not formally equate it with *hayula*, it certainly appears to be synonymous. This aspect of *madda* is also demonstrated by al-Farabi's refusal to use *hayula* in his serious work, *The Book of Letters*.

A Latin commentary bears out the synonymy of *hayula* and *madda* for Ibn Sina. This commentary, written by Ibn Sina's Latin translator Alpago and published in the sixteenth century, treats this part of the definition in the following manner: "Materia quandoq; dicitur etc. Ex dixis Avicennæ patet, q' materia dicitur synonyme de hyle, & de omni subiecto, qd' simul cum re alia eiusdem specie, aut alterius speciei cum eo recipit aliquam perfectionem, aut formam."[63] Not only has Ibn Sina given *madda* and *hayula* as synonyms – as Alpago also asserts – but he has also listed the same characteristics for each of them, indicating a true coincidence of these terms and their meanings. Arabic acquired useful and interesting words from other languages, such as *hayula*, although Ibn Sina, following al-Farabi's lead, takes the process a step further and uses *madda* in a technical sense. The strongest evidence that al-Farabi uses *madda* in a technical sense is his use of the expression *al-madda al-ula* for prime matter, discussed above.

Ibn Sina states that matter is said of every subject, in other words matter is part of the structure of everything. In this, too, *madda* is similar to *hayula*. *Madda* must also receive its perfection, in the sense of completion, by the joining of different things in it. The idea of joining things together to form a species also implies that matter is a compound substance; it is not a simple substance. Ibn Sina uses the example of an animal formation by the coming together, little by little, of blood and sperm. With the definition for *madda* he uses a more material vocabulary including: *al-dam* (blood), *al-minan* (sperm) and *al-hayawan* (animal), all physically existing, material objects. Ibn Sina uses "perfection, completion" (*al-kamal*) in the sense of "form" in this definition. He says "it receives the perfection," meaning "it receives the form." This is an ellipsis: form is what perfects matter. Ibn Sina is stating the result of that form's combining with the subject (*mawduᶜ*) which received it. When the form combines with the substrate, perfection results. This is very similar to al-Farabi's ideas. The idea here is amplified to say that perfection accrues slowly, as the forms are being built up on the substrate, little by little.

The specific examples here deal with the types of matter which take form to produce an animal, so that it may become one species or another. In a roundabout manner Ibn Sina is also stating that a species is a species because of the kinds of form and matter which comprise it. Perfection is attained by the combination of other things in a substrate; these things are bound together a little at a time. Al-Farabi's physical example was wood which forms a bed. Al-Farabi uses an inanimate object, and Ibn Sina uses an animate thing, but both examples are concrete physical objects. Ibn Sina states that the confluence of physical matter may or may not result in a member of a species. Such an assertion indicates an awareness that results cannot be predicted. This may refer to another aspect of the problem of matter – causation. It may be helpful in understanding Ibn Sina's meaning here if one takes him to say that every time the natural process known to cause generation of an animal occurs, an animal does not necessarily come into existence. However, when the effect occurs, it is too regular to be explained by chance.

The careful study of these terms indicates a development of the philosophical vocabulary in the Arabic language. In the first Chapter the outlines of the problem of definition are given. In Chapter 2 the pioneer of Islamic philosophy, al-Kindi, was discussed. He was the first philosopher writing in Arabic, who would be forced by circumstances to write in a less technical manner than his successors. Al-Kindi found an elegant solution to the problem of philosophical definitions by defining the most complex terms concisely in simple language, thus allowing a phrase to be substituted for a term in subsequent definitions and leading the reader to an initial understanding of philosophy. Although one may be tempted to quibble with al-Kindi's choice of definitions – either in their words or concepts –the modern reader must continually remember that he wrote for an audience inexperienced in philosophical thought. To a larger degree than those who followed him, he had to depend on intuition.

In Chapter 3 the discussion focused on the way in which the translation movement continued contemporaneously with philosophy becoming a more familiar science, enabling al-Farabi to move beyond al-Kindi's definitions. In al-Farabi one finds a work more self-consciously Aristotelian, incorporating the newer translations of Aristotle unavailable to al-Kindi. There is also an appropriation of native language Arabic terms to designate the concepts expropriated from Greek thought.

The work of Ibn Sina, reviewed in Chapter 4, shows a philosophy employing the fully formed philosophical vocabulary. While he has internalized and quotes Aristotle on occasion, Ibn Sina's own work is a synthesis, which results in a new interpretation. Ibn Sina is not a slavish imitator. The philosophical vocabulary is so much more familiar to the *failasuf* at this point that he is comfortable using transliterated Greek words like *al-hayula* and *al-ustuqas*, either in addition to or instead of the Arabic terms al-Kindi had appropriated, such as *al-sura* and *al-ʿunsur*.

In Chapter 5, the comparisons show al-Kindi in a favorable light, more of an innovator than is often realized. One sees how he influenced the subsequent development of Islamic philosophy; in the above-mentioned discussion of the short definition of *sura*, the reader observes his direct influence on Ibn Sina's work. It can also be seen that Ibn Sina directly rebutted the views held by the natural philosophers, which included al-Kindi, in his treatment of *mabda' haraka al-shay'*. In his discussion of the four causes, al-Kindi says it is "the principle of motion of a thing, which is its cause. ..."[64]

On the other hand, Ibn Sina states that by the efficient cause he means something more than a principle of movement. He says,

> That is because the metaphysical philosophers do not mean by the efficient [cause] the principle of setting in motion only, as the natural philosophers mean; rather (they mean) the principle and giving of existence, like the Creator [is] to the world; as for the efficient natural cause it does not give existence other than setting in motion in terms of one of the modes of setting in motion; thus the giving of existence in the natural philosophers is the principle of movement.[65]

Here Ibn Sina mentions the efficient cause as bringing existence to a thing, not merely principle of motion. Whereas, in contrast, al-Kindi described the efficient cause as being only the principle of motion.

Here is a sharp contrast between the efficient cause as setting a thing in motion or as the principle of giving existence. Al-Kindi, who was in the category of natural philosophers, only had to explain motion in natural terms, while Ibn Sina does not mean merely the principle of motion, but the metaphysical idea of giving existence to a thing. By isolating natural from metaphysical ideas, he is able to direct attention to the cause at a deeper level, not only the visible natural level.

Part 2

IBN SINA'S
BOOK OF DEFINITIONS

6

THE SOCIO-POLITICAL MILIEU OF IBN SINA

In the late tenth century the Central Asian city of Bukhara was a hotbed of cross-cultural influences brimming with new ideas as an intellectual center, as well as a frontier outpost through which bands of marauding raiders traveled on their way someplace else. One poet, Abu Ahmad b. Abi Bakr al-Katib, described its rank fetid canals, and crowded and unhealthy conditions in scurrilous terms.[1]

In dynastic terms, the last independent Samanid amirs ruled Bukhara. As an outpost on the eastern fringes of Abbasid power, Bukhara was far from the major center in Baghdad. At the same time in Central Asia, Chinese influence remained strong, along with the remnants of Buddhism and Zoroastrianism. In fact, the Tang Chinese had combined with the Uighurs to control the Tarim Basin and the Silk Road through Bukhara a couple of centuries before Ibn Sina's birth. Shortly, the Samanid dynasty would face conquest from the south and east as the brutal Ghaznavid Sultan Mahmud steamrollered through Khurasan. By AD 705 the Muslim Arab armies had nominally conquered the provinces of Central Asia. But as the Arabs pushed their conquests, language, and religion, the inhabitants of Khurasan proved resistant.

Part of Khurasan's resistance was expressed in the beginning of a Persian literary renaissance, known as the Shu'ubiyya. Its most famous intellectual, egotist, doctor, and philosopher was Ibn Sina. Another spectacular member of this renaissance was al-Firdawsi, poet and author of the *Shahnamah*, the epic Book of Kings, which recorded the ancient mythology of kings and heroes in the New Persian language. Like Ibn Sina, al-Firdawsi was a native of Bukhara; unlike Ibn Sina he went happily to the court of Mahmud of Ghazna, a town in the eastern part of Afghanistan, 90 miles southwest of Kabul. In a manner common to many aristocratic Muslim courts Mahmud, a tyrant, collected artisans and intellectuals to add luster to his court. A Samanid conqueror who had come to Ghazna earlier founded the Ghaznavid dynasty, of which Sultan Mahmud was a descendant.[2]

Ibn Sina (b. 370 AH/AD 980) trained as a physician, studied law and became famous as a philosopher. He treated the Samanid Amir Nuh II in his first professional endeavor. For payment, the amir allowed him to use the Saminids' extensive library.

Ibn Sina's intense self-conscious streak is evident in his autobiography. Even if there is little personal information in it, an autobiography was still unusual for a man of his times. Ibn Sina, the philosopher, appears to have been driven by intellectual curiosity and the need to know, expressed within an Islamic framework. Early in his life, when his father and his brother espoused Isma^cili doctrines, Ibn Sina distanced himself from them. He flatly states in his autobiography, *Life*, that his father tried to interest him in such beliefs, but claims he would have none of it. Certainly, Shi^cism became politically unpopular earlier in the tenth century when the Samanid Nuh I encouraged Sunnism at the behest of his vizier.

Ibn Sina, however, appears to have generally avoided court politics despite his employment as a physician and minister for rulers. At the end of the 990s or the early 1000s he fled from Bukhara across the Karakum Desert to Gurganj to escape the clutches of Mahmud.

Interestingly enough, Ibn Sina was usually religiously conventional in his writings, whatever his private convictions. In *al-Ilahiyyat*[3] he gives a synopsis of how to treat women that would not be out of place in the writings of one of the more rigid law codes. He recommends that women should be kept home, veiled. Promiscuity is bad in either sex, he says, but in men it only leads to envy, while great shame will befall women. He states that divorce should only be originated by men, because women have inferior rationality. Other than this brief chapter he does not appear to speak about women, or men's relationship with them, in his work. In fact, as is the case in studying many medieval philosophers, one receives the impression that there exists some parallel universe, where no beings have gender.

Although Ibn Sina had a devoted disciple, al-Juzjani, who completed his life story, he seems to have left behind little information about his personal relationships. Thus, when al-Bayhaqi says that – unlike Plato, who was abstinent – Ibn Sina was of a different temperament, being extremely fond of wine and sexual excess, readers may wonder at his historical accuracy. (He wrote, after all, 150 years after Ibn Sina.[4]) Or, for that matter, what was the accuracy of al-Bayhaqi's information about Plato? Al-Bayhaqi's insults may be regarded as more of a general smear campaign than as historical fact. Many famous courtiers and writers were imprisoned or suffered other indignities, on the whim of a patron or when their royal patrons fell from power, and Ibn Sina was no exception. (An earlier philosopher, al-Kindi, even lost his library when the political scene shifted.) In about 440 AH/AD 1023 in the city of Hamadhan (western Iran), Ibn Sina was imprisoned for four months. However, it was Ibn Sina's good fortune to be released by ^cAla' al-Dawla, who then became his patron.

^cAla' al-Dawla Muhammad (d. 433 AH/AD 1041–2), the Kaykuyid prince, ruled in western Persia fighting off the raids of Ibn Sina's old enemy Sultan

Mahmud of Ghazna in northwestern Persia. ᶜAla' al-Dawla lost occasionally – he even lost Isfahan once – but he recaptured that city when Ghaznawid authority collapsed. In 429 AH/AD 1037–8 ᶜAla' al-Dawla built a wall around Isfahan to protect it against future raiders.⁵ His perspicacity was validated ten years after his death, when another conqueror razed the walls and made Isfahan his capital.

Ibn Sina may have felt that in ᶜAla' al-Dawla he had finally found a patron worthy of his talents. For about thirteen years until his death in 428 AH/AD 1037, Ibn Sina lived in Isfahan under the patronage of ᶜAla' al-Dawla. Ibn Sina, already in poor health, undertook a trip to Hamadhan with ᶜAla' al-Dawla; he died there. His *Daneshnamah-i ᶜAla'i* (*Book of Knowledge for ᶜAla'*) was written for this prince, in Persian; it is a short encyclopedic work of essential philosophical knowledge.

Ibn Sina wrote numerous books, primarily in Arabic, the lingua franca of the medieval Islamic period. Among his most famous works are the philosophical encyclopedia *Kitab al-shifa'*, and *Kitab al-qanun fi al-tibb*, a description of the diagnosis of disease and its cure. The *Shifa'*, which literally means "healing," includes sections on the soul, logic, physics, and metaphysics. *Kitab al-qanun fi al-tibb* (which translates into English as Avicenna's *Canon*) refers to the "laws of medicine." As a result of the Latin translation of this latter work in the European Middle Ages, Ibn Sina became famous as "Avicenna," and the translated version of his book continued to be used as a medical textbook for centuries after his death. Thus the *Shifa'*, which is a healing of the soul, serves as a counterpoint to the healing of the body found in *Kitab al-qanun*. He relied heavily on a complex system from China of reading the pulse to make the diagnosis. The physician not only counts the number of heartbeats per minute, but notes their type and character.

Characteristically in *Kitab al-qanun* Ibn Sina zealously guards the turf of philosophers from intrusion by physicians. Of course, many of the most famous philosophers were also physicians, among them Aristotle, al-Kindi, and Galen. Many of the same terms occur in both medicine and in philosophy; often with related meanings. For example the word ᶜ*illa* in medicine means "disease." The physician was the one to look for the cause of the disease in order to cure it. Perhaps as an ellipsis, ᶜ*illa* came to mean the cause of something in philosophy; and the cause in a direct sense. The practice of medicine in classical times really necessitated the physician's contemplating the world in philosophical terms, as health was understood to be the result of a balance in the human organism. And that human organism stood in as a microcosm for the universe. Ibn Sina states that the philosopher is the one who investigates natural science, just as the legal scholar does, when he attempts to prove the soundness of the obligation of following consensus. Then it is not in his role as legal scholar, but in his role as mutakallim (theologian) that he understands consensus. The legal scholar only follows the law; it is in his role as theologian that he discusses consensus. The legal scholar as legal scholar cannot offer proofs irrevocably. Neither can the physician offer proofs irrevocably as physician, or the system fails.[6] The warning is offered to physicians who were not philosophers. Ibn Sina makes an example of Galen, whom he said attempted to establish proofs from the vantage point of being a philosopher, not from that of a physician. Ibn Sina sums up his position bluntly, "It is not appropriate for physicians to research in these matters, when it is not their art; rather, it is appropriate for the philosophers, so we have turned away from these matters."[7]

Ibn Sina's position is that it is inappropriate for physicians to worry about such matters. For example, he claims that in regard to the elements, physicians need only know how the elements affect the conditions of sickness and health in people. They do not need to know the ultimate nature of the elements. Consequently, Ibn Sina will avoid discussing these questions in his medical textbook, as an example to physicians. Such questions as the ultimate nature of the elements are covered in his philosophical works.

When the Arabs translated Greek texts, both philosophical and non-philosophical, into Arabic, philosophy was for them a self-conscious science.[8] And, since this translation movement occurred simultaneously with a tremendous intellectual awakening and curiosity brought on in no small way by Qur'anic exegesis, cultural conditions were excellent for the birth of Islamic philosophy. With curiosity abounding about theological questions, such as the nature of God, the afterlife and the place of human beings in the universe, it was a natural step to move to metaphysical enquiry about the nature of reality and the universe.

However, one problem early philosophers confronted when working in Arabic was the lack of a philosophical vocabulary. This lack demonstrated a need for books of definition of the type found in other disciplines such as grammar. Definition books were usually short, with concise, pithy definitions; sometimes short enough to be easily memorizable. But philosophers established the technical vocabulary by using words from other sciences and foreign loan words, and they required lists of vocabulary for their readers. The reader was then supposed to observe how these words were to be used in purely philosophical discourse.

Ibn Sina's *Kitab al-hudud (Book of Definitions)* is the second known philosophical book of definitions. (Al-Kindi's *On the Definitions and Descriptions of Things* was the first.) Ibn Sina writes an Introduction in which he discusses why he writes the treatise. In the Introduction he begins with his usual disclaimer: he is writing this for those who have demanded definitions, and he does so despite the difficulty. There is a nod to Aristotle, whose definition of definition he repeats from the *Topics*, and a disagreement with al-Kindi over al-Kindi's definition of passionate love (ᶜishq).[9] Once the preliminaries are out of the way, Ibn Sina proceeds in a logical order, defining definition, description, the Creator, and other terms, moving from the obviously important to the less important. All told, he defines about 70 terms. In his long definitions, such as intellect (§ 21), soul (§ 25), and form (§ 28), he begins with several popular definitions of the term, and then gives the limits of philosophical usage. This style is reminiscent of al-Farabi's definitions, as he also frequently began his definitions with the popular or common usage, and moved on to the technical.

Although *The Book of Definitions* is not dated within Ibn Sina's career, it is hard to imagine it as an early work, since many of the definitions are repeated from his longer works. They may be written in less detail in *The Book of Definitions*, but Ibn Sina repeats the same or similar terms as in his other works. Taken in conjunction with those other works, the definitions in *The Book of Definitions* are consistent. Some of Ibn Sina's works, such as *Mantiq al-mashriqiyyin* (*Logic of the Easterners*), were lost even in his lifetime. Many scholars find it hard to consider his work complete but in spite of some gaps there remains an impressive body of work.

In many ways, Ibn Sina reads like a modern author. His language is clear in expression; the text is stripped down and clean, not flowery or encumbered with extraneous ideas. Moreover, although the text is frequently difficult for a modern reader to comprehend, this has more to do with the reader's presumptions and expectations than with the form of Ibn Sina's expression. Once the reader overcomes her or his predispositions and lets the text speak for itself, the reader will be rewarded with real ideas that have flowed, alive and intriguing, from the eleventh century to the twentieth century. Ibn Sina also does the reader the great favor of refusing to patronize. He may indulge in formulaic exaggeration of his own ability and brag about his mental feats, but he expects the reader to be able to follow him (which is, after all, the greatest compliment any author can pay a reader).

The goal of the current project is to re-imagine Ibn Sina, so that by imagining the past it becomes understandable. One reason to research the past is to research and translate antique authors, to recreate their times, their lives, their thoughts. If the scholar cannot attempt to re-imagine their times, that scholar is only engaged in academic taxidermy – mounting stuffed philosophers with dried thoughts.

Islam began in the seventh century AD with God's message to the Prophet Muhammad, a reiteration of the message to earlier prophets. This message, sent via the Prophet, is for all people. It took the form of the Qur'an, God's message of love and duty to his creatures.[10] Unlike the Christian New Testament and the Hebrew Bible, which claim only to be inspired by God, rather than literally word-for-word the word of God, the Qur'an is believed to be the literal word of God. In the Qur'an's creation story (according to one commentator) the first thing God created was the Pen, which writes the destiny of the world.¹¹ The Qur'an is eternally existent and uncreated, according to orthodox theory. The Qur'an was given to Muhammad in Arabic – a clear and pure Arabic (S. 26.195 and S. 46.12) – which is inimitable and untranslatable. Thus, the Qur'an itself is also a miracle; it serves as the witness to the truth of Muhammad's mission (S. 29.15). So, although the Qur'an can be explained in other languages, there can never be a complete translation.

In the belief of the Qur'an's nature, there is already a strong emphasis on words, since the Qur'an carries the divine words. This led to the need, felt early in the Muslim community, to fully understand the words. Although the message seemed simple and clear in the seventh century, as time went on questions arose over the correct interpretation of various verses.

The first theologians dealing with such questions included a group called the Mu'tazili, sometimes referred to as the "rationalizing theologians." They attempted to investigate questions and apparent inconsistencies using the rules of logic. A verse such as "To Allah belong the East and West. So whichever way you turn, there is Allah's face. Indeed, Allah is Omnipresent and Omniscient." (S. 2.115),¹² raised the question, "What is meant by God's face?" Other verses referred to God's hand in similarly problematic terms.

The Ash'arites, another school of theology, developed an inspired response to the question of the face of God and the hand of God.¹³ God's face and hand exist, but without knowing how. In other words, Muslims must believe that God has a face and a hand, but further speculation is discouraged; it is beyond the powers of human reason to understand. Thus, believers know that God has a face and a hand because the Qur'an tells them so, but they do not know what God's face or hand might look like.

In Islamic theology, speculation was particularly difficult because it was generally and emphatically agreed that God is nothing like creatures. God is an absolute unity. God cannot have parts, and – in contradiction – it appears self-evident that a face or a hand is a part. This immense divide (plus the insistence on the absolute oneness of God) increased the complexity in the question of just what the face or hand of God might be. By affirming the existence of God's face and hand, without discussing the "how" the Ash'arites had hoped to avoid such arguments.

Another disparagement of the philosophers was that they depended on human reason, rather than on faith, which is a divine gift. However, the faithful have other documentation: Muslims have the "hadiths" in addition to the Qur'an, the direct word of God. Hadiths are reports of the sayings and practice, or acts, of the Prophet and the Companions. As such they are an aid to interpreting the Qur'an and the duties it requires. Although human beings are required to pray five times a day by Qur'anic law, the details are needed, such as what the prayer will consist of, as well as the time of performance and ritual purity. The details of these injunctions may be found in the hadith literature.

Debate also arose over the question of whether the Qur'an itself is eternal or was created by God. In a short time, rational or logical speculation about the nature of God aroused suspicion in orthodox circles. Al-Ghazali (d. 505 AH/ AD 1111) rejected philosophical enquiry, and in doing so dealt Islamic philosophy a body-blow from which it never recovered. After al-Ghazali, speculative thought became more mystical and focused on Illuminationist ideas rather than pure intellectual speculation. By writing in terms inaccessible to the uninitiated such mystical philosophers hoped to evade the critics.

One way to read the history of Islamic thought is as the history of tension between rationalism and faith grounded in intuition. For all that critics object to the heathen qualities of Islamic philosophy — falling into the snares set for them by the theologians — the philosophers were generally Islamic in their public, social, and cultural outlook. Ibn Sina may have drunk wine — as other Muslims have been known to do — but he did not make philosophic demands that would be totally out of place in medieval Islamic culture. He did not demand, for instance, that women should be able to work professionally, or be able to ask for divorce on equal terms with men, or — heaven forbid — be philosophers.

The Islamic philosophers affirmed creation and the existence of one God, and they did so in terms unknown to the Greeks. Thus, when modern scholars describe Islamic philosophy as a pale continuation of Greek philosophy, they are making themselves into Islamic theologians and following the complaints of those theologians, rather than looking at the full world view as actually described in Islamic philosophy.

Now, look at Ibn Sina and an instance of his scandalously "prohibited" behavior. Ibn Sina drank wine, which is expressly prohibited in the Qur'an. What is most interesting is that he admits it. Ibn Sina states in *Life*, in his revery of youthful study habits, "Whenever sleep overcame me, or I became conscious of weakening, I would turn aside to drink a cup of wine, so that my strength would return to me."[14] But before quickly judging Ibn Sina an unbelieving Muslim, it is worth remembering that in all cultures the actions of many people do little to reflect their religious beliefs. Christians who attend Church only on Christmas and Easter are a common phenomenon in the West, although presumably these people still consider themselves Christians. Religious identity is a very private and unknowable thing.

If in considering Ibn Sina with fresh eyes, his geographical and cultural origins are borne in mind, in addition to his philosophical and medical education, then influences on his thought beyond Islam and Hellenistic philosophy may appear. Buddhism, which began as an offshoot of Hinduism in India, traveled north and then spread to China and Japan in the east. For a time, Buddhism was widespread in Central Asia, although it had to compete with Zoroastrianism, the official religion of the Persian dynasties.

Although the influence of Buddhism in Central Asia dried up by AD 980, remnants and traces of its influence continued. Earlier in the millennium it had been a major force in the area, as shown by various manuscript caches of multiple language texts found in storehouses. Perhaps western scholarship on Islamic philosophy today tends to focus on Greek influences, but a lack of awareness of Chinese or Buddhist philosophical force does not negate that considerable influence. In the following commentary there is a detailed discussion of some possible instances of eastern influence, such as the ancient method of pulse diagnosis that Ibn Sina appears to have learned from the Chinese. Buddhist ideas which have parallels in Islamic thought, such as triads, are also discussed.

The Asian world was hardly isolated. Both goods and ideas traveled back and forth continually between China and Central Asia throughout the first millennium AD, as foreign courts lusted after eastern luxuries, most particularly Chinese silk. Central Asia is an ultimate peripheral region, peripheral not just to Europe, but to India and China as well. Discovering exactly what the early Chinese historians knew about their neighbors, and coordinating Chinese histories with either Muslim or western histories has been left mostly undone for several reasons. These difficulties were well summed up by a nineteenth-century French scholar, Remusat, who said that the methods of the Chinese historians in writing history, their geographical perspective, and their dating vis à vis Central Asia and Europe, prevented a coordination of Chinese history in the matrix of world history.[15] To give one example, at first the Chinese took the name "Tajik" and gave it to the Muslim lands in general as *Ta-shih*. When they learned later to differentiate among different inhabitants of the Muslim world, they limited the term Tajik to the inhabitants of one region.[16] Sadly, in the end Central Asia became a backwater for two reasons. It never recovered from the depopulation visited on it by the Mongol conquerors in the seventh/thirteenth centuries. Juwayni, Persian historian of the Mongols, describes the desolation of Nishapur after all the inhabitants were massacred and states that even the dogs and cats were killed, following Genghis Khan's capture of the city.[17] Questions may arise at the enormity of the numbers reported – 700,000 massacred at Marw, 1.7 million at Nishapur and 1.6 million at Heart – but the possible inflation of their numbers should not diminish the severity of the catastrophe for the region.[18]

The Mongols preferred pastures for their flocks to a settled population and this is one possible reason for their policy of genocide. Even so, their devastation of the rural areas was more serious, as these were irrigated lands which are tremendously difficult to reclaim once they have been lost. Not only that, but without an agricultural surround, a large city could not be supported. Cities do sometimes recover from such terrors, if there is an economic reason for them to rebuild. But, in the case of Bukhara, as the sea routes became better known, it became much more economical to ship goods by sea than to travel by land. The passing of the Silk Route, as the primary highway for commerce between east and west, ended the importance of the Central Asian cities. Amir Timur did, indeed, build Samarkand, using imported craftsmen, building a monument to his power and glory, but Timur was the last to take the area seriously.

Taking into consideration all the influences on Ibn Sina, the challenge should be accepted to think of him as a real person, in complex terms, and not as a stuffed philosopher. It has generally been accepted that Ibn Sina was ethnically Persian, but what does this mean? He lived in a place where multiculturalism was the norm. The English translation of Ibn Sina's *Life* begins, "My father was a man of Balkh."[19] A more literal translation might say "My parent was from the folk of Balkh."[20] Arabic has its own poetry and strength, but the emphasis of the original writing is different than its accepted English translation. Ibn Sina's father served as a kind of local governor, according to his remarks. But of the generations before his father, it is hard to know if they were of Balkh or if they immigrated from the Central Persian lands. Modern-day Balkh is in Afghanistan and was formerly one of the most important cities of Khurasan. Khurasan itself was the home of many important intellectuals in this period. Ibn Sina's mother was from Afshonah, a small town near Bukhara, so she was a local Central Asian woman. This situates Ibn Sina firmly in the Central Asian milieu, which means that ethnically he was one-half Central Asian. His father's name remains unknown, while some manuscripts give his mother's name as Sitara. Scholarly speculation has raged for years as to the origin of the name "Ibn Sina." "Ibn" means son of, and is frequently used as a module in names, yet no reasonable explanation of Sina is forthcoming. The family moved to Bukhara when Ibn Sina was young, and Bukhara in those days was a place rife with many influences, but resistant to the central Abbasid authority. In reading Ibn Sina's *Life*, perhaps one is most struck by the range of knowledge, represented in the array of authors, available to Ibn Sina. Part of this accessibility of a broad range of knowledge was a function of the international scope of Bukhara as a center of learning, while part, no doubt, was also the result of his family's influential position.

Ibn Sina studied medicine among other sciences as a young man. He says it was not difficult. He emphasizes that philosophy is more difficult, especially more difficult than medicine. Ibn Sina appears to equate difficulty with value, and consequently devalues the practice of medicine. On the one hand, he states that he began to treat the sick at an early age, and indeed, when he was about seventeen he cured the Amir Nuh ibn Mansur (d. 387 AH/AD 997). Ibn Mansur showed his gratitude by allowing Ibn Sina to use the Samanid library at Bukhara, which was evidently a tremendous resource. On the other hand, he emphasizes the difficulty of philosophy. First, he frequently stayed up all night working on philosophy problems and when he was in danger of falling asleep, he either drank wine to stay awake, or fell asleep and dreamed about the questions which perplexed him – they often became clearer in his sleep. Second, he claimed to have read Aristotle's *Metaphysics* forty times without understanding it. (This number may be understood in the sense of "dozens" of times.) It was not until he read a commentary on the *Metaphysics* by al-Farabi (d. 339 AH/AD 950–951), probably *The Book of Letters* (*Kitab al-huruf*) that he understood Aristotle's book.[21] This story makes two points: it emphasizes the difficulty of philosophy and thus its superiority, as well as the need for a commentator. The idea of having a commentator or guide to direct the student to the right path of understanding is central to both philosophy and Islamic society, especially on religious questions.

The idea of a guide is particularly strong among Sufis, the mystics of Islam. The guide of a Sufi disciple does not necessarily have to be living or human; rather, the Sufis have a tradition of those who do not have living visible human guides. The most famous Sufi guide is Khidr, a mysterious figure who guided the thirteenth-century Sufi mystic, Ibn al-ᶜArabi, among others.[22] Ibn Sina, by stressing his dependence on his guide, shows he is following tradition. He authenticates his own philosophical search, demonstrating that he too is dependent on the guidance of an authority. Up to this point by his own admission Ibn Sina had been arrogant and independent. He had recounted the shortcomings of his teachers in philosophy, one, a man named al-Natili, who was hired to teach him the *Eisagoge*, Porphyry's introduction to Aristotle's logical works. Ibn Sina quickly surpassed this tutor in logic, and was left to study on his own. The *Metaphysics* is the first text he admits to reading so many times he had nearly memorized it without understanding it. Thus, to see Ibn Sina crediting al-Farabi with explaining this text increases al-Farabi's stature as a guide. As mentioned previously, in the *Qanun*, Ibn Sina objected to physicians who think they are equipped to be philosophers, and able to think in philosophical terms, even though medicine and philosophy deal in some similar terms; medicine does not have the dimensions of philosophy.

Finally there is the question of Ibn Sina's reputation as a libertine. Al-Juzjani asserted this characteristic in his continuation of Ibn Sina's *Life*. Ibn Funduq al-Bayhaqi developed and amplified this idea, accusing Ibn Sina of all-around lack of abstemiousness. Throughout his life Ibn Sina worked for various princes, as a minister or physician, often writing at night. His output was prodigious, which would not appear to leave him that much time for attending parties and carousing. On the other hand, the princes did expect socializing from their companions. At one time Ibn Sina served as vizier to Shams al-Dawla. Al-Juzjani gives this picture of Ibn Sina's working habits, "The instruction took place at night, because of the lack of free time during the day on account of his service to the Amir."[23] Al-Juzjani also states specifically that at this time Ibn Sina was working on the *Qanun* and the *Shifa'*, teaching from both of them each night in shifts. These are his two most important works the *Qanun*, on medicine, and the *Shifa'*, on philosophy. Apparently his work and personality aroused envy in the biographers after al-Juzjani. Whatever his personal habits, Ibn Sina's output was staggering.

There are several ways of looking at Ibn Sina. First, he may be seen as a Peripatetic Aristotelian/neo-Platonic philosopher. This is frequently done. He may also be seen as being heavily influenced by the Persian Shuʿubiyya movement, a populist movement, the renaissance of Persian literature by Persians, sometimes in the Persian language, like Ibn Sina's contemporary al-Firdawsi, the poet and author of the Persian nationalistic epic the *Shahnamah* (*Book of Kings*). Like Ibn Sina, al-Firdawsi was from Khurasan. Evidence for this interpretation includes a major book written in Persian *Daneshnamah-i ʿAla'i* (*The Book of Knowledge for ʿAla' al-Dawla*), and Ibn Sina's continual residence in Persian territories, no matter how far he moved. He may be seen as a Sufi, although his interest runs in the line of rational mysticism, or union with God through the intellect. Evidence for this perspective includes treatises such as *Risala fi al-ʿishq* (*The Treatise on Love*). In the end, Ibn Sina is perhaps best viewed as an intelligent, independent and original thinker, who used the ideas of his predecessors or discarded them as he found it convenient to do. Even this small, and perhaps insignificant treatise, *The Book of Definitions*, points to a scholar with a wide range of interests and exposure to many ideas, without undue concern as to their orthodoxy – whether political or religious. The first as he spent his life fleeing Mahmud of Ghazna, whose patronage al-Firdawsi accepted; and the second as he appeared unconcerned with the orthodox reaction to his claims to drink wine and to disbelieve in jinn.

7

TRANSLATION:
THE BOOK OF DEFINITIONS[1]

1. In the name of Allah, the Compassionate, the Merciful.
2. The eminent shaykh Abu ᶜAli al-Husayn ibn Sina,[2] may Allah Most High have mercy on him, said:
3. Friends asked me to dictate the definitions for things to them; they requested me to define specific things.[3] Knowing from experience that definition is practically impossible for anybody – whether it is definition or description – I kept putting them off. In fact, anyone who is so foolish as to stay with it and who has the confidence in their ability to give definitions in a suitable way must be ignorant of those passages in books, which are corrupted and then taken to shape false descriptions or definitions. Nevertheless there is no way to stop my friends, who continuously importune me. They appeal for my assistance and have even redoubled their efforts over time. Even though I have demonstrated to them the mistakes in definitions found in these same passages, their importuning continues. They still believe I am able to assist them in grasping after knowledge. No matter that I am willing to acknowledge my shortcomings in helping them seek the truth, they still catch me unawares, particularly in the way they pester me to give them definitions on the spur of the moment. I seek help from Allah, the Giver of the intellect.

   Therefore I will record whatever comes to me through recollection, so that at least some of my audience may agree on the soundness and accuracy in my remarks. Before I begin this project, allow me to present some difficulties in this art. Success is with Allah.
4. Concerning the difficulty connected with giving an actual definition, while we do not usually concern ourselves with error, in this case, we may say there is a difficulty greater than that imposed by other situations. This difficulty is a severe obstacle. Imagine, for instance, that among the lowly and dissolute guests at the court, one were to absent himself from royal affairs, not out of modesty and consideration for social customs, but because he fears being taken advantage of by the sovereign;[4] such a man withdraws from galas and the other festivities. In much the same way, we

are fully aware of our shortcomings. We beg pardon for our shortcomings in managing to realize descriptions in their real actualities in undertaking this task, and we seek protection from whatever definitions are not true. Such is our fortune, and may Allah protect us from error.

5   According to our knowledge of the art of logic, for a definition to be actual, it is necessary for it to be an indication of the essence of a thing. It is the completion of its essential existence so that nothing from the essential predicates is left out, unless these predicates are included in it whether in actuality or in potentiality.[5] "In potentiality" includes every one of the individual expressions which are subsumed in it. When the individual expressions are broken down and dissolved to the parts of its definition, this break-down into component parts, effects the parts of a definition loosening them to the end of the matter, into parts with no other essential parts remaining. It is a definition when it is thus: a definition of a thing defined in actuality is equal to it in intention. It is equal to it in intention just as it is equal to it in common usage. It is not the case [in actual definition] for concepts like "sentient being" and "animal" to be equivalent, when sentient being is equal to the other term in common usage, but sentient being is not equal to animal in intention, because the purpose of the expression sentient being is a thing which senses only, while the purpose of the expression animal is another thing, such as, for example, it is a body possessing a soul to nuture it, being sentient and moving at will. The concept of animal is more developed in intention than sentient being (*al-hassas*), although they are equivalent in common usage.

6   Philosophers only intend in that case to give a definition, not an essential distinction where it may sometimes derive from a high genus and a low differentia – like our expression "a human being is a rational, mortal substance" – rather they want in definition to impress on the soul an intelligible form equal to an existing form. In the same way an existing form becomes what it is by the completion of its essential attributes, either in actuality or in potentiality. If philosophers were to make this change in the distinction then they would seek the definition of the distinction. It would be like seeking knowledge of one thing in order to learn about another.

7   Therefore it is stipulated in defining terms, that one give the nearest genus so that all the common essentials may be included in it. It was enjoined to add all the differentiae, although one of these differentiae is sufficient for distinction. It can be said that the definition of terms should not be limited to the formal differentia without the material differentia, or to the material differentia without the formal differentia. If either one of the two is sufficient as a means of distinction, then one would think how does it come to a person to make distinction present in defining carefully? For if he

takes as a concomitant something which is not individuated, then it will not be possible to raise it in the imagination to the level of the essential. Moreover how will he be able to pick the nearest genus in every passage; and he will not be careless so that he takes the farthest genus over the nearest genus. For the composition does not indicate which genus; and division in a way that is not damaging to understanding is the hardest part. Finding this through demonstration is very difficult. Next we assert that definition has already attained the sum of what it should essentially attain; there is nothing in a definition of non-essential concomitants; the nearest genus has been taken.

8 How does a human being manage to obtain all the substantive differentiae of the term defined until they are equal? How shall the distinction among some of the differentiae not make him careless about seeking the rest? How will he find in each one the aspect of the thing sought? Thus, in respect of the divisions which consist of the intrinsic differentiae, how will he keep that in mind when they are part of the genera which are above the near genus? Will he divide that genus into two kinds of intrinsic divisions? And how is it possible for him to keep every part in its place, that he may seek the nearest genus from the first of two divisions; and with that he will not lose the differentia which belongs to another division, if it is essential. If it is as some people say that essential differentiae are not intrinsic, and the essential differentiae incorporate only the inessential, then how is it possible for a person to guard against mistakes in every case? He will begin with what he must for the essential division without the inessential (*ghayr al-dhatiyya*). These reasons and those currents that flow from them are what causes us to go on at length here, giving us solace that, except in a few cases, we will master bringing true definitions up to the standard.

9 In regard to insufficient definitions and descriptions, many reasons for our weaknesses are mentioned in the *Topics*, although they were not mentioned from this point of view.[6] There is a difference between an insufficient definition and a description. An insufficient definition is of the essentials, which means it discusses the genera and differentiae, from which follow logically the equivalence to the thing in popular usage, but it does not attain equivalence in true meaning. In such definitions the ensuing statement falls short of the genus or the differentia or what is common to both.

10 This kind of common failure may also be seen in insufficient definition and description. It is a mistake to put the differentia in the place of genus, like the one who says that yearning love (*ʿishq*) is the excess of love (*mahabba*)[7] rather it is love overflowing. Likewise matter may be put in the place of genus – for example, one may say of a chair that "it is wooden-ness upon which to sit;" or of a sword that "it is iron which cuts."

In these two definitions matter is put in the place of the genus. Similarly it is like their statement that ashes are "wood burned." Or, they may put the part in place of the whole, like saying "ten is five plus five." The Sage quoted another example of this – it is the saying that an animal is body with soul. This only leads to obscurity in the subject.[8]

11 Putting the habitual intellect in the place of the potential is the same kind of mistake, while the potential has its place among the genera, like their saying that upright person is the one who has the ability to avoid lustful desires, since the profligate is also able to do so, yet he does not do so. Therefore the potential is put in place of the habitual due to the resemblance of the habitual to the potential, because the habitual is an established potentiality. This is like saying that the one possessing the power over injustice is the one who tends by his circumstances and his nature to grab what is not his from the hand of someone else.[9] Here a habitual trait has replaced a potential trait, because the one who is capable of injustice may be just, he may be not be evil, and his nature may not be thus.

12 A metaphorical or ambiguous word is of the same type of mistake, such as a statement that "understanding (*fahm*) is agreeable," or "the soul is a number."[10] Or, one may put a thing among the concomitants instead of the genera, such as the one and the existent. Similarly, the species may be put in place of the genus, such as their saying that the evil person is one who wrongs people; and wrongdoing is a type of evil.

13 In regard to the differentia, one may take the concomitants in place of the essentials, and the genus in place of the differentia. One may consider the passions[11] as differentiae. And while the passions are strong the thing is stabilized, and it is strong.[12] We may take the accidents as differentiae of substances. We may take the differentiae of quality in the sense of not-quality; and the differentiae of the relative in the sense of the not-relative, rather than what it is related to.

14 As for the common rules, for example, we may define a thing through what is more hidden than it, such as, the definition of fire as an entity resembling the soul; here the soul is more hidden than fire. Or a thing is defined by what is equivalent in knowledge, or of what is subsequent to it in knowledge. The statement that number is a multitude, which is composed of ones, is an example of a thing which is equivalent in knowledge. Since number and multitude are one thing, this is saying the same thing in its definition.

15 Of this class, one uses a contrary in the definition of its contrary, such as saying a pair is a number greater by one than one. Next they say the single number is a number less by one than a pair. Thus if one takes the relative in a definition of the relative, it is the same thing as Porphyry[13] has done, when he reckoned that one should take into account genus in

the definition of the species, and species in the definition of genus. But this is an obscure matter.[14]

16 Regarding the contraries in relation to negation and non-existence, it is necessary that one take into account the affirmative and the habitual in their definitions, without conversion.

17 As for the one who takes the subsequent in the definition of a thing, it is like saying that the sun is a star which rises in the daytime. It is not possible to define day except with the sun, because it is the time of the rising of the sun. In such a way the well-known definition of a quantity is that it is receptive of equivalence and nonequivalence; and of quality that it is receptive of resemblance and nonresemblance. In summary, these mistakes and what resembles them in meanings turn us away from true definitions.

18 The definition of definition (*hadd*) is what the Philosopher mentions in the book, *Topics*; definition is a statement indicating the quiddity of a thing,[15] that is, definition is a statement in regard to the perfection of a thing's essential existence. The nature of something is what the thing acquires from the near genus and its differentia.

19 About description (*rasm*). A complete description is a statement composed of the genus of a thing and the accidents concomitant to it, so the description becomes equivalent to the thing. In absolute terms, the description is a statement which defines a thing in terms of inessential knowledge – but which is particular to it. It is a statement which distinguishes a thing from whatever may be its equal, but not essentially.

20 The Creator[16] (*al-bari*) – may He be glorified – has no definition, and no description, because He has no genus and no differentia. There is no composition in Him, and no accidentals attach to Him, but there is a saying about Him explaining His name, He is the Existent, the Necessary Existence, about whom it is not possible that His existence comes from any other, nor is there any other existence equal to Him emanating from His existence. This explains His name. Following this explanation is the statement that He is the existent who is not increased by number, nor by extent, nor by parts of the constituent, nor by parts of the definition, nor by parts of the relationship. There is no change, not in His essence, nor in the concomitants of His essence which are unrelated, and not in the concomitants that are related to Him.

21 The definition of intellect (*ʿaql*).[17] Intellect is a common term[18] having many meanings. Thus one says intellect belongs to the health of the first innate disposition (*al-fitra*) in a human being. The definition of intellect is, intellect is a faculty for distinguishing between repugnant and worthy matters. One says intellect is part of what a human being acquires of the knowledge of the universal judgements through experience. Then there is the definition with the meaning that it is a sum total of premises in the

mind, which are used for extracting good purposes and aims. Intellect is used in another meaning; its definition is that intellect leads to praiseworthy conduct in a human being, resulting in their motions, rest, words and choices. These three meanings are the meanings which the general public designates by the term intellect.

22 There are eight meanings which the term "intellect" indicates to philosophers. One meaning of intellect is that of which Aristotle speaks in his book *Posterior Analytics*.[19] He differentiated between intellect and knowledge. Aristotle said its meaning is: this meaning of intellect consists of conceptualizations and beliefs arising within the soul by its innate disposition,[20] but knowledge is what arises by acquisition. The other meanings are spoken of in the *Book of the Soul*. These include the theoretical intellect and the practical intellect. The theoretical intellect is a faculty of the soul by which it receives the quiddities of universal things in so far as they are universal. Practical intellect is a faculty of the soul, serving as the moving principle for the desirous faculty toward whatever it chooses among particulars, for a supposed end.

23 Intellect is also said to belong to many faculties of the theoretical intellect. These include the material intellect, which is a faculty of the soul, preparing it to receive the essences of things, stripped of matter. Next there is the habitual intellect, which is the perfection of this faculty insofar as it may become a faculty close to actualization by attaining what he called intellect in the *Posterior Analytics*. Next, there is the actual intellect, which is a perfection in the soul of a certain concept or of an intelligible concept, so that when intellect wishes, it thinks a concept; it causes that concept to be present in actuality. Next, there is the acquired intellect, which is an essence stripped of matter, imprinted in the soul by way of what has reached it from the outside.

24 Next, there are intellects which are called active intellects, which are all quiddity, stripped of matter totally. The definition of the Active Intellect is as follows. With regard to its being intellect, it is a formal substance; its essence is a quiddity stripped down in itself, not by stripping anything else of matter or of the bonds of matter. Intellect is the quiddity of every existent. But with regard to its being an Active Intellect, it is a substance of the previously-mentioned type, by its nature the Active Intellect brings the material intellect out of potentiality into actuality by illumination.

25 The definition of soul (*nafs*). Soul is a common term which refers to human beings, animals, and plants according to a common meaning, and there is another meaning common to human beings and heavenly angels. The definition of the first meaning is that the soul is the perfection of a natural body instrumental for the living being in potentiality. The definition of soul in the other sense is that the soul is an un-embodied substance which is the perfection of a body, having motion by choice

according to a rational principle, that is, an intellect in actuality or potentiality. The potential intellect is a differentia of the human soul, but the actual intellect is a differentia or property of the universal angelic soul.

26 The universal intellect and intellect of the universe,[21] and the universal soul and the soul of the universe are the expressions used. Thus the universal intellect is understood in the meaning consisting of the intellects, including many different ideas by the number of intellects which belong to individual people. The universal intellect does not exist alone as an established state; rather the universal intellect exists in conceptualization. As for the intellect of the universe, it is said in two meanings for the same reason "the universe" is said in two meanings, in one universe means the sum total of the world,[22] and in the second universe refers to the ultimate body[23] which is said to be the body of the universe, and its motion is said to be the motion of the universe, since the universe is under the influence of its motion. As for the intellect of the universe and the universe in it, in consideration of the first meaning let us explain its name as being the sum total of essences stripped of matter in all aspects, which do not move by themselves or by accident; there is no movement except by longing. The last one of this series is the Active Intellect present in human souls. This series is made up of principles of the universe subsequent to the first principle. The first principle is the Creator of the universe. As for the universe in it in terms of the second meaning, it is the intellect which is a substance stripped of matter in all aspects, and it is the mover which causes the movement of the universe by way of longing for itself.[24] Its existence is first, an existence received from the First Existent.

27 Next we will consider the expressions the universal soul and the soul of the universe: the universal soul[25] is understood as referring to different individuals, in answering the question, "What is it?"[26] For each of these individuals, a particular soul belongs to an individual. The soul of the universe is analogous to the intellect of the universe; it is the sum total of noncorporeal substances which are perfections; it is the governing agent of heavenly bodies, moving them by reason of intelligent choice. The noncorporeal substance which is a first perfection of the ultimate body is moved by it, like the motion of the universe by reason of intelligent choice.

The relationship of the soul of the universe to the intellect of the universe is the same as the relationship of our souls to the Active Intellect. The soul of the universe is a principle close to the existence of physical bodies. Its rank in attaining existence comes after the rank of the intellect of the universe. The soul's existence is an emanation from the intellect's existence.

28 The definition of form (*sura*). Form is a common term, said in different meanings according to the species and according to each essence of a thing, whatever it may be. It is also said of the perfection by which the species completes its second perfection. It is also used for the reality which establishes the substratum it has, and for the reality which establishes the species. The definition of form in the first meaning is species; indeed, form is the answer applied to many things in reply to "What is it?" It is also used in answering "What is it?" in common with another.

The definition in the second meaning is that it is every thing existing in something not as a part of it, nor is its constitution sound without it, whatever it may be.

The definition of form in the third meaning is that a thing exists in something else, not as a part of it, nor can its constitution be sound without it, and for its sake a thing exists;[27] for example, the sciences and virtues belonging to a person exist in this meaning of form.

29 The definition of form in the fourth meaning is that a thing exists in something else not as part of it, nor is its existence sound apart from it, but an existence which is particularly in it in actuality, for example as the form of fire is in matter as fire. The material aspect of fire in actuality is established only through the form of fire, or through another form governing the material which governs the form of fire. The definition of form in the fifth meaning is that it is a thing existing in something, not as a part of it; nor is its constitution sound apart from it; and form establishes a certain constitution in a thing, without which the natural species would not attain form. This is like the form of humanity or of animality in the natural body which is the subject for it. Sometimes form is said of some individual perfection (*al-kamal al-mufariq*), for example, the soul. Then its definition is: form is the incorporeal part of an individual, by which it is distinguished and by its corporeal part it is a natural species.[28]

30 The definition of matter$_1$ (*hayula*).[29] Absolute matter$_1$ is a substance which exists in actuality only when it receives a corporeal form from the potentiality of matter$_1$ to receive forms. Absolute matter$_1$ does not have in itself any form particularizing it, except in the sense of potentiality. The meaning of my statement, "There is a substance belonging to matter$_1$," is that the existence which comes to matter$_1$ in actuality belongs to it in itself. One also says that matter$_1$ belongs to everything from the point of view[30] that it receives a certain perfection or something which it did not have. Therefore it will be matter$_1$, in relation to what is not in it and it is a subject in relation to what is in it.

31 Concerning subject (*mawdu*^{c}). Subject is said of what we mentioned above. It is everything in consideration that it has some perfection

belonging to it, which it already had. It is also said that subject is in every substratum³¹ that is constituted in itself, and in terms of what is constitutive in it, just as matter₁ is said of the substratum, but not in self-subsisting terms, and not by itself, but through what constitutes it. Subject is also said of every idea which is judged by affirmation or negation.

32 About matter₂ (*madda*). Matter₂ may be said to be a term, which is synonymous with matter₁. Matter₂ is also said of every subject which receives perfection by its being joined to another subject, and accruing to the subject little by little, the way sperm and blood accrue to the form of an animal. Sometimes what it joins with is of its kind, and sometimes it is not of its kind.

33 About element₂ (*ᶜunsur*).³² Element₂ is a term for the first origin of subjects. Next, element₂ is said to belong to the first substratum through whose transformation an element₂ receives forms; from which beings are variegated, either absolutely (as matter₁) or on condition of embodying (as the first substratum of bodies which the rest of generated bodies are from) by receiving their forms.

34 About the element₁ (*ustuqas*). The element₁ is the primary body by whose coming together with other bodies different kinds of primary bodies are formed. Element₁ is said of the final result after the bodies break down, where there is no further division except into similar parts.³³

35 About the building block (*rukn*).³⁴ A building block is a simple body. It is an essential part of the world, such as the spheres and the elements₂. A thing in relation to the world is a building block, and it is an element₁ in relation to what it is compounded of; it is an element₂ in relation to what it is generated from, equal to what it becomes through compounding and transformation taken together, or by its transformation. Therefore air is an element₂ of clouds by condensation, but air is not an element₁ of them. There is element₁ and element₂ of plants. The sphere is a building block, but it does not have an element₁ nor an element₂ belonging to form. There is a subject to its form, which subject has neither element₂ nor matter₁. This is the case when the substratum of something existing in actuality is what is intended by subject. We would not mean by it a substratum established in itself; but we mean by matter₁ and element₂ a substratum, which is a thing in potentiality from which it is. Matter₁ does not mean that the actualized substance is through the perfection of its substratum. Of these things, matter₁, subject, element₂, matter₂, element₁ and the building block, some of them may be used in place of others.

36 The definition of nature (*tabiᶜya*). Nature is a first principle in itself of motion and rest, which are in something essentially. In the whole universe it belongs to each essential change and stasis. One group has expanded this definition by saying it is energy flowing (*quwwa sariyya*) through

bodies; that it is such-and-such a principle, but in this case they have made an error already, because the definition of useable energy in this situation is only as a principle of change in the changeable. This is like saying that nature is a principle of change, which is a principle of change. This is gibberish.

37 Nature is sometimes said of an element$_2$, of a form (essential and acquired), or of motion, each of which, although none is of nature in itself, has a resemblance in name. Physicians use the term nature in dealing with the humors, innate heat, and the conformation of limbs, motions, and the vegetative soul. We will define each of these terms.

38 About disposition (*tab^c*). Disposition is each conformation by which a particular species is perfected, whether active or passive. Its use in these terms is more general than nature. Something may exist by nature, but not by disposition, such as the additional finger. It seems that this is so by disposition in relation to the individual nature, not by disposition in relation to the universal nature.

39 The definition of body (*jism*). Body is a common term with several meanings. Body is said of every continuous, limited thing measured by three dimensions in potentiality. Body is also said of a form in which it is possible to determine the dimensions as you like, such as length, breadth, and depth; it has assigned limits. Body is also said of a substance composed of matter$_1$ and form having this description.

40 The difference between a quantity and this form[35] is such that if the shape of a drop of water or of wax changes, its limited measurable dimensions change. One of these drops in itself will not remain numerically the same. The form capable of receiving these states remains. It is bodily one, numerically without change, and unchangeable. That is why even if something becomes condensed or rarefied, its bodily form is not transformed, but only its dimensions. That allows for the difference between the bodily form which is in the category of quantity and the form which is in the category of substance.

41 The definition of substance (*jawhar*). It is a common term. Substance is said of the essence of every existent, such as a human being or whiteness. Substance is also said of every thing existing in itself, because its essence does not need another essence associated with it for it to be subsisting in actuality. This is the meaning of their phrase "substance is self-subsisting."

42 Substance is also said of whatever has this attribute and is such as to receive opposites in succession. Substance is also said to belong to every essence whose existence is not in a substratum. Substance is said to belong to every essence whose existence is not in a subject. Ancient philosophers since the time of Aristotle have adopted the usage of the expression "substance." We have already differentiated previously

between subject and substratum. The meaning of their phrase "an existent not in a subject" is: the existent is not associated[36] with the existence of the substratum; it is self-subsistent in actuality; self-establishing in itself; it does not matter that it is in a substratum, although the substratum does not subsist without it in actuality, for even though it were in a substratum, it would not be in a subject.

43 Every existent, whether it is whiteness or heat or motion, is a substance in the first sense. The first principle is substance, in regard to the second, fourth, and fifth meanings; it is not substance in the third sense. Matter is substance in the fourth and fifth senses. It is not substance in the second and third senses. Form is substance in the fifth sense, but it is not substance in the second, third, and fourth senses. It is not necessary to squabble over the terms.[37]

44 The definition of accident (ᶜarad). Accident is a common term. Accident is said of every existent in a substratum. Accident is said of every existent in a subject. Accident is said in the meaning of the universal individual. Accident is predicated of many individuals as a predicate that is not self-establishing; that is, accidental. Accident is said to belong to every idea which is an existent of an external thing in terms of its disposition. Accident is said of every idea, which is predicated on a thing because it has existence simultaneous with another in it. Accident is said of every idea which exists in a thing, but at first was not, and in this case, the form is an accident only in the first sense.

45 Whiteness in anything which has whiteness as a quality predicated in itself, such as the phoenix and snow, is not an accident in the first or second aspect, but is an accident in the third, because this whiteness which is a predicate is not self-sufficient in a substance, not in a subject, or in a substratum; rather whiteness is such that it completes a white thing, and it is not predicated of the phoenix and snow except by derivation, is not predicated just as it is. The motion of the earth to the lowest point is an accident in the first, second, and third aspect. It is not an accident in the fourth, fifth, or sixth aspect. Rather its upward motion is an accident in all these aspects, and the motion of a passenger in a ship is an accident in the fourth and sixth aspect.

46 The definition of angel (malak). It is a simple substance, having life, rational speech, and immortal. It is an intermediary between the Creator – may He be glorified – and the earthly bodies. It has rational, spiritual, and bodily [character].

47 The definition of the celestial sphere (falak). It is a simple round substance, not receptive to generation and corruption, having motion naturally toward the center, enfolding it.

48 The definition of a star (kawkab). It is a simple round body, its natural place is the soul of the celestial sphere; its condition is that it shines,

while not being receptive to generation and corruption; moving to the center, not enfolding it.

49 The definition of the sun (*shams*). It is a body, the greatest of all the stars. It is the brightest of them in light, and its natural place is in the fourth sphere.

50 The definition of the moon (*qamar*). It is a star. Its natural place is in the lowest celestial sphere. Its condition is to receive the light of the sun on different shapes. Its essential color tends toward blackness.

51 The definition of *jinn*. It is an ethereal animal, speaking, a transparent mass. Its condition is to assume different shapes. This is not its description, rather it is the meaning of the term.[38]

52 The definition of fire (*nar*). Its nature is a simple mass which is hot, dry, and moving naturally away from the center, in order to be firmly settled under the sphere of the moon.[39]

53 The definition of air (*hawa'*). Its nature is a simple mass that is hot, moist, transparent, and delicate, moving to the place which is under the sphere of fire, and above the sphere[40] of earth and water.

54 Water (*ma'*). Its nature is a simple substance that is cold, wet, and transparent, moving toward the place which is under the sphere of air and above the sphere of earth.

55 Earth (*ard*). Its nature is a simple substance that is cold, dry, and moving toward the center, subsiding in it.

56 The world (*ᶜalam*). It is the sum total of all simple, natural bodies. The world is also said to be a whole totality, an existing homogenous essence, as in the expressions, the world of nature, the world of soul, and the world of intellect.

57 Motion (*haraka*). It is the first perfection of what is in potentiality in respect to what it is in potentiality. If you wish, you may say that it is an emergence from the potential to the actual, not in one instant. As for the motion of the universe, it is a motion of the farthest body around the center, including all motions around the center, and it is the fastest of them.

58 Eon (*dahr*) resembles the Creator. It is the concept understood from relating permanence to the soul in all time.[41]

59 Time (*zaman*). It resembles the created world. It is the measure of motion in respect to before and after.[42]

60 Instant (*alaan*). It is an imagined ultimate in which past and future time share. It may be said that instant is a small measure connected in the imagination by means of the real instant with its kind.

61 The end (*nihayya*). It is that which quantifies a thing until it does not exist, and nothing more of it can be seen.

62 The infinite (*ma la nihayya lahu*)[43] is a quantity such that if any of its parts are taken from it, you will find something beyond it and never repeated.

63 A point (*nuqta*) is an indivisible entity; a point has position. A point is the end of a line.

64 A line (*khatt*) is an extension, which does not accept division, except in one direction. A line is also an extension whose aspect cannot be divided in any other direction. A line is the edge of a plane.

65 A plane (*sath*) is an extension on which it is possible to create two intersections, on the constituent bases. A plane is the limit of a body.

66 Space (*bu'd*) is what lies between two end points which are unconnected. Space is a symbolic expression indicative of its direction. It is in the nature of space that one can also imagine end points of the kind of these end points.[44] The distinction between space and the three dimensions is that there may be a linear space[45] without a line or a planar space without a plane.

67 For example, if two points are fixed in a body without separation in its interior in actuality, there would be a space between them, but there would not be a line between them. In the same way, if two opposing lines are imagined in it, there would be a space between them, but there would not be a plane between them, because there would be a plane only if it were separated in actuality in some respect of its separation. There would only be a line in it when there is a plane in it. So there is a difference between length and line, width and plane, because the space between the two previously-mentioned points is length and not a line. The space which is between the two previously-mentioned lines is width and not a plane, although every line has length and every plane has width.

68 Place (*makan*) is the interior plane of an encompassing mass contiguous with the visible plane of an encompassed body. Place is also said of the lowest plane on which a heavy body rests. Place is said in a third meaning, but this meaning does not exist; it is the dimensions equal to the dimensions of something positioned into which the dimensions of the positioned penetrate. So if it were possible for it to remain without the positioned, this would be the void in itself and if it is not possible for it to be unoccupied by a body then it will be the dimensions, other than the dimensions of the void; but this meaning of the expression place is not existent.[46]

69 The void (*khala'*) is a space in which it is possible to suppose three dimensions, subsisting, but not in matter; it is in its nature that a body fills it and is emptied of it.

70 A filled (*mala'*) volume is a body in respect to its dimensions which prevent another body from entering into it.

71 Nonexistence (*'adam*), which is one of the principles, is that the essence[47] of a thing is not in a thing in terms of the thing receiving existence; existence is not in a thing.

72 Rest (*sukun*) is the cessation of movement in which its natural propensity to move is such that it is in a single condition of quantity, quality, place, and position at a particular time, and then it continues in such a way that this condition exists for two instants.[48]

73 Speed (*surʿa*) is the generation of movement, broken up in such a way that one covers a long distance in a short time.

74 Slowness (*but'*) is the generation of movement, broken up in such a way that one covers a short distance in a long time.

75 Leaning (*iʿtimad*), and also inclination (*mayl*), is a condition in which a body resists that which prevents it from moving in a particular direction.

76 Lightness (*khiffa*) in regard to weight is a physical potentiality by which a body moves from the center naturally.[49]

77 Heaviness (*thiql*) is a physical potentiality by which a body moves toward the center naturally.

78 Heat (*harara*) is an active quality which moves in an upwardly direction to whatever there is, owing to its generating lightness (of weight). It makes homogeneous things come together, and different things become isolated, and it generates rarefaction in the category of quality in a dense body. It generates condensation in the category of position in it, by dissolving and evaporating body.

79 Coldness (*buruda*) is an active quality which makes homogenous and non-homogenous things come together by concentrating and binding them together, which are both in the category of quality.[50]

80 Moistness (*rutuba*) is a passive quality. Moistness is receptive to cohesion and to taking on a strange shape easily. Yet a thing does not keep that shape, but rather it reverts to its own shape and position, which is in accordance with the movement of a mass according to its nature.

81 Dryness (*yubusa*) is a passive quality, making it difficult for things to be receptive to cohesion. An unnatural shape reverts to its natural shape with difficulty from a dry state.

82 A coarse (*khashin*) body is a mass whose surface is divided into atoms, which are unequal in size and different in position.

83 A smooth (*amlas*) body is a mass whose surface is divided into atoms of the same size, equal in position.

84 A firm (*sulb*) body is a mass in which the surface is unyielding in the face of pressure exerted on it, unless pressure is applied forcefully.

85 A soft (*layyin*) body is a mass of which the surface yields to that pressure easily.

86 A supple (*rakhw*) body is a soft mass, which breaks slowly.[51]

87 A fragile (*hashsh*) body is a brittle mass, which breaks quickly.[52]

88 A transparent (*mushiff*) body is a mass which does not have color in itself, and from this condition one sees the color behind it by using the transparent body as a medium.

89 Rarefaction[53] (*takhalkhul*) is a common term. It is said that rarefaction is due to a movement of the mass from some particular expanse to a greater expanse; it follows that its constitution becomes thinner with its continuing existence. It is said rarefaction is also due to a quality of this constitution. Rarefaction is also said to belong to the movement of atoms in the shrinking of the mutual distance between them, then a body becomes rarefied; it is thinner than it was. This movement is in position, which is first in the quality. Rarefaction is also said to belong to the pattern according to which atoms are laid down.

90 One understands the definition of condensation (*takathuf*) from the definition of rarefaction. One learns that it is a common expression, having four meanings opposite to those of rarefaction. One meaning of condensation is movement in terms of quantity; the second is in the quality; the third is that of movement in position; and the fourth is position.[54]

91 Sum total (*ijtima^c*) is the existence of many things in which one may embrace all of the things in one idea. Separation is its opposite.[55]

92 Contiguous (*mutamasan*) is the term for any two things which have their limits in common, taking up one position in space, such that it is not possible to put anything else having a position in the space between them.

93 The intermingled (*mudakhil*)[56] is one thing coming together with another thing in its totality, until one place suffices for what was previously two entities.

94 Continuity (*muttasil*) is a common term. To be continuous is said in three meanings. One of these meanings is whatever is said to be continuous within itself; this is a differentia of quantity. The definition of a continuous body is that there is a shared border between its parts, but the description of a continuous body is something receptive to division in infinity.

95 The second and third meanings of the continuous are these. The first of them belongs to the accidents of a continuous quantity in the first meaning, with respect to what is a continuous quantity. The boundaries of the two continuous bodies are as one. The second meaning is the movement of a body in a position, while it is in position. So everything in which the boundary of a body and that of another body are one in actuality may be said to be continuous, such as the two lines of an angle.

96 The third meaning is one of the accidents of a continuous quantity insofar as it is in matter$_2$. According to this meaning, two continuous bodies are those where the limit of each one is a concomitant of the limit of the other in movement, even if it were something else in actuality, such as the continuity of organs, with each other, or the continuity of ligaments and bones, or the continuity of the glued substance with glue, and in general, whatever is in contact and concomitant, which resists the reception of the opposite of contact.

97 Unity (*ittihad*) is a common term. Unity is said of the participation of things in a single essential or accidental predicate, like the unity of the substances the phoenix[57] and snow in the predicate white, and the unity of the substances ox and human being in the predicate animal.

98 Unity is also said of the participation of several predicates in one subject like the unity of taste and flavor in an apple. Unity is also said of the assembling of subject and predicates in one essence like the personification of a human being from the unity of body and soul. Unity is also said of the coming together of many bodies either one after the other, such as all the bodies making up a city or by contact like the components of a chair or a bed, or continuously like the limbs of an animal. The most truly worthy of the term "unity" in this context is an occurrence of one body out of many, from the summing up of many by nullifying their properties, due to the elimination of their common boundaries.

99 Succession (*tatali*) is a condition where things have a position, such that there is no other thing of that kind between them.

100 The consecutive (*tawali*) is a condition such that things of a certain type come one after the other, in relation to a defined principle; such that there is not anything else of that type between the two things.

101 Cause (*ᶜilla*). Every being which exists has existence from another essence in actuality. This being has existence in actuality and existence of this being in actuality is not from the existence of that one in actuality.[58]

102 The caused (*maᶜlul*) is every being[59] whose existence in actuality comes from the existence of another being, but the existence of that other being is not from its existence. The meaning of our phrase "from its existence" is not the same as the meaning of our phrase "with its existence." Indeed, the meaning of our phrase "from its existence" is that a being is, in consideration of itself, a possible existent, and its existence only becomes necessary in actuality, not from itself; but rather because another actually existing being makes the existence of the second being necessary on its account. A being has possibility in itself. Thus it has in itself possibility without condition; and it has existence in itself by condition of the necessary cause. A being has existence in itself on condition that there is no cause to prevent it.

103 The difference between our phrase "without condition" and the phrase "with a condition of not" is like the difference between our phrase "there is no white stick" and "a stick is not white." As for the meaning of our phrase "with its existence," it means that if one of the two beings is presumed existent, it follows logically that one knows the other is existent. If one is supposed removed, it follows that the other is removed. The cause and the caused come together in the meaning of these two concomitants. Aspects of the concomitants are different;

because one of the two, which is the caused, if one supposes it existent, it follows logically that the other was already itself in existence, therefore this being existed. As for the other, which is the cause, if one supposes it existent, it follows logically that its existence will be followed by the existence of the caused. If the caused is removed it follows logically that the cause had been removed first; it is sound that this one could be removed, but not that the removal of the caused necessitated the removal of the cause. As for the cause, if we abstract it, the caused will be abstracted by necessity of the abstraction of the cause, which abstracts it.

104 Origination (*ibda^c*) is a term understood in two meanings. One of them is the founding of something not from another thing and not through the intermediary of anything else. The second meaning is that absolute existence comes to a thing from a cause without intermediary, while existence is to a thing in itself, if it is not an existent, and it has already been deprived, it is a complete deprivation of what belonged to it in itself.

105 Creation (*khalq*) is a common term. Creation is said of giving existence, whatever it may be. Creation is also said of giving existence, coming out of matter and form, whatever it may be. Creation is said of this second meaning when a thing becomes necessary in the concomitance of matter$_2$ and form in existence, after not being preceded by existence in potentiality.

106 Generation (*ihdath*) is said in two respects. One of them is temporal and the other is non-temporal. The meaning of temporal generation is bringing forth a thing after it did not have existence previously. The meaning of non-temporal generation is giving a thing existence when it did not have that existence in itself, not at one time excluding another,[60] but rather in every time in both cases.[61]

107 Eternity (*qidam*) is said in different respects. Thus it is said "eternal in relation to" and "absolutely eternal." The eternal in relation to is a thing whose time in the past is greater than the time of another thing; it is eternal in relation to it. As for the absolutely eternal, it is also said in two aspects. It is said in regard to time and in regard to essence. As for that which is eternal in regard to time, it is a thing, which exists in an infinite past time; and as for the eternal in regard to essence, it is a thing that has no necessitating principle for the existence of its essence. So the eternal in regard to time is that which does not have a temporal principle, and the eternal in regard to essence is that which does not have a principle[62] on which it depends. He is the One, the True, may He be exalted well above what the ignorant say.[63]

108 Thus ends the book. Praise be to Allah for his blessing always.

8

COMMENTARY

Originally this translation was planned without a commentary. However, the obscurity of medieval Islamic thought without the benefit of a context and references to some of the ideas has been demonstrated repeatedly. Coming upon an English translation of an Arabic text without a commentary is like joining the spectators for a murder trial two-thirds of the way through – the spectator has no idea what issues have been raised, who the participants are, and, particularly, what strategic lines of argument opposing counsels are developing. All medieval Arabic treatises are part of a continuing conversation held among players interested in a particular subject, and consequently much background is assumed by the author to be in the consciousness of the reader. Although on one level *The Book of Definitions* seems obvious, it is more obvious for those who have read such treatises before. When Ibn Sina gives definitions he merely gives the word to be defined and a short definition. He does not use some formula such as "the term x."[1]

The Commentary is meant both to explicate some of Ibn Sina's ideas and to raise questions for thought in the reader's mind. This form was suggested by the medieval Scholastics, such as Thomas Aquinas, who pose questions that will allow them to discuss issues in an interesting way and escape the rigidity of a line-by-line commentary. This format allows the author to bring together issues found in different parts of *The Book of Definitions* and to bring in related ideas that Ibn Sina discusses in his better-known works. *The Book of Definitions* in itself is so concise as to be nearly telegraphic in places. Classical Arabic has the fascinating ability to be elegantly repetitious, extremely terse, and opaque all at the same time. Many of the definitions and philosophical ideas are found in similar form in his other works. In this treatise Ibn Sina refers to God as the Necessary Existence; however, he does not discuss the logic behind this name for God in *The Book of Definitions*. His line of argument is fully discussed in *al-Ilahiyyat* (*Metaphysics*).[2] What is even more interesting is that this name for God, which was, in effect, a shorthand reference to the rational, philosophical argument, was then appropriated by the theologians as a name for God. Even as the theologians scorned Ibn Sina as a philosopher and a *kafir* (unbeliever), and excoriated him for his life-style, they followed him in one of the most fundamental concepts – the idea of God. In doing so, they paid him the ultimate tribute: they read his books.

By using a wider-ranging Commentary, instead of a line-by-line exegesis, the author hopes to show the reader something of the scope and delight of Ibn Sina.

General questions

Question 1 Why is Ibn Sina offering a *Book of Definitions*?

Response The major originating push for Islamic philosophy was the translation of Greek philosophical texts, especially the works of Aristotle. This process spanned the eighth to tenth centuries, and received a strong boost in 217 AH/AD 830 with the founding of the *bait al-hikma* in Baghdad for the translation of scientific texts under the khalif Ma'mun.[3] Philosophy texts comprised only a small percentage of the translations. Philosophy texts were usually translated into Arabic by way of Syriac. When the translators began their task, they faced a dearth of philosophical vocabulary in Arabic, the same problem which the Greeks had faced centuries earlier.[4] Liddell and Scott's Greek lexicon gives the linguistic history of many common words which the philosophers, especially Aristotle, adapted for a technical use, for example, *hyle*.[5] *Hyle* began as a word for forest, firewood, brushwood, timber, and then the material something was made of. Aristotle used it as technical term for unformed matter.

A similar situation existed in Arabic, and the translators and philosophers begged, borrowed, and stole terminology wherever they found it. Thus, the Persian word *jawhar*, meaning jewel, was used for "substance." Al-Kindi took the Arabic word *tin*, meaning clay, and in his book of definitions, *On the Definitions*, tried to imbue it with a philosophical sense of unformed matter. However, this usage was not widely adopted; instead *hayula*, the Arabic transliteration of the Greek word *hyle* became the preferred term. There seems to be a certain amount of tension regarding which word should be used for matter: Ibn Sina gives a definition for two terms, *hayula* (§ 30) and the native Arabic word *madda* (§ 32). His opening remark on the definition of *madda* is that it is synonymous with *hayula*. In this case, the remark that *madda* is synonymous with *hayula* is a prescription for usage and an attempt to influence terminology on Ibn Sina's part. However *madda* did not generally replace *hayula*, even in Ibn Sina's own writings.[6]

In his *Book of Definitions* Ibn Sina is indicating to his readers not just lexicographical terms, but the philosophical ideas they embrace. *The Book of*

Definitions brings together definitions from his major works, particularly *al-Ilahiyyat*, the metaphysical portion of *al-Shifa'*, and *Kitab al-najat*, his own abridgement of the *Shifa'*. So, to an extent, *The Book of Definitions* serves as a shorthand guide to his philosophy. In this way, *The Book of Definitions* is similar to an introductory philosophy course, beginning with an Introduction explaining his reasons for writing the work, and an analysis of many common mistakes in giving definitions. Because so many of his definitions are found in his other works, *The Book of Definitions* may date to later in his career, as it seems unlikely that he would first write the definitions and then write books for them to appear in. Again, Ibn Sina mentions the name for God "the Necessary Existence" (§ 20) in the discussion of the Creator, but he does not give the reasoning behind this name. By contrast, it takes him a whole chapter of *al-Ilahiyyat* to discuss this name, and the reasons for it, which involves a formal metaphysical analysis of the ontology of both the Necessary Existence and possible existents.[7] Likewise, in *al-Najat*, he analyzed the Necessary Existence in a major discussion in Part III.[8] While he does not discuss these issues in *The Book of Definitions*, his discussion of the Creator (§ 20) in philosophical terms would set the student of philosophy on the right path for an investigation of the Creator and His relationship with the cosmos. As much as actually giving definitions in this work, Ibn Sina directs the reader to the concerns of philosophy and how to look at them. His definition of *jinn*, being of the word only, sharply delineates the concerns of philosophy from theology, since the existence of *jinn* is attested in the Qur'an, but not in philosophy.

Al-Kindi's *On the Definitions and Descriptions of Things*[9] from the ninth century was an earlier attempt at a philosophical lexicon. However, al-Kindi's definitions were very short, often only a phrase, and in this sense, Ibn Sina's definitions might have been more useful. Al-Farabi's *Book of Letters*, although much longer, is sometimes considered as a philosophical lexicon. In one particular way, Ibn Sina follows al-Farabi – he gives the common usage of a term, like al-Farabi does, before giving its philosophical usage in his major definitions, such as those for soul and intellect.

Question 2 What were the major precedents for this *Book of Definitions* which had an influence on Ibn Sina?

Response Ibn Sina quotes Aristotle exactly from the *Topics*, saying that definition "is a statement indicating the quiddity of a thing."[10] But even more influence is shown from al-Kindi (d. circa 260 AH/AD 873), the author of the earlier Arabic-language book of definitions, *On the Definitions*. Al-Kindi's influence is apparent in Ibn Sina's word choice and the order of his definitions. The similarities in word order occur in the early definitions.[11] The order of al-Kindi's definitions is: the First Cause, intellect, nature, soul, body, beginning, matter, form, element, act, deed, and substance. The order of Ibn Sina's definitions is: the Creator, intellect, soul, form, matter, subject, matter (second term), element, element (second term), building block, nature, disposition, body, and substance. Ignoring Ibn Sina's definitions of terms for definition and description, which are lacking in al-Kindi, they both begin the text proper with terms for God. The term for God is the First Cause in al-Kindi's work and the Creator in Ibn Sina's. Following the definition of God, both lists fall into the same relative order for these early terms: intellect, soul, form, element, and substance. Nature comes third in al-Kindi's list and eleventh in Ibn Sina's. Matter (*hayula*), comes after soul in al-Kindi, but after form in Ibn Sina, however in either case matter (*hayula*) and form still fall together. Thus eight of the early terms occur in a very similar order in both philosophers.

It appears by the close correlation of terms that Ibn Sina deliberately selected the same word order as did al-Kindi. In the definitions of nature, soul and matter there is a similarity of terms and ideas, with Ibn Sina repeating phrases from al-Kindi's definitions. As a further example of Ibn Sina's familiarity with al-Kindi's work, it can be seen that Ibn Sina inserts a definition based on al-Kindi's in his definition of form in the *Physics*. Ibn Sina says, "Its form is the essence by which it is what it is." In al-Kindi's definition of form he says, "The form is the thing by which it is what it is."[12]

The most tantalizing clue that Ibn Sina has read al-Kindi is the former's casual reference to the meaning of terms for love. In an introductory paragraph (§ 10), Ibn Sina uses a previous scholar's definition as an example of mistakenly taking the genus for the differentia, saying that "yearning love (*cishq*) is the excess of love (*mahabba*), rather it is love (*mahabba*) overflowing." The anonymous author whom Ibn Sina quoted as saying "yearning love is the excess of love" is al-Kindi in his *On the Definitions*.[13] Al-Kindi makes the opposite point from that of Ibn Sina. Al-Kindi considered *cishq* excessive, and passionate; while *mahabba* was acceptable love. For Ibn Sina *cishq* is a fervent love of God. However Ibn Sina's opposite view on the terms for love is a red herring; his interest is in the displacement of genus by differentia. It should be noted here that it is not unusual for these authors to refer to each other anonymously when they are speaking about another's work. Everyone in the audience knows of whom they speak. Even Aristotle is usually not referred to by name, but as "the Philosopher" or "the Sage." Since the in-crowd had read all the same books, names were an unnecessary reference. Ibn Sina has quoted al-Kindi's definition of *cishq* exactly, before critiquing it. Many scholars believe that Ibn Sina was a Sufi – although of a more rational sort – and this off-the-cuff remark validates that position.[14]

Therefore, this evidence indicates that Ibn Sina had read and remembered al-Kindi's *On the Definitions*, both because of the congruence of his word order with his predecessor's and his quoting al-Kindi.

COMMENTARY

Question 3 How did Ibn Sina pick the words he defined?

Response Philosophy needs both metaphysical and physical terms. Metaphysics is considered to consist of what is beyond the physical world of appearances, and the terms in it must be able to deal with abstractions. The metaphysical world includes God, the heavens and their inhabitants; human souls; and such intermediaries as may communicate between the invisible and visible worlds. Philosophers must also discuss the physical world, both in itself and as it serves as the springboard for metaphysical questions. Later philosophy is sometimes seen as totally dependent on Greek thought, but this is because it was the early philosophers who first framed metaphysical questions. Since the world remains the same – with fellow human beings also subject to human nature – the same questions remain to be discussed.

In looking at his word list, one would do well to remember that Ibn Sina was a physician as well as a philosopher, and the author of a famous medical encyclopedia, *Kitab al-qanun fi al-tibb* (Book of the Laws of Medicine). In his philosophical lexicon Ibn Sina defines different classes of terms, primarily medical terms, philosophical words, and religious terms, as well as a few transliterated Greek words. The medical terms are words also found in medical terminology. They include the four elements – *nar* (fire), *hawa'* (air), *ma'* (water), and *ard* (earth § 52–54). The four elements are not defined in the same way in philosophy as in medicine, but they are similar. In both the medical and the philosophical definitions, Ibn Sina begins the definition of each element by saying, "It is a simple substance" (*jirm basit*).[15] They come under a section called "*arkan*" (elements).[16] In the *Qanun* he uses or defines many of the terms which are found in *The Book of Definitions*, including dry (§ 80) and wet (§ 81), light (§ 76) and heavy (§ 77). These words appear in the discussion of the four humors under "Elements." In his long discussion of diagnosis by pulse, Ibn Sina uses and discusses these terms also found in his *Book of Definitions*: stillness (or rest, § 72) and motion (§ 57), fast and slow (§ 73–74), hot and cold (§ 78–79), hard and soft (or compressible and incompressible § 84–85), rarefaction (§ 89) and continuous (§ 94). Many of these terms are pairs of opposites that the physician will consider when taking a pulse for diagnosis.[17]

The next set of terms in *The Book of Definitions* is heavily philosophical. They are words with other uses which are given specific philosophical meanings: *ʿaql*, used for intellect or reason, but which in its verbal form originally meant to hobble a camel; the word *jawhar*, originally a Persian loan word meaning jewel or gem, which was pressed into service to mean substance; and the word *nafs*, which meant self, and is now the word for soul. From religious usage Ibn Sina takes *jinn*, a term found in the Qur'an and used for desert sprites who are creatures created by God, just as humans are. However, the fact that one is reading a philosophical text is emphasized when

Ibn Sina says explicitly that he is giving merely the meaning of the word *jinn*. This is the sole definition in which he makes this statement and appears to indicate he does not believe they have real-world existence. Ibn Sina also defines *al-bari*, the Creator, using a philosophically-preferred name for God as Creator. The most common religious expression for God's activity of creating is found in the verb *khalaqa* and its derivatives. Ibn Sina's definition of the Creator bears this out, in that he defines the Creator in philosophical, not theological terms. This is a case of parallel universes – both philosophy and theology use a Creator in the world scheme, but the Creator's attributes are expressed differently.

A different set includes a few words transliterated from the Greek: they are *hayula* and *ustuqas*. *Hayula* is a transliteration of the Greek word *hyle* meaning matter, in the sense of raw, unformed matter, as mentioned previously. *Ustuqas* is from the Greek equivalent *stoikeion* meaning element. The interesting thing about this pair is that Ibn Sina also defines the Arabic words with similar meanings, namely, *madda* for *hayula* and *ʿunsur* for *ustuqas*. He goes so far as to state in the definition of *madda* that it is "a term which is synonymous with matter$_1$ (*hayula*)." (§ 32) The Greek forms of these two words would not be readily understood by his readers without explanation. In this period Islamic philosophers used vocabulary to move philosophy away from theology. Thus, one no longer finds a definition of *tin* (clay, matter), another word defined by al-Kindi and also appearing in the Qur'an. While everyone was familiar with the Arabic words for fire, air, water, and earth, readers were more unlikely to be familiar with their use as the four elements from Greek philosophy, or in medicine.

Question 4 What are Ibn Sina's first principles?

Response All philosophy begins with assumptions. Philosophers operate on two kinds of assumption, those which are cultural and those which are professional. Cultural assumptions are basic ideas so embedded in the cultural matrix a person lives in as to be invisible to that person. Since the philosopher is unaware of them, it does not occur to him to mention them. However this does not excuse the reader from making every effort to find them. As examples of cultural assumptions in ancient Greek society, one might consider their acceptance of slavery as a normal way of organizing society; the strong patriarchal bias that allowed each man to run his household as he wished; and that everyone who was not a Greek was a barbarian. None of these ideas are unusual for the time or appeared to merit any attention in the philosophical discourse of the day.

A change in the cultural assumptions occurred in Islamic times, however. Muslims, like Christians, assumed the existence of a Creator in their thinking. No matter how secular the philosophy was (for its time) one understands that there is a Creator behind the metaphysical scheme. Thus, it is not surprising to find Ibn Sina's discussion of the Creator couched in philosophical terms; while the terms are philosophical, the thought complements religious thought. In contrast, Aristotle believed that a First Mover set the world of eternal matter in motion. There is no Creator in Hellenistic metaphysics. Aristotle looked for change of any sort, which he classified as motion. The First Mover is removed from the universe, and there is no need for an afterlife with its Last Judgement and Resurrection, literally or metaphorically. Since the First Mover is cast in impersonal terms, there is no point in worshiping him. Many of Ibn Sina's conclusions resemble those of the theologians, demonstrating that they are all members of the same cultural milieu.

Ibn Sina also considers the life of the soul, its nature and its immortality in his treatises. This, too, shows the Islamic theme of the Last Judgement and the immortality of the soul. Islamic philosophers did not always reach the same conclusions about the soul and the resurrection of the body, but, then, neither did all the Islamic theologians. Once again, philosophers form part of a whole continuum of ideas about what happens to the soul after death.

The second type are professional assumptions, meaning that philosophical systems need a starting point so the intellectual process begins with assumptions; these are called first principles. They give a starting point to philosophy. As a professional assumption Aristotle said, "All men by nature desire to know."[18] This is a riveting statement in view of consistent evidence to the contrary. Aristotle ascribes the need to know to a universal appetite for knowledge in itself, like hunger or lust. Based on the amount of time he spent pursuing it, Aristotle also assumed that there was such a thing as knowledge which a human could acquire and that ultimately the world will make sense, it is only a question of discovering more knowledge. One of Aristotle's definitions of knowledge is knowledge of the causes; this appears to serve as a template to organize scientific (in its most general sense) knowledge.

Like Aristotle, Ibn Sina refused to allow an infinite regress in terms of cause. Inherent in this attitude is the subscript that the world must make sense. All of Ibn Sina's arguments are advanced in light of the assumption that the universe can be comprehended by reason. In the Sinawiyyan perspective, the universe is a logical, not absurd, place.[19] If one accepts an infinite regress, the world will remain incomprehensible, although he does not claim human reason can fully and entirely understand the universe. If one accepts an infinite regress, each cause throws the seeker back to another cause, without finally giving knowledge of the First Cause. By assuming an infinite regress is impossible, one also assumes knowledge is possible.

Ibn Sina also assumes that humans understand basic concepts intuitively, and that knowledge of them is innate. His basic concepts are the existent, the thing, and necessity.[20] He says these concepts are impressed on the soul, intuitively understood. It is not possible to arrive at any knowledge without these primary concepts.[21] No true definitions are possible of these concepts. Primary concepts give philosophers a starting point. Circularity in thinking is no more acceptable than the regress.[22]

Another important assumption is that humans have souls. Ibn Sina also takes for granted that the soul is punished or rewarded. His opinion of the body's rising appears to have been fluid; however he does state that souls are immortal and he believes that they will be punished or rewarded for their actions.

A definition must be the definition of a class, not of an individual. In contrast philosophers appear to assume the individuality of members of a class as another unacknowledged first principle. Definitions use species and differentia, that is, the class and its defining characteristic. However, when Ibn Sina quotes Aristotle that definitions point to the essence[23] of a thing, one questions whether the essence is individual or universal. Matter is capable of change. Through the interconnected working of form in matter, numerically different individuals arise. Matter appears to be the medium through which beings acquire their individuality, their separateness from other members of the same class. Of all the philosophical questions, that of individuality is confronted the least. A related question for the philosophers is how the soul is individuated and what is its relationship with the body.

Ibn Sina assumes souls are individual, although he falls back on saying the mechanism for individuality is obscured from humans.[24]

Question 5 How are philosophical terms defined?

Response In philosophy, one frequently finds what is called "a technical term." This refers to the employment of an ordinary word in a particular sense. It is the professionalization of the word. The Arabic word *hadd* has many meanings, which can be understood from the context. It can mean "limit," or "border," such as the border of a country. It can mean the edge of a knife. In its Qur'anic context the plural of this term, *hudud*, is used for specific punishments, meant to limit people's behavior by deterrence.[25]

In philosophy *hadd* is used as a technical term for definition. The word for definition *hadd* comes from the root *hadda* meaning to limit and border, to sharpen; another derivative *hadid* refers to iron. Thus using the word *hadd* as a technical term for definition removes it from the daily language and gives it a complex of related ideas indicating the limits to meaning and the borders of meaning. What do definitions do? They limit words. They set boundaries between one word and the next. Good definitions give the reader a sharp sense of what they mean. Thus, if one thinks of philosophy and theology as two fields of knowledge lying contiguously, one can also see the boundary between the two concepts. Each of these two branches investigates God, but each reports on the results of the investigation in different ways. In Ibn Sina's definition of the Creator (§ 20) he is closely approaching the theologians' turf.

A philosophical treatise called *The Book of Definitions* will let the reader know she or he is to expect certain kinds of statements. Many of the words defined have an ordinary language meaning as well as a technical meaning. The word for intellect, *caql*, comes from a root relating to tethering a camel, or restraining it with a rope; in philosophy it means intellect. This appears to have derived from the idea that this capacity restrains and prevents the person having it from doing unsuitable acts. Thus the intellect restrains the body and the passions.[26] Seen in this light, the intellect is a metaphor for the rope that hobbles the camel, hobbling the body on a metaphysical level. Words can also have various technical meanings depending on the science. Thus while *hudud* (plural of *hadd*) means definitions in philosophy, in law it means the limits set on behavior and secondarily the officially proscribed punishments set out for specific offenses. By the example of the punished criminal, others are restrained from criminal behavior. It is precisely because the words are taken from ordinary language and pressed into philosophical service that a *Book of Definitions* is needed.

Question 6 Does Ibn Sina distinguish between definition and description?

Response Al-Kindi did not differentiate between definition and description in his treatise *On the Definitions and Descriptions of Things*.[27] The title of this work may be evidence that al-Kindi considered them equivalent expressions. Arabic-speaking authors frequently emphasize an idea by using synonyms joined with a conjunction to convey a single idea. For example in *al-Adhawiyya fi al-macad* (*On the Afterlife*), Ibn Sina employs a double pair of near-synonyms for a stylistic emphasis of ideas. "Grief and pain, and happiness and delight" are the pairs he uses, where each noun is connected to its companion with "and" (*wa*), as is each pair to the other, but the noun pairs are used as intensifiers to reinforce an idea, rather than to differentiate ideas.[28] Furthermore, al-Kindi did not define either definition or description in his work – or if he did that part of the manuscript has been lost.

However, Ibn Sina formally defines both terms. Definition shows the quiddity of a thing; it states a genus and a differentia (§ 18). This indicates definition is abstract, because it refers to the essence of a thing, which can be referred to, but which cannot be seen or described.[29] Definition does not relate to an individual, but to a member of a class. Description, on the other hand, "is a statement composed of the genus of a thing and the accidents concomitant to it, so the description becomes equivalent to the thing. In absolute terms, the description is a statement which defines a thing in terms of inessential knowledge – but which is particular to it. It is a statement which distinguishes a thing from whatever may be its equal, but not essentially." (§ 19) It is notable that Ibn Sina says description includes the accidents and the genus of a thing, but not its essence, and becomes equivalent to the thing. Therefore description is much more concrete and may in fact be of an individual. That it makes reference to additional knowledge of a thing which is non-essential and gives particular details also points to the object of description as an individual, rather than the faceless member of a class, which is the case for definition. Finally when Ibn Sina states that a description distinguishes one thing from another which is equal, this is another indicator that he is discussing particular individuals in a class. Thus for Ibn Sina a definition is more abstract than a description, gives the essence, and refers to a whole class of things. Definition identifies the thing in theoretical terms. Description describes a thing in real world terms, but does not describe its essence. It would be possible not to recognize a thing from its formal definition alone, unless one already knew what the thing defined was. Ibrahim Madkur believes that in using *rasm* for description, the Islamic philosophers were ultimately following the Stoics.[30] Description gives the accidents, not the essence of a thing, the reverse of Aristotelian definition. The Stoics had formerly believed that only the accidents – in the sense of the appearances of things – could be known and these things did not have essences apart from the accidents. Aristotle believed in essences, which functioned as the underlying realities of thing, and definition must pinpoint them. According to Madkur, *rasm* is a translation of the Greek term *hypographe*, which describes the physical state.[31] The word used for description – *rasm* – comes from a root, *rasama*, meaning to sketch or draw. This indicates a physicality to the term. Ibn Sina's analysis of the term *bari* (Creator) is neither a definition, nor a description: in fact he states, "He has no definition and no description ..." (§ 20). It is not a definition because the Creator has neither genus nor differentia, the two items required for definition; since the Creator has no accidents – which Ibn Sina lists by negation – this cannot be a description either. Thus the paragraph on the Creator stands as an anomaly in the art of definition. It will later lead Ibn Sina in a mystic direction.

Ibn Sina's treatment is more sophisticated than al-Kindi's because he assumed the need to discuss the nature of definitions. Furthermore, as mentioned earlier, he delineates *hadd* – definition – as a technical term.

An idea of the distinctions Ibn Sina will draw throughout his definitions comes when he discusses the similarities and differences of the terms "sentient being" (*al-hassan*) and "animal" (*al-hayawan*). Animal is more specific than sentient being, because it means more than sensing, it includes a soul, and it has independent locomotion. The animal soul perceives and has locomotion. The rational soul speaks and thinks (§ 5).

While the terms for definition and description may be equal in common usage, they are not equal to those who analyze thought.

COMMENTARY

Questions on God

Question 7 How does Ibn Sina's definition of the Creator differ from the prevailing views?

Response The underlying approach to the definition of God is very similar in Ibn Sina and the Mu'tazili position as reported by al-Ash'ari. The Mu'tazilites, who might be considered the early speculative theologians[32] of Islam in the ninth century, attempted to show there was no conflict between reason and revelation. In their negative statements the Mu'tazilites say God is not connected with a body, and has no shape, no body,[33] no form, no human form,[34] no blood, no individuality, no substance, no accident, no color, no taste, no breath, and no touch. Ibn Sina begins by discussing the possibility of a definition of God, called the Creator, and he immediately says there can be neither definition nor description of the Creator. In his negative statement Ibn Sina says God has no definition, no description, no genus, no differentia, no composition, and no accidents connected with him. The only immediately apparent overlap is that both the Mu'tazilites and Ibn Sina deny that God has any accidents. Why do the Mu'tazilites list the characteristics they do? These negative attributes are the factors relating to their investigation of the physical cosmology of the world. They are the kind of words found in Abu al-Hudhayl's ninth-century discussion of atoms. Ibn Sina's terms come from the discipline of philosophy; he is using standard categories and denying their applicability to God. By not having genus or differentia, Ibn Sina demonstrates that God is not a member of any class. Ibn Sina appears to have dealt with the concerns of the Mu'tazilites by the issues raised in his other treatises. These issues, such as aspects of predestination, showed the interest Ibn Sina took in their concerns.[35] The Ash'arites did not become a concern until later in Persia, where Ibn Sina lived.

The Mu'tazilites are primarily concerned with a discussion of the unity or oneness of God. Al-Ash'ari (d. 324 AH/AD 935–6) reports in his book[36] that the Mu'tazili say God is "hearing and seeing, but not with a body." As noted above, these two lists of non-characteristics or non-attributes are discontinuous; there is no overlap, except for "accidents" (*awarid*). Accidents are mentioned in both the theological and philosophical lists, but that is the only real similarity in word choice. By the list of attributes negated in addition to accident, it becomes apparent what the Mu'tazilites mean by accident and how it differs from what the philosophers mean by accident, since vocabulary items such as shape, color, and taste are considered accidents in philosophy. Here is an example of Ibn Sina's use of a deliberately different vocabulary. Like al-Kindi, Ibn Sina distinguishes philosophy from the realm of religion through vocabulary. Al-Kindi referred to God as "the First Cause;" he also used the Persian loan-word *jawhar* for substance. These usages distinguished him from the theologians. Many of the most significant "professionalized" philosophical terms are not found in the Qur'an, allowing for a cleavage between revelation and philosophy. The major vocabulary items Ibn Sina uses to state that God does not have attributes are technical philosophical terms: definition, description, genus, differentia, composition, and accident. If God does not have genus and differentia, it follows he cannot have a definition in the Aristotelian sense, since they are the components of definition. The relevance of this fact is shown by Ibn Sina's placement of Aristotle's definition of definition immediately before the discussion of God in terms of definition.

Ibn Sina's sole positive statement occurs later in his discussion, when he says, "God is the Necessary Existence." This is the expression used at the end of philosophical arguments on the nature of God by Ibn Sina in *al-Ilahiyyat*,[37] but *The Book of Definitions* lacks these explanations. Since *The Book of Definitions* was meant to be an introductory text and therefore a less technical text, Ibn Sina apparently did not see the appropriateness of giving a long reasoned discussion of the Necessary Existence. In the definition of the caused (§ 102–3) he makes a few remarks about the Necessary Existence and possible, or contingent, existents but the discussion would be of limited use to those who were not familiar with his longer explanation. Specifically, he remarks that possible things are not necessary in themselves, but come from something else, which makes a possible thing necessary on account of the other. The necessary cause is what brings it into existence. This is a very abbreviated and telegraphic description of the Necessary Existence and its relationship to the world. And in this case, he may not have been in a hurry to try to explain this concept to outsiders. The name Necessary Existence (*wajib al-wujud*) is taken over by those theological writers who succeeded him as a name for God. Thus the Necessary Existence was frequently employed as a name by such luminaries as the mystic Ibn al-ʿArabi.[38]

Question 8 What does Ibn Sina say about God as the Necessary Existence?

Response The one positive statement that Ibn Sina makes about the Creator (§ 20) is that He is the Necessary Existence.[39] In this discussion of the Creator the word he chooses is *bari*, a word used more by philosophers than theologians. The few lines given here are a précis of his longer argument in *al-Ilahiyyat*.[40] It is uncertain where this name for God originated. A century earlier al-Farabi appears to have used the term, the Necessary Existence, in his *al-Taʿliqat*, which in any event is a work of uncertain authorship; however, al-Farabi did not explain it.[41] Ibn Sina discusses the term in great detail and thoroughly explains the philosophical derivation of the name. The key distinction between a necessary being and a possible being is cause. A possible being, or a contingent being, is one that is dependent on another to cause it to exist. A necessary being is one that exists without a cause beyond itself. A necessary being is one that is necessary in the primacy and simplicity of its existence. Ontologically, all beings must be necessary, possible, or impossible, according to Ibn Sina. There can be only one necessary being, existing without a cause. In his discussion, the only criterion that Ibn Sina focuses on is cause. To analyze existents, one must look at everything that exists and determine whether or not it has a cause. All existing things must either have a cause or be without a cause. Cause here means cause for coming into existence. If things have a cause they are possible existents, and are also known as caused. Finally, there can only be one Existence that all others derive from. If the situation were otherwise, one would have either circularity or an infinite regress. Neither of these situations is acceptable, because humans only have knowledge through the knowledge of the causes of things. In a system with an infinite regress, knowledge is not possible, since there is no knowledge of the cause of something. The intellect demands that there should be an ultimate cause. This cause itself is without another cause. Thus it is the one being without which nothing else could exist and it is known as the Necessary Existence.

Furthermore, the Necessary Existence has no quiddity other than its existence. It is the ultimate, simple, indivisible entity. This remark, and its imprecise Latin translation would lead Thomas Aquinas into the error of thinking that Ibn Sina believed God had no essence. From this text, Ibn Sina does think God has an essence, which is the same as his existence. God (the Necessary Existence) does not have a quiddity (*mahiyya*), a term which Ibn Sina reserves for essence in creatures.[42] Once more the view of an Islamic philosopher is that God is unique and that there is nothing like Him. This view reflects the Muʿtazilite doctrine that there is nothing like God.[43] By being the only entity that has *anniyya* for his essence, God is separated from all of creation, but he has a kind of higher essence; nothing else shares in this essence. God alone is not divisible into essence and existence, either in mental or in ontological terms. He has both essence and existence, in a singular situation, which is called *anniyya*. With this statement Ibn Sina demonstrates the distance of his thought from the Hellenistic philosophers who preceded him. Perhaps he only mentions the Necessary Existence briefly in *The Book of Definitions* to avoid the many complications that would arise were he to discuss it.

He does not define "necessary" or "possible" in the body of his definitions. The structure of the discussion of the Creator, shows an interesting mix of the Aristotelian with the non-Aristotelian.

In Aristotle, one source of knowledge comes from the causes; these are formal, material, efficient, and final. Aristotle is very firm in limiting the number of causes to avoid an infinite regress.[44] In terms of the cosmos, it is eternal; the Unmoved Mover only sets it in motion. Thus, following Aristotle,

Ibn Sina demands an end to the chain of causation, but he pursues this end in a different way. Furthermore, he implicitly acknowledges the idea of knowledge coming from the knowledge of the causes by insisting on a cause that is known. The negative discussion of the Necessary Existence does not contradict the claim that knowing the cause of everything is knowing that the Necessary Existence is the cause. While humans do have limited knowledge, they do have knowledge of the efficient cause.

Questions on the soul

Question 9 How does Ibn Sina describe the soul?

Response In his remarks Aristotle said that the soul is the perfection of the body, but he left open questions about the nature of individuality in the soul and how it becomes individual.

In *The Book of Definitions*, Ibn Sina actually says very little about the human soul. He does say a soul is particular to each individual (§ 27). In the previous definition of intellect, Ibn Sina located the intellect – in both its practical and theoretical functions – in the soul. He also says there is a vegetal, an animal, and a rational soul. In the hierarchy of faculties, Ibn Sina includes functions such as reproduction, growth, and nutrition in the vegetative soul. The most important functions of the animal soul are motion and perception. In higher creatures, such as humans, the lower functions co-exist with higher functions; reason is the highest function. Thus humans are able to process food and nourishment because of the vegetative soul, and they have the capacity for motion from the animal soul, which adds movement to the qualities of plants. The rational soul is found in humans. The human qualities which differentiate human beings from animals are the ability to think and to speak; interestingly enough the Arabic root (*n-t-q*) implies both functions.

Ibn Sina, following Aristotle, also gives as the definition of soul the perfection or completion of the body. Ibn Sina says that a soul is a non-corporeal substance (§ 25). Once a soul is determined not to be physical, the unavoidable problem of individualization appears. Generally, non-corporeal substances are not considered to be individuated. Matter gives the distinction by which one knows individuals, such as size, hair color, and other incidentals. While one may recognize that a person's individuality is more trenchantly shown by intangibles, such as behavior and personal traits, by being intangible these are also difficult to quantify. While one may state that an individual has a specific shade of hair color, such as strawberry blonde; and one may identify the texture as silky, curly, or frizzy; non-material factors are much harder to quantify in terms understandable by a larger audience. Non-material factors are also difficult to describe in terms that distinguish one person's trait from another's. Person A's stinginess cannot be described as different from person B's stinginess, except through anecdotes. Once again, the behavior in material circumstances gives the observer the meaningful description, although one knows the material circumstances are merely symptoms of the trait in the soul.

In *al-Najat*,[45] Ibn Sina tackles the question of whether the separated soul is individual and what connects it to the body. In this passage he states that it is the soul's attraction to the body and union with it that generates a unique individual. The soul possesses an attraction for one particular body, and this causes the two entities – soul and body – to bind together. Thereafter it acts as a unit and becomes individual in its nature through its connection with the material body and their shared experiences. The temporal difference of its generation also differentiates one soul from another. The interesting question for Ibn Sina is, Do souls pre-exist bodies? It is interesting because of the implication that pure, noncorporeal form does not have distinguishing characteristics (differentiae) but only its genus to distinguish it. And if all souls have the same genus, all souls are one. Thus, for Ibn Sina, unembodied souls by their very nature cannot have an individual identity; as noncorporeal entities they cannot be separate. Therefore souls as separate noncorporeal substances cannot pre-exist the bodies. Behind this question one can see lurking the issue of individuality. And there is a related issue: Even if souls are not numerically one, why aren't they interchangeable? If souls gain an individual identity only through a connection to their bodies, shouldn't they be interchangeable when they are stripped of the bodies? How does one explain their differences? Frequently the reader may observe a philosopher shirk the question of individual differences within a genus. While it is understandable for the philosopher to uphold definition as belonging to a species and not to an individual, a reader perceives in this the hand of the philosopher ducking an analysis of individuality. Ibn Sina is finally driven to state that how a soul is individualized and its relationship to the body is hidden from us.[46] For all his bluster, at least Ibn Sina admits that a problem exists here, and although if it is understood that it takes the soul and body to generate an individual through their interaction, the mechanism is still not known. This may be the philosophical equivalent of the Ashᶜarite theologians saying that God has a face, without our knowing how (that is, the type of face).

Evidently, Ibn Sina has only considered part of the problem – individuality in life. If the living soul-body unit is one individual, and the incorporeal soul develops its individuality through by its connection and interaction with the material body and its temporal aspect, how does the soul maintain an individual nature after the death of the body? In such a scheme is there really individual immortality? In one sense a life force continues, but if it has no individual characteristics – memory or emotions – how can one consider this as bringing a person immortality? If an individual soul goes back to the one great world soul on the death of an individual body, does anything of the soul that is individual survive? Since matter and form are so connected for Ibn Sina at the human level, it is hard to imagine that he really understands the individual soul as surviving without a body. The body gives individuality; the soul can't exist before the body; and to be certain, the soul is immortal and immaterial. But can it exist alone in the Sinawiyyan world? In one sense he does not have a philosophical answer for this question. He has already refused to accept reincarnation, so the soul alone, without the body (matter), is necessary for a meaningful existence. Furthermore he states on several occasions more or less forcefully that only the soul, not the body, is resurrected. Throughout his writings he states that perfection of the soul is necessary in order for it to enjoy the rewards available to it. In his "Essay on the Secret of Destiny," Ibn Sina objects to the idea that God subjects humans to physical punishment throughout eternity for their misdeeds, claiming the desire for vengeance is human, not divine.[47] Rather he believes the purpose of this much promised suffering and punishment is to deter vicious actions.

On the level of the whole, the cosmos has a intellect and a soul. Here the universe is an analogy of the individual person. Thus there is a macro-intellect and a macro-soul: these reflect creation. Just as human beings have individual intellects and souls, the whole universe has one intellect and one soul. In this manner the universe manifests itself as a microcosm as well as a macrocosm. Ibn Sina came closer to confronting the problem of individuality of the soul than Aristotle – or at least admitting the problem existed – but individuality remains an unsolved problem. A similar problem persists in his view of knowledge as being delivered by the Active Intellect. One may sum the problem up as: "If I know what I know through the Active Intellect, why does my knowledge differ from yours? Why don't we all know the same things?"

Question 10 How does Ibn Sina describe the intellect (*ᶜaql*)?

Response The Arabic term *ᶜaql* is a general term which refers to the thinking organ that processes material, whether inductively or deductively, and whether the knowledge is innate or acquired. It can be used to refer to the center which intuits information or develops scientific learning. In this use there are two types of knowledge which can be processed: the intuitive and the learned. The intuitive is innate and already embedded in the thinker's soul; it is brought out by the efforts of the Active Intellect. The second type, which is properly called "scientific" knowledge, results from encounters with the experiential, external world. Scientific knowledge must be understood in the broadest sense, as anything entering the intellect from the external world.

COMMENTARY

The term intellect, as used in Islamic philosophy, refers to a metaphysical entity, which is the locus for various non-material processes – both active thinking (intellection) and intuitive thought-processing. On occasion mysticism is included under intuition. The term *caql* has been variously translated as mind, intellect, reason, and so on; it is, however, broader than what one is accustomed to think of as only reason.

In his discussion of intellect Ibn Sina distinguishes between popular and philosophical usage. He does this in the same way his predecessor al-Farabi did. First, Ibn Sina gives the common usage and then states a formula such as, "These three meanings are the meanings which the general public designates by the term intellect," which indicates the technical meaning will follow.

Before giving the three non-technical definitions, he states that intellect is part of the intrinsic nature of a human being; and it forms part of the composition of a healthy human being. In recalling conventional aphorisms, such as Juvenal's, that health is a sound mind in a sound body, one may understand the reference here. This represents the mental component of health. Defining humans as rational animals conveys another popular idea. Human beings have both a rational, intelligent nature and an animal nature. This, too, is not a technical definition.

The three specific divisions of the common usage of definitions that he gives are: (a) Intellect is what distinguishes right from wrong. It recognizes that good acts are attractive and bad acts are ugly or repugnant. Through experience in the daily world, people learn to make these universal judgements. (b) The intellect is what a person uses to bring together premises, that are the evidence used to set aims for their lives and ethical standards which must be followed in reaching those aims. Again, there is reference to the function of the intellect in discovering good and bad. (c) Intellect is what enables a person to conduct her or his life in a praiseworthy manner, leading to good choices. When a person conducts herself or himself in a good manner, all the actions (including rest, which is a cessation of action), words, and so on, which follow from such conduct will be good, and hence she or he will be good.

After the general usage of the term intellect, Ibn Sina investigates the philosophical usage. He finds eight distinctions in the term for intellect. They have some overlap. Once again Ibn Sina does not refer to Aristotle by name, while indicating the reference by mentioning a specific book, or by calling him "the First Philosopher."

The philosophical definitions of intellect are: (i) First, there is a distinction between intellect and knowledge. Intellect is the locus of thoughts occurring in the soul. It is in the nature of the soul that these ideas come to the intellect. Knowledge must be acquired, it is not innate. This definition is found in Aristotle's *Posterior Analytics*. The following two meanings are mentioned in *The Book of the Soul*. (ii) The theoretical intellect is a faculty, that is, a capacity, of the soul to understand the essences of universal things, insofar as they are universal. This means it can select the essences or ideas of objects and comprehend their universality. (iii) The practical intellect, another faculty of the soul, is what gives a soul motion. An individual moves in the way she or he does in order to work toward its desires. After an individual chooses from among possible ends, the practical intellect tries to actualize the choice by desire. This appears to relate to choices in the physical world. (iv) The material intellect, which exists in human beings, perceives matter and is able to strip away the material aspects of an object to reveal its non-material core, or essence. (v) The habitual intellect refers to the faculty which enables the soul to gain knowledge. It is the intellect possessed by human beings, and it was also mentioned in the *Posterior Analytics*. This is similar to the function of the Active Intellect, albeit on a lower, human level. (vi) The actual intellect, in the next meaning, is defined as the function of the intellect thinking. It produces a concept and makes it present in the soul. (vii) The acquired intellect receives its data from the external physical world. Acquisition here means that it takes data and processes it. This external world leaves the imprints on the intellect, which the intellect transforms into essences denuded of matter. Then it can manipulate the data. (viii) The Active Intellect brings things from potentiality into actuality by illuminating them. Individuals understand and comprehend things or ideas through the illumination of the Active Intellect on the human intellects. With this view of the universe, philosophers promulgate the idea that ultimate truth and ultimate reality are one and the same, but it does not explain why individuals think different thoughts. If there is one reality, people should comprehend reality the same way and they do not.

When Ibn Sina makes a distinction between the universal intellect and the intellect of the cosmos, he is distinguishing between the abstract intellect and the physical intellect. This universal intellect is the sum total of expressions of the intellects of all people throughout creation. The universal intellect does not have a real, separate existence, yet its existence is manifest throughout the world in all the individuals. It functions in the forming of an individual's concepts. Thus the universal intellect is an imaginary concept, in that one imagines lifting away the individual intellects of all persons and amalgamating them into the combination of all intellects in the universe, and therefore holding all ideas in the corporation of intellects. Here the faculty of imagination perceives this idea, it is a real faculty; "made-up" has nothing to do with imagination in this sense. The intellect of the cosmos is both everything in the world and the ultimate intellect, in the same way that the cosmos has an ultimate body. The universal intellect shows the interdependence and connectedness of the world. Its status is the commonality of everything in the world; it is all created. In the second meaning, the intellect of the cosmos is the profoundest part of the cosmos.

COMMENTARY

Questions on physics (nature)

Question 11 What does Ibn Sina say about matter and form?

Response The major point Ibn Sina makes about matter in his *Book of Definitions* is that matter only comes into actuality when it receives form.

In Aristotelian doctrine, matter and form – that is, the material of something and its shape – could *not* exist separately in the real world. There is no raw unenformed matter.[48] For this reason it appears to be incorrect to translate *hayula* as primary matter, although some commentators believe Aristotle required a primary matter, even if he refused to acknowledge it. Plato held an opposing view, that ultimate reality is a set of shapes or essences, the Forms which exist in disembodied splendor on another level. This otherworldly existence is a truer existence than that of objects in the physical world. Objects in our world participate in the heavenly forms. Aristotle denies that the Forms have real-world existence by themselves, that is, without matter. Another way of stating their two perspectives is to describe Aristotle as an empiricist and Plato as an idealist.

One discerns a continuation of this discussion in Ibn Sina's remarks on matter. The Arabic term *hayula* is a transcription of the Greek word *hyle* used by the philosophers for matter in its straight material state. First, in his definition of *hayula*, Ibn Sina states that matter as an absolute stratum has no existence until it receives the forms which bring it into actuality. Thus he denies the idea of a raw stuff, raw matter having a pre-existence before it is enformed. Pure matter is only the potentiality to receive form, and form here is what gives a thing its essence and its actuality. Thus, if one talks about matter and form separately it is only talk; it does not give matter existence separately. Likewise form serves the purpose of giving matter a perfection. So as can be seen, in this case, Ibn Sina equates form with what gives something its perfection, perfection being used in the sense of completion.

Neither of these words for matter (*hayula* or *madda*) is used in the Qur'an, that term is *tin*, which means a primary type of matter, such as clay. At S. 23. 12 and S. 32. 7, for example, God creates human beings out of clay. The emphasis of these verses, it should be noted, is not the particular type of clay or other matter from which creatures were created; the emphasis is on God as the Creator. The mind focuses most naturally on considering the majesty and power of the Creator as agent. In S. 7. 12 there is slightly more emphasis on the matter a human being is created from, where the point of the verse is that Iblis (Satan) claims to be superior to human beings, because of their respective raw materials. Iblis is created of fire, human beings of clay.

In the typical verses describing creation of the heavens and earth in general terms, where description of matter might logically be expected, the material of creation is not mentioned at all, only the act of creation. (S. 2. 117.) Thus there is a different focus – theologically the focus of how things come to be is on the agent, that is God, whose power and might creates the world; while philosophically, the emphasis is on the fact of things existing, what they are composed of and, in immediate terms, where they came from. In his second definition of matter, Ibn Sina describes the slow development of a thing with the example of sperm and blood gradually forming an animal.[49] When one reads this definition, there is an echo of Ibn Sina's occupation as a physician with an empirical bent, interested in how things work on a physical level. Such a description does not deny the existence of a Creator; it is a parallel description in physical terms of a theological reality.

Ibn Sina's idea as found in the definition of *hayula* (matter), that the potentiality which receives the form leads to the actual existence of a thing, is repeated in al-Qashani's definition of *hayula*. ᶜAbd al-Razzaq al-Qashani (d. 730 AH/AD 1329) defined matter in his *A Glossary of Sufi Technical Terms*. He says, "Matter (*hayula*): this is the name among Sufis for a thing in relation to what appears in it of forms; so they call '*hayula*' every hidden thing which a form appears in."[50] Therefore, al-Qashani says what is brought out by form is matter. This is another instance of Ibn Sina's thought being reflected in the Sufi tradition.

Question 12 What does Ibn Sina have to say about change and its opposite?

Response Change refers to the conditions of an object, and its passing from one condition to another. A reference to condition can be to an object's most basic condition – that is, its existence – or to a (relatively) more minor change such as growth or change of location. At this point the philosopher's metaphysical assumptions about the nature of the world come into play. If the philosopher believes the world to be eternal and matter uncreated, change does not begin with things coming into existence, in a pure sense, but with motion.

For Aristotle, change is the basis of movement. Since matter is eternal and uncreated in this metaphysical view, the universe begins when matter is set in motion, when it is no longer merely existing in a frozen, static condition. For Ibn Sina in *The Book of Definitions* the point is not whether or not matter is eternal, but whatever comes out of matter is given its existence from God (§ 105). It is interesting that Ibn Sina does not define creation (§ 105) as from nothing, as al-Kindi does in his *On the Definitions*. One wonders if Ibn Sina intends a major distinction from al-Kindi, who stated creation is "the appearance of a thing from what is not,"[51] whereas Ibn Sina states that origination (*ibda*ᶜ) "is the founding of something not from another thing and not through the intermediary of anything else" (§ 104).[52] Ibn Sina's definition sounds as if he is saying it is not from something else, whereas al-Kindi's terminology is generally accepted to mean "from what is not," expressing the idea of "nothing" – a notoriously difficult idea in Arabic, as much because of the thought process involved as the words. Some theologians used "not a thing," which led to the idea of something else behind thing-ness, rather than a void.[53] Words such as nothing and non-existence or privation may engender the idea that they have some positive content – rather than referring to nothingness.

For the most part, Ibn Sina avoids the question of whether or not matter is eternal. He does not state explicitly the ontological condition of matter prior to creation in *The Book of Definitions*. This gap is noticeable in his definitions of origination, creation, and generation (§ 104–106), where the medium for creation is important. Also, as mentioned before, because Ibn Sina pairs (§ 104) "not of/from a thing" with "not by the intermediary of a thing," the reader's focus is on a thing as a possible agent or facilitator, rather than a thing as matter.

Furthermore, it is noteworthy that corruption (*fasad*) is among the words that Ibn Sina did not choose to define, although he has defined its opposite: various kinds of generation (§ 106) and creation (§ 104 and 105). He does not even mention that corruption is the opposite of creation. He also omits change (*al-taghayyur*) from his list of definitions, although he defines motion (§ 57).

The definitions that come closest to discussing change are those like smooth and coarse, that deal with physical properties. In looking at Ibn Sina's definition of the smooth, the coarse, and so on, one sees the influence of atomism. For example, the idea that the texture of a body's surface occurs as a result of the size and regularity of atoms resting on the exterior side of the object is very interesting. One then imagines these atoms rearranging themselves to produce a different effect. After large-scale conditions, the philosopher's attention moves down to smaller scale conditions and changes, such those of texture and body.

Throughout Ibn Sina's discussion, and in the Arabic translation of Aristotle's *Physics* by Ishaq bin Hunayn, the emphasis is placed on the potential and the perfect, or the becoming and the complete. Arabic easily lends itself to this interpretation in the grammarians' view of tense. The Arabic language has two aspects – the complete and the incomplete.[54] The first, the perfect, states a completed action. The second, the imperfect, states an event that is underway or in progress or may occur at some future time but is not completed. Thus the primary focus is on completion of the act, rather than the temporal aspect. This view of the world is mirrored in philosophy: potentiality, which is an incomplete state, appears to correspond to the imperfect tense, and actuality, the complete state, corresponds to the perfect state.[55]

Question 13 What does Ibn Sina say about cause?

Response The issue of cause is connected with the realization of things in an actual existence, and with the meaning of actual versus potential. It is also connected with change in the sense, that if there were no change there would be no cause either. Without a cause, things are.

Among the principles implied in Ibn Sina's views of causation are: nothing comes into being by itself, that is, things are not self-generating; things either exist or do not exist, there is no interim state of "pre-existence;" and there must be an end, that is, an infinite regress is not acceptable. An infinite regress refers to the idea that things can go back forever, *a* being caused by *b*, which is caused by *c*, and so on, interminably, without any final agent of cause.

To have a meaningful theory of cause one needs these assumptions, or else one may posit either a world with a chain of causes going back infinitely, or a world with the peculiar doctrine that things pre-exist on some level before they exist. The first necessitates accepting the infinite regress which is, in logical terms, the same as no cause; since one can never pin the cause down, it continually regresses to the next level. The second leaves one in the position held by certain Islamic theologians who claimed non-existence was an accident, like existence, and God must will a thing to be non-existent for it to go out of existence.[56] This is a logically repugnant idea, for how can one accept the requirement for God to perform a positive act (willing) to achieve a negative result (non-existence)? Implicitly Ibn Sina accepts Aristotle's assertion that the knowledge of things comes from the knowledge of causes. This is shown by Ibn Sina's rejection of the infinite regress. One must know a thing's causes in order to know it. For Aristotle cause is not understood in the ordinary language sense. Cause is understood in the sense of responsible for. In Aristotle the causes are four – formal, material, efficient, and final. In his system the final cause is usually regarded as the most important – it is the explanation of a thing's purpose, that for which it is. In Islamic philosophy and later in medieval Christian philosophy, there is a tendency to make the most important cause the agent, that is, the efficient cause through which a thing came to be. This emphasis exists in Ibn Sina and is emphasized by the Scholastics, such as Thomas Aquinas.

Ibn Sina deals with the problem of agent by defining one existent as the Necessary Existence from which everything else flows. Only the Necessary Existence has pure, actual existence; everything else was originally potential and possible, and as such it is still corrupted with elements of non-actuality, that is potentiality. There is only one Necessary Existence, because if there were two necessary existences an infinite regress would again exist. When the Necessary Existence creates things they become necessary. If the Necessary Existence wills something, it must come to be. But this kind of necessity is not a self-fulfilling necessity. Only the Necessary Existence is self-subsistent.

Although many commentators perceive Ibn Sina to be defining other existents as necessary once they are brought into existence, this is necessity of a totally different order from that of the Necessary Existence. The Necessary Existence's necessity is part of its unique essence (*anniyya*), and nothing else participates in this existence. Created things are only necessitated when the Necessary Existence (God) brings them into existence. Only then are they necessary – at the time of creation – because God has willed them and what God wills must happen. The unavoidability of God's will is shown grammatically by using the perfect tense for acts God will perform in the (human) future to show how definite they are. Human time has no meaning for God. There is no potentiality with God, God is pure actuality. In this scheme potentiality is inferior, because it indicates something not yet perfected. Its very incompleteness indicates its imperfection. And no imperfection can attach to God.

One knows the cause, that is, the Necessary Existence, exists because the product of this cause, which is the caused, or creation exists. By their very existence created things manifest the existence of a Creator. But if there were no Creator, no created things would exist either.

Confusion arises over Ibn Sina's view of possible or potential things before they actually exist, although he vehemently denies the pre-existence of potential things.[57] However, in his vocabulary throughout *al-Ilahiyyat*, he consistently refers to everything except the Necessary Existence as "possible things;" there are also impossible things, but it seems his emphasis is on what may come to be through one thing, which is the Necessary Existence. Perhaps if the phrase "in potentiality" is understood as referring to a state or condition, rather than a pre-existence, this confusion will be escaped.

His use of the word *dhat* meaning "essence" as a shorthand for "an existing thing" or for "a created thing" is further evidence of the meaning attached to these terms. As seen previously, this word is used only for essence in a created sense. This is a usage of the term which emphasizes the second-class quality of existence for created beings. There are two classes of beings for Ibn Sina, and they can be identified equally by either type of cause or existence. There is the cause (One) and the caused (everything else), or there is the Necessary Existence (One) and possible existents (everything else). These concepts are coextensive. No matter whether one defines the referents by cause or by existence, the same result remains the same.

As mentioned previously in the discussion of matter, there is no pre-existence of matter without form. Therefore things come into being all at once. Non-existence is not a state. This is another reason why it is incorrect to say, as some commentators have, that Ibn Sina views existence as an accident added to substance. He does not. Things exist or do not exist. Since things do not have a pre-existence they cannot have existence added to them and come into existence. To take the view of existence as a super accident added to an essence which then brings that essence into existence contradicts Ibn Sina's most basic principles.

Relationship with other philosophical traditions

Question 14 How does Ibn Sina's treatment of physical conditions refer back to the pre-Socratic atomists?

Response The remnants of atomist views lie behind Ibn Sina's construction of the theory of the physical, visible world. Topics such as space, atoms, continuity, and the duration of a body interested Islamic atomists, as may be found in the writings of the theologians, especially the Mu'tazilites. They considered that bodies were composed of atoms; accidents were attached to these atoms; and their duration was created by God.

The smallest parts were known in Arabic as "the parts which are not divisible" or atoms. These theologians thought that a certain number of atoms was required to compose a body. Thus Abu al-Hudhayl (d. circa 226 AH/ AD 840–1) thought the smallest body possible was composed of six atoms, which took the position of left and right, back and front, high and low. Together, these six atoms formed a body in the shape of a plane which was a unit.[58] He also made the interesting claim that God could make an atom exist separately so that the human eye could see an individual atom.[59] Mu'ammar (d. 215 AH/AD 830), a contemporary of Abu Hudhayl, considered that at least eight atoms were needed for a body. He saw eight atoms arranged as a cube, with length, breadth, and depth, positioned in groups of four atoms by four atoms.[60]

One should note that Ibn Sina does not define the word usually translated as atom, *juz'*, although he does use the plural form in § 82 and 83, in the sense of atoms. In defining coarseness (§ 82) he states that coarseness is caused by atoms clumping together unevenly over the surface of the body. Such a remark implies that atoms must be able to exist in different sizes, since the difference in their sizes causes the surface to be irregular and therefore coarse. The pre-Socratic philosopher Democritus also thought there were different sizes of atoms.[61] While Democritus thought some atoms were very small, a large atom would still be as small as a mote of dust visible in sunlight.[62] The next definition, smoothness (§ 83), suggests that a body is smooth because it is covered by atoms of homogenous size, resulting in an even surface texture.

Another idea of atomists is that accidents adhere in the individual atoms. Thus a thing is not a white thing, but it appears white while each atom carries the accident white. In this view, the sum of accidents is what forms a substance, not an underlying stratum. In his definition of unity (§ 98) Ibn Sina says that taste and flavor come together in an apple. This sounds very much like accidents inhering in atoms.

Al-Ash'ari quotes a definition of the intermingled (*mudakhilah*) from Ibrahim al-Nazzam, a theologian, that says, "The meaning of the intermingled is that a place for one of two bodies is a place for the other and one of two things is in the other."[63] By comparing this with Ibn Sina's definition of the intermingled (either *mudakhil* or *mutadakhil*) it is evident that Ibn Sina certainly reflects al-Nazzam's ideas. Ibn Sina says, "The intermingled is one thing coming together with another thing in its totality, until one place suffices for what was previously two entities." (§ 93) Al-Nazzam says that a second body occupies the same place as the first, and this occurs to such an extent that one of them can be said to be in the other in effect. Ibn Sina repeats the idea that one meets and comes into another in its whole being, and that in the end a single place holds what was previously two separate entities. If one thinks in terms of two liquids mixing, which become totally blended, such as water and wine, or two gases in the atmosphere, the reference is evident.

Al-Nazzam (d. circa 230 AH/AD 845) was among the most important early theologians. It seems very likely Ibn Sina would have been familiar with Mu'tazilite views, as he dealt with Mu'tazilite objections in another treatise, as George Hourani has pointed out.[64] If Ibn Sina was familiar with the Mu'tazilite work *al-Mughni* of 'Abd al-Jabbar, a slightly older contemporary, he would have been equally familiar with Mu'tazilite views on physics. Since 'Abd al-Jabbar was the chief justice of Rayy, he was active in the same region as Ibn Sina.[65] A Persian theologian certainly seems to be just as likely a source of influence on Ibn Sina as the Hellenistic philosophers. As will be reviewed later in *Mantiq al-mashriqiyin* (*The Logic of the Easterners*) Ibn Sina states that he gained much knowledge from non-Greek sources, so Ibn Sina is avowedly eclectic in his sources.[66]

Some of his explanations, particularly coarseness and smoothness, appear to be taken from atomists. Therefore it may seem that Ibn Sina is explaining the opinions of many philosophers and theologians, not only Peripatetic Greek thought. In the selection of terms describing the physical properties of bodies, he discusses terms which were of interest to atomists like Abu al-Hudhayl: sum total, contiguous, intermingled, continuity and unity (§ 91–97).[67] It is noteworthy not only that he discusses them, but that these definitions fall together, as they might in considering the physical attributes of an entity, such as a material body. Ibn Sina defines resting, that is a body at rest (§ 72), as a body continuing at rest for two instants. The speculative theologians define resting as the state when a body comes to a place where it remains for two instants, and its motion becomes rest.[68] In both statements the time elapsed is two intervals, where the word for instant is understood as the smallest amount of time. The two instants are this one now and the next. The difference is that

Ibn Sina defines rest as the cessation or absence of motion, while the theologians define rest as a type of motion, that is, remaining in one place for two instants is the act of rest.

In these definitions one sees many references to the Mu'tazilite view of the physical world, that demonstrate Ibn Sina's awareness of their point of view.

Question 15 How does Ibn Sina's discussion of time compare with the theologians' discussion of time?

Response This point is raised in order to understand why Ibn Sina mentions "not in one instant" in his discussion of motion (§ 57) and "in two instants" in his discussion of rest (§ 72). What does Ibn Sina mean by these references to the duration of motion? The theologians – in general – viewed creation as a continuous act of God's. In this view, known as occasionalism, the world persists because God is continually re-creating it, from one instant to the next. God continually causes the world to endure. The created world has no power of its own to act, or even to endure, without the continued will of God to that end. A phrase such as "to endure" may be used to describe the condition of the world, and sometimes a time element is given which may be translated as for "two instants" or for "two seconds." This is because the theologians have reduced the duration of time under discussion to two intervals: they have focused on the present moment where creation exists (the first interval) and the next moment of time immediately coming when the world will cease to exist, unless God continues it. Thus time is the duration of "two instants," this moment and the next.

It is intriguing to see Ibn Sina utilize the theologians' terminology in this respect. Generally Ibn Sina refrains from using theological terminology, using technical terms which are philosophical, not Qur'anic. He follows al-Kindi in pointedly distinguishing himself from the theologians by vocabulary.

In this case, Ibn Sina does a reversal and follows the theologians. Why? The time element in his definition of motion (§ 57) and rest (§ 72) also sets him apart from Aristotle.[69] In the *Metaphysics* for example, while Aristotle talks about the process of things being made as movement – such as a building, – he does not put in the time element, whereas Ibn Sina gives the limit "not in one time."[70] Ibn Sina is in agreement with Aristotle in defining rest as the absence of motion. However, rest continues specifically "for two instants" for Ibn Sina, while for Aristotle no time is mentioned.[71] In the mention of time and the specific way in which it is mentioned (two instants) gives evidence of the Islamic cultural matrix. Discussions of change and accident were so commonly framed in terms of time that it is hard to imagine them otherwise. Events on earth could only be conceived as happening in time. Implicitly this acknowledges the Creator, who makes things happen in time.

COMMENTARY

Question 16 Is eastern influence, particularly Buddhist, apparent in Ibn Sina's works?[72]

Response The reasons for suggesting eastern or Buddhist influence on Ibn Sina's thinking are: first, he was from Bukhara, a vital east-west crossroads of ideas; second, in various works he refers to having read authors not known (to readers of Arabic) and to non-Greek sources of knowledge; and third, there are ideas of Ibn Sina that parallel Buddhist ideas and may show Buddhist influence, as demonstrated in his idea of triads. Unfortunately, subsequent invasions and plunder by the Mongols and by Timur (in the fourteenth century) devastated Central Asia so thoroughly we cannot expect much evidence of the historical record to remain. Even so, overall there appears to be a deep and enduring undercurrent of Buddhist culture throughout Central Asia.

To demonstrate this, first Bukhara should be understood in geopolitical terms. One of the factors demonstrating Buddhist influence is the material remants of language, especially Sanskrit. While many Buddhist texts were composed in Sanskrit, the local language was Sogdian, named after the region Sogdia. This region includes modern-day Uzbekistan, Tajikistan, and Kirghizia, and was centered around Samarkand. The translation of Buddhist texts into local languages, especially Sogdian, shows that they were available to local populations. Evidence for Sanskrit being understood by some of the learned classes includes a Sanskrit grammar found at Turfan.[73] Pilgrims such as Fa-Hsien and Hsuan Chuang reported that the monks of Central Asia were studying the language of India (Sanskrit).[74] Buddhist, Manichean, and Christian texts in Sogdian have also been found.[75] In the seventh century T'ang power spread as far west as Bukhara, where the Chinese joined the Uighurs to control the Tarim basin area.[76] In fact, some scholars think the name of the city of Bukhara had as its former name *vihara*, a Sanskrit word meaning shrine or monastery, attesting to its Buddhist roots.[77] The Islamic polymath al-Biruni, a contemporary of Ibn Sina, went to India, where he studied Sanskrit and the culture, including Hinduism and such Buddhism as he found, although by this time Buddhism was nearly extirpated from India. In material terms over 20,000 manuscripts have been found in storage at Tunhuang. This group of manuscripts includes those written in many scripts and languages, including Brahmi, Persian, Uighur, and Tokharian.[78] Scholars have also identified Buddhist manuscripts from Central Asia, dating from the fifth to sixth century AD, now located in the St. Petersburg Branch of the Institute of Oriental Studies of the Russian Academy of Sciences.[79] One Buddhist manuscript, written in early Turkestan Brahmi script, gives early physical evidence of the circulation of Buddhist ideas in Central Asia.

Ibn Sina's birthplace Afshonah, a town near Bukhara, is located in modern Uzbekistan. At that time Bukhara was a famous trading center located on the

Silk Road, connecting China with the Mediterranean Sea by way of Central Asia; the route to India breaks off and runs due south from Bukhara through the mountain passes. These routes were traveled not only by traders, but by Buddhist pilgrims. It is commonly accepted that religious ideas were brought in a deliberate way as well as incidentally with the merchants. While Ibn Sina is usually considered to have been Persian on the basis of his father's nationality, he is ethnically Central Asian, as his mother was a native of Afshonah, a point whose importance is frequently ignored.[80] The fact that he does not speak of her does not negate her influence, it only demonstrates the cultural fact that women were phantom participants in history, who were not spoken of.

Having taken into account the environment of Bukhara as a cross-cultural site, one may look for evidence of eastern influence in Ibn Sina's own writings. In his autobiography Ibn Sina says that he read books in the library of the Samanid Amir Nuh ibn Mansur at Bukhara. "I saw books whose names had not reached very many people and which I had not seen before that time, nor have I seen since."[81] Considering this statement both in light of the many manuscripts that have been discovered in different languages and in terms of Ibn Sina's various tutors, it is safe to assume that some of these works were in one or more of the eastern languages – including Sogdian, the language centered around Samarkand – and that they included ideas not known in the West, such as the works of eastern sages. Despite such evidence, this statement has often been interpreted as a reference solely to Ibn Sina's reading of Greek works. Yet he cannot mean Greek authors, such as Aristotle and Plato, as every one of his contemporaries would have been familiar with them. Furthermore, in *The Logic of the Easterners* Ibn Sina discusses his education a second time and states, "And often we gained knowledge from non-Greek sources."[82] Ibn Sina further states that in studying logic the Easterners "probably had another name for it."[83] Considering the geography of his birth the likeliest non-Greek sources would have been these Hindu or Buddhist sources which came from India or China.

Furthermore, Ibn Sina mentions in his autobiography that among his tutors was a vegetable grocer who knew and taught Indian mathematics to Ibn Sina.[84] This grocer could well have introduced Ibn Sina to some additional ideas from Hinduism and Buddhism, and perhaps some Sanskrit as well, or at the very least instilled in the young scholar an interest in pursuing other learning from Indian sources. By the tenth century Indian ideas had been well established throughout the Islamic world. The Sufi mystic al-Hallaj traveled to India before 290 AH/AD 902 and later returned to Mecca and Baghdad. It has often been suggested that the ideas of Hindu mystics on love and devotion considerably influenced the development of the devotional ideas in Sufism. In the centuries before Ibn Sina's birth, Mahayana Buddhism had heavily influenced Central Asia and China, having spread out from northern India. By the late tenth century Islamicization, although begun, would not have been complete. On reading the history of the province of Khurasan, which includes Bukhara, one understands it is at the eastern edge of the former Persian empire, subsequently overrun by Chinese and Uighurs, Zoroastrians and Buddhists. In later centuries the Mongols also charged through. These waves of influence and destruction have left incomplete and confusing records on the ground, requiring scholars to speculate on what influences may have existed. From the tone of his books, Ibn Sina was ravenous for knowledge from many sources, not only Greek and Muslim ones. Some of his terminology, like "sentient being" (*al-hassas* § 5), suggests that he can be read for eastern, as well as western influences.

Another intriguing avenue of influence can be found in Ibn Sina's *Kitab al-qanun*, in which he presents a thorough delineation of pulse diagnosis. This is the method, thought to date back to Chinese physicians, of carefully measuring the type and strength of a person's pulse, in other words, its qualitative as well as its quantitative measurements. The physician takes the pulse by laying fingers on the wrist of the patient, who extends his or her arm, wrist up with palm upturned. The fact that the pulse description takes up nineteen chapters in Ibn Sina's discussion in the *Qanun* shows the thoroughness of his discussion and the depth of his interest. Some of the descriptions given for pulse types translate as: wavy, continuous, serrate, gazelle-like, and twisted.[85] In the *Qanun* Ibn Sina shows that through a thorough analysis of the pulse, the physician will be able to find whatever imbalance causes disease and then to recommend treatment. The method of taking the pulse is similar in the *Nei Ching*, in which Ch'i-Po recommends taking the pulse at dawn, before the patient's energy has been disturbed, before the patient has had food or drink; that the doctor should take the pulse on the wrist, palm upturned, using three fingers. The pulse is influenced by the changing seasons. Also, anger, motion, and rest all cause changes in the pulse.[86] Ibn Sina makes the same recommendations, including the observation that the change of seasons affects health.

In addition to his remarks indicating he read about eastern sages, Ibn Sina's treatise on the afterlife, *Adhawiyya fi al-ma{c}ad* (*On the Afterlife*), suggests that he was familiar with reincarnation, including ideas that are similar to Buddhist ideas. In this treatise Ibn Sina presents many differing opinions on the afterlife, differences in opinions not only among Muslims, but among many religions. He mentions ideas of the Manicheans, the Christians, and the Zoroastrians (Magians).[87] Then he mentions that many people believe in the transmigration or reincarnation of souls.[88] First he says that some believe human souls can be reincarnated in any body, whether plant or animal; some think reincarnation in animals is possible and some think human souls can only be reincarnated in other human bodies. Of this last group there are two subsets: (a) those who think vicious souls will be reincarnated until the soul perfects itself, at that time it is ready to be freed from matter, and (b) those who think both vicious and fortunate souls are reincarnated – the vicious to burdensome bodies and the fortunate to prosperous, or agreeable, bodies.

This description of reincarnation demonstrates a familiarity with the concepts in Hinduism or Buddhism, since in these religions the level of a soul's reincarnation depends on its deeds in the previous life. Furthermore, the idea that with the perfection of the soul it escapes reincarnation and becomes free of matter is known from Buddhism.

In Buddhist literature, a discussion explains the relationship of the Three Bodies of Buddha, in which the Body of Essence makes manifest the Body of Bliss (or Experience) which, in turn manifests the Transformation Body. A passage on the Three Bodies in a Mahayana sutra says:

> The Body of Essence, the Body of Bliss, the Transformation Body –
> these are the bodies of the Buddhas.
> The first is the basis of the two others.
> The Body of Bliss varies in all the planes of the Universe, according to the region,
> In name, in form, and in experience of phenomena.
> But the Body of Essence, uniform and subtle, is inherent in the Body of Bliss,
> And through the one the other controls its experience, when it manifests itself at will.[89]

One finds a parallel instance of ontological triads in Ibn Sina. In *Kitab al-najat* he uses the triad of intellect, thinker, and thought.[90] Whatever words are used to translate the Arabic, they show their connection all in being from the same root – *ᶜaql*. There is a Sinawiyyan idea parallel to the Buddhist idea in that each of the other two entities arise from the first, and are closely related. This is a different idea of triplicity, from the Christian idea of the trinity. There is another triad, also in the *Najat*, in which Ibn Sina describes the way each sphere arises from the longing of each intellect.[91] This approach is similar to the Buddhist idea, and is particularly notable, because Islam is so steadfastly and profoundly unitarian. Any idea of God as tripartite in the substance of the godhead is anathema to Muslims, Ibn Sina among them. However, Ibn Sina's idea here represents the triad in extrinsic terms, not interfering with the unity of the substance of the First Entity. In form, if not content, this is similar to the Buddhist idea of the Transformation Body, which is the Buddha as he appeared on Earth, emanating from the Body of Bliss, which in its turn emanates from the Body of Essence.

Although scholars often describe these triads as "of course Plotinian" and "of course neo-Platonic,"[92] the argument that inspiration comes from persistent Eastern and Buddhist ideas is more persuasive. This idea, particularly when combined with love as the moving force, takes on an interesting stripe in Ibn Sina's scheme. Everything moves with love (*ᶜishq*). God is the Beloved whom everything moves toward; God (*al-maᶜshuq*) is the good for the lover (*al-ᶜashiq*) and the longing or love (*shawq, ᶜishq*) which moves everything.[93]

If Ibn Sina the physician used Chinese techniques in medicine, surely Ibn Sina the philosopher would have been equally open to other Buddhist ideas which he found useful. So, in summary, arguments can be made that Buddhist culture and ideas had been in the cultural air of Bukhara at the time of Ibn Sina's birth, 370 AH/AD 980.

Question 17 Why does Ibn Sina mention the phoenix as an example of whiteness (§ 97)?[94]

Response In the definition of unity, he says, "Unity is said of the participation of things in a single essential or accidental predicate, like the unity of the substances phoenix and snow in the predicate white."[95]

The phoenix is a fabulous bird. The eastern and western depictions of the phoenix are very different. The West conceives the phoenix as purple or red; some authors derive its name from the Latin word *pheniceum*, which means purple. In this case, of course, one must also imagine the phoenix itself as purple. As will be recalled, the phoenix immolates itself at the end of a life-cycle and is reborn from its ashes. Although many different life-spans are given for the phoenix, five hundred years is frequently given.[96] On the other hand, the eastern idea of the phoenix, which may be conflated with Simurgh, is a radiant, wondrous bird, whose color is white. There are suggestions that the eastern concept of the phoenix was derived from a Chinese-inspired mythical bird, the Feng-huang.[97]

Ibn Sina mentions the phoenix only in passing, which argues for this idea being familiar to his readers, who would understand the reference. Furthermore, the white phoenix, as opposed to the purple or western phoenix, was an emblem of reborn Persian nationalism and pride. Whether or not Ibn Sina intended it as a nationalistic symbol, it was used this way by others, such as al-Firdawsi. When Islam arose, Muslims would claim superiority over non-Muslims. The earliest Muslims were Arabs, and the Qur'an had been revealed in Arabic, so such claims often included the notion of the cultural superiority of Arab culture over the converted indigenous cultures. This claim was particularly anathema to Persians, whose culture is much older than that of the Arabs. The Shuᶜubiyya Movement formed as a reaction to the Arabs; it took the form of a Persian literary renaissance. Writers of non-Arab descent, writing in either Arabic or Persian, took great delight in extolling the superiority of the Persian civilization, frequently at the expense of Arabs.

Against this backdrop the phoenix persists as a symbol from the mythology of the old Persian empire. The word for phoenix used in *The Book of Definitions*, *qaqnus*, is Persian, not Arabic.[98]

The phoenix appears to be synonymous with Simurgh, a fabulous bird living in the mountains, and found in al-Firdawsi's nationalistic epic *The Shahnamah* (*The Book of Kings*), which presents the mythological history of the early Persian kings.[99] Simurgh appears primarily in the story of Zal. Zal's mother gives birth to a beautiful baby, except for one quality: Zal has white hair. Al-Firdawsi's description is: "All the hair of his body was white like the snow."[100] Fearing this abnormality, his father exposes the baby to the elements. Simurgh takes him to her mountain fastness, on the Alborz Mountain, and raises him with her own brood. When she returns him to human company, she leaves Zal with one of her feathers. In time of need he is to the burn the feather which will summon Simurgh to aid Zal and his family.

The continuity of feathers and fire – whether the burned object is Simurgh's feather or the entire phoenix – demonstrates a certain genetic relationship between the Simurgh and the phoenix. By extension, beauty and radiance are equally part of those things which participate in the attribute of whiteness. The other emphasis on the examples given here (snow and the phoenix) is on the beauty which is part of the white thing. Snow is a shorthand for whiteness in the sense of a beautiful characteristic, and whiteness is the most obvious characteristic of snow. Snow has whiteness, not just as a dull thing, like a chicken, but a radiant whiteness. To imagine snow is to think of radiance and sparkle. The phoenix also is considered beautiful, supernatural, and white. Goichon's preference for the word "phoenix" (*qaqnus*) paired with snow, for examples of whiteness is more sensible than "soul" (*nafs*), given in the Constantinople text.[101] Souls may be described as pure, but this transforms the quality of whiteness to a metaphorical level as an attribute, rather than the essential or accidental participation in the predicate, which he mentions. The parallel example for whiteness is "that the ox and the human being participate in the predicate of animalness."

Simurgh puts in a later appearance in ᶜAttar's poem, *The Language of the Birds*, about a century after Ibn Sina.[102] This poem describes a Sufi quest by a group of birds, including a hoopoe and a nightingale, a parrot and a bittern, and others who journey to find the famed Simurgh, who in this instance is a bird of untold wonder. The feather that Simurgh had shed flying over China resulted in many paintings of that lost feather which will summon up Simurgh's essence. After harrowing adventures the pilgrim birds realize they are seeking themselves. ᶜAttar plays on the pun found within the Persian word Simurgh: *si* means "thirty" and *murgh* means "birds," so the name means "Thirty birds." The metaphor in this poem is the Sufi idea of annihilation of the soul in God, where the birds represent the souls. Just so, at the moment of the soul's annihilation it finds itself living in God. When the birds ask what they are looking for, the answer comes: "Without speech came the answer from that Presence, saying: 'This sun-like Presence is a mirror. / Whosoever enters It sees himself in It; in It he sees body and soul, soul and body'."[103] Perhaps a better derivation for Simurgh would be from *sim* meaning silver or silvery and *murgh* meaning bird.[104] In line with this interpretation, Simurgh's wish to save Zal and her sympathy with the baby's plight could be based on the similar color of his hair and her plumage – both radiant white or silver. cAttar's Simurgh is radiant.

In conclusion it seems likely the ideas of Simurgh and phoenix were syncretized in the word *qaqnus*, to mean a marvelous, radiant, bright bird. Using the more neutral word *qaqnus* instead of Simurgh allows Ibn Sina some subtlety in his use of a symbol understood as nationalistic. In spite of the existence of a wholly Arabic word, cauq, for phoenix, rather he uses the Persian word. This allows Ibn Sina to refer to the phoenix's eastern connections, but without instantly alienating an audience in large part composed of Arabs.

Question 18 Should we interpret Ibn Sina's use of cishq for "love" as showing Sufi influence?

Response Sufis, the mystics of Islam, emphasize the individual's interior states and approach God through love. Broadly speaking, in Sufism the adept loses himself or herself in God, being joined with God in unity through love, although what the *self* is that one loses varies with the commentator. Whatever word is used to describe the soul's contemplation of the Beloved, that is God, it is a radical state, as the individual eventually experiences obliteration or annihilation (*fana'*) of the self. What kind of love was appropriate and legitimate, and how the soul should view its relationship to God, was part of an ongoing – and not only academic – debate. Al-Hallaj had been executed for his exuberant ravings, such as "I am the Truth." The orthodox saw this assertion as blasphemous. The Truth is one of the Ninety-nine Beautiful Names of God. So when al-Hallaj said "I am the Truth," his enemies interpreted this as a claim to one of God's names, or claiming to be God. In the century after Ibn Sina, al-Ghazali made Sufism orthodox and respectable, but the climate was more ambiguous in Ibn Sina's day.

Sufis represent their position as a reaction against what they see as the legalism of orthodox Islam, which emphasizes a pattern of exterior behavior, rather than the interior state. Sufism's primary attention is fixed on the inner state of God's servant and that servant's journey back to God. Thus Jesus, according to Ibn al-cArabi, was one of the best models for focusing on the interior state of love for God.[105]

In the ninth century the word *mahabba* meant "love" in the positive sense and was used for the love of God, while the word cishq meant passionate love, with the emphasis on desire and excessiveness, according to the evidence of al-Kindi's definitions.

By the next century (309 AH/AD 922) the authorities would execute al-Hallaj for blasphemy. However, in his vocabulary ᶜishq took on new meaning. Al-Hallaj identified desire – that is ᶜishq – with the essence of God, according to Louis Massignon.[106] He used the term for love, ᶜishq, which includes the sense of desire. In al-Hallaj's rapturous Sufism, the soul longs and pines for God's essence, desiring only to be reunited with God and obliterating itself. Other Sufis, sometimes known as "drunken Sufis", pursued this idea with even greater abandon, describing a wild and drunken craving for God. The love of God is described in human terms, with the Beloved being understood as standing for God, and intoxication as love of God. When the authorities chose to interpret such wantonness in material terms, the Sufis frequently encountered persecution.

Thus, in Ibn Sina's time, there is a transition in the formation of ideas concerning the love of God. Al-Hallaj was executed over fifty years before Ibn Sina's birth. As proof of the change in the term's (ᶜishq) associative meanings, Ibn Sina wrote a treatise on love called *Risala fi al-ᶜishq* (*The Treatise on Love*), choosing the term ᶜishq rather than *mahabba*, and in which he describes the soul's journey back to God. Ibn Sina identifies God's essence with His existence in other treatises; considering God's essence as love parallels this thinking. Love is a force, perhaps the ultimate positive force; and being or pure existence is also the most positive force.

There is another apparent difference between ᶜishq and *mahabba*. *Mahabba* is a static term, while ᶜishq indicates motion toward something.[107] The picture that the Sufis draw of the soul's movement to God is essentially active and dynamic; it represents love as yearning. Although the soul reaches different stations, at which it may remain for a time, it continues to move to a higher level, seeking God as the lover seeks the Beloved. *ᶜIshq* is a technical term for the highest station in the soul's journey to intimacy and union with God.

Ibn Sina's terminology and metaphysics were widely employed by the Illuminationist philosophers of Persian heritage who succeeded him, such as Mulla Sadra. Mulla Sadra's metaphysics shows a great debt to Ibn Sina. The use of *wajib al-wujud*, the Necessary Existence, became common among Sufis and theologians as a name for God. In Ibn Sina's metaphysical scheme he used this name after a long discourse on how he arrived at it to refer to the ontologically necessary First Existence. Subsequent theologians employed this name in the way Christians might refer to God as "the Almighty," without reference to his argument; presumably they had internalized and agreed with his argument, and their use of his term implied agreement with his existential idea. Overall Ibn Sina appears as a rationalist mystic, but not a visionary mystic, in that none of his surviving works encourage the rapturous state of loss of self in order to merge with the One; nevertheless, he is interested in the Sufis' description of union.[108]

Question 19 One of the Sufi views of God is as the Pathetic God, longing to be known. It is expressed in the hadith, "I was a hidden treasure." Can we see Ibn Sina's comment on the movement of the universe by longing as an influence on this view?[109]

Response In the definition of soul, Ibn Sina says that the universe moves by longing. He says, "The cosmos does not move except by longing of the soul." (§ 26) This is the movement belonging to movement of the whole universe by way of longing for itself. The idea of longing as one of a pair of forces setting the universe in motion is an old one. Empedocles, the pre-Socratic philosopher, propounded the theory that the twin forces of love and war, or desire and dislike, caused the motion of the universe. The force of love brought things together by attraction, and the force of strife drove things apart and fragmented them. This was a constant cycle. After Ibn Sina, in the mystical philosophy of Ibn al-ᶜArabi (d. 638 AH/AD 1241), the hadith is found, "I was a hidden treasure longing to be known, so I made humans."[110] This hadith is among the hadiths known by unveiling to Ibn al-ᶜArabi.[111] This means that although the hadith (tradition) is not found in the major collections of sound hadiths, Ibn al-ᶜArabi considered it to be revealed directly to him and consequently valid. Such personal revelation is called unveiling. While not considered an orthodox hadith, the hadith did continue to be attested to by the Sufis. It conveys the idea of God as the Pathetic God, that God is lonely in his splendor and almightiness, and therefore he created human beings so that creatures would know him. By their knowing him, he knows himself. One may interpret this idea as a reworking and redefining of the Empedoclean idea of the universe working on the principle of attraction, and love making the whole world come together. Thus the idea of an emotion which started at the human level expands upward to the divine level. Unlike most theories of creation, it is satisfying inasmuch as it provides an emotionally satisfying reason for God's creation of the cosmos, which usually tends to be a problem without any solution.

Al-Qashani quotes this hadith in the *Glossary of Sufi Technical Terms*.[112] Under the letter *nun* (*n*) he gives a definition for "The marriage penetrating for all descendants" where he quotes the saying, attributed to God, "I was a hidden treasure, so I longed to be known." This demonstrates the persistence of the idea, frequently expressed in Sufism, that God created humans so he would have company and someone who would know him.

One presumes Ibn Sina wrote *The Book of Definitions* for beginning students of philosophy, and consequently the emphasis is on the rational use of terms. But hints of mysticism are still found and a world view that is not strictly reason-based peeks out. The mention of the cosmos moving by longing for itself (§ 26) can only be interpreted as a mystical explanation for the world.

On its surface *The Book of Definitions*, like Ibn Sina's other works, is very rational, that is, based on intellection. But the Sinawiyyan universe is based equally on love, as it is on reason and intellect. The love mentioned is usually described in rational terms, rather than mystical terms; but it is there. This may reflect Ibn Sina's training in both philosophy and medicine; it may also reflect the tenor of the times – mysticism as a somewhat dangerous pursuit, while orthodoxy was valued on all fronts.

Concluding questions

Question 20 What is the difference between Ibn Sina's treatment of angel (§ 46) and jinn (§ 51)?

Response Theologically the reality of both angels and jinn is attested by the Qur'an. Ibn Sina defines angels, saying they are simple living substances with rational speech, immortal. He does not mention that angels do not have bodies; this is implied, however, since he stated that they are simple substances – form only. Jinn, on the other hand, are called ethereal animals, but he does not indicate what they are composed of – only saying they are a mass (*jism*). He also says that jinn can take on different shapes. But Ibn Sina states that he is giving only the meaning of the name jinn and not describing it. By this device he informs us that he has given a verbal description of the name, thus making no claim of a real-world existence for jinn; this is the only definition which he states is "the meaning of the term." A definition that defines a name is a nominal definition. Generally speaking, Ibn Sina's other definitions are of essences and are called essential definitions. When Ibn Sina gave the definition of definition as "indicating the quiddity (or essence) of a thing," this means he is making a claim for the truth or validity of things so defined (§ 18) in Aristotelian terms. They are not just terms; there are real existing things behind the words.

From numerous passages in the Qur'an where angels are mentioned one may note their position in the universe as messengers sent by God to human beings. For example, they are called beings created by God, as messengers with wings and, in fact, having various numbers of wings (S. 35.1). The angel frequently speaks to human beings to warn them to fear God (S. 16. 2 and S. 26.193). In his definition Ibn Sina emphasizes the function of angels, which is to communicate in their position as intermediary between the heavens and the earth – between Creator and humans. In this sense angels are the metaphysical bridge that allows humans to communicate with the higher level; otherwise God is metaphysically isolated. Angels function on a mystical level; they can give knowledge directly to prophets. Angels allow God to send messages to earthly beings without compromising His oneness or unity. Otherwise God is so far beyond humans as to prevent communication. Although the Qur'an does not specify the material, tradition says that angels are created from light.

In pre-Islamic Arabia, jinn were viewed as spirits of the desert, frequently hostile to humans. In Islamic times the jinn continue to exist; they are mentioned in the Qur'an as created from part of fire (S. 55.15). Like angels, jinn are created from a substance that shines and creates light. Some say Iblis was created as a jinn, others that he was an angel. According to some traditions, Iblis lost rank when he refused to bow down to Adam as God ordered. He refused to bow down before Adam out of pride, because Iblis said Adam was made of clay or mud (S. 15. 29–34). The thirteenth-century Qur'an commentator al-Baydawi demonstrates in his remarks on S. 2. 32 how much the philosophers had influenced the theologians. In this section al-Baydawi discusses the nature of angels and the question of whether Iblis is an angel or a jinn. There was precedent for both viewpoints. Finally, al-Baydawi states that perhaps Satan differs from the angels not in his essence, but only in accidents.[113] This remark shows strong philosophical influence, both in the idea behind it and in the terms used to discuss it. The words al-Baydawi uses for essence, *dhat*, and for accidents, *cawarid*, are philosophical. Accidents had been discussed by theologians in the theory of occasionalism.[114] To see a commentator speculating on the essence of Iblis is extremely suggestive, in that although the theologians scorned philosophy they did not hesitate to use philosophy as a tool when it was convenient.

While the existence of jinn was posited religiously, Ibn Sina approached the philosophical problem of their existence head-on by stating that they only existed in verbal terms. His treatment of angels and jinn in *The Book of Definitions* shows a change in the metaphysical landscape under Islam from that of the Greeks. Aristotle believed that matter is eternal; there is no need for a Creator. All that was needed in the Greek metaphysical scheme was a First Cause, beyond the world, to set the world in motion. In the Islamic view of the world, a Creator created the world and humans celebrated their place in creation by worshiping him. The First Cause was no longer an impersonal, faceless force, which it makes no sense to worship, but a Creator, God, whose hand and face (S. 2. 272) also exist, although in an unspecified way. As Creator God is worthy of worship and attains a link with the created world. However this generates another problem: God is so far removed from creation, so far above creatures, that there is no common ground, hence provoking the need, both religiously and philosophically, for intermediaries. Angels fill this need; they are non-corporeal substances who can take on shapes visible to humans in order to bring God's message to humans. They can talk to humans in language that humans understand. The Qur'an ascribes its message as being brought by the angel Gabriel (S. 16. 2).

Thus Ibn Sina's definition emphasizes the important points: angels are simple substances – not body and form – but simple, living, immortal, and having rational speech. The angels serve as a conduit for messages and grace from God. As usual, in Ibn Sina's metaphysical structure the simple is more actual and more real than the complex or compound. God is the ultimate simplicity.

One of the continuing mysteries of Ibn Sina's *Book of Definitions* has been the order of his definitions. These can be clarified, at least partially, once one notices that the definition of angel is before that of sphere, and the definition of jinn before that of fire. The angel is an intermediary from the heavens to earth, so it is appropriate that the definition of angel occurs before sphere. The major attribute of the term jinn both here and in the Qur'an is that it is made of fire or some part of fire, so the definition of fire follows the definition of jinn. After that are the other three elements. Thus the order develops logically and conversationally, leading to related definitions – from angels to spheres, from jinn to fire, then air, water and earth.

By contrast, in al-Kind's book *On the Definitions* al-Kindi defined angelicity, but not jinn. His definition is "angelicity consists of living and articulating."[115] Ibn Sina repeated these two characteristics and added others.

Question 21 What can we glean about Ibn Sina's metaphysical viewpoint from this work?

Response For Ibn Sina, the purpose of metaphysics is to reveal the connections between the material world and the unseen, but no less real, world. The major premise of Islamic thought, inasmuch as it took the position God is totally above the world and beyond humans' comprehension, led philosophers to recognize that this position was metaphysically untenable. Although it was philosophically necessary that God be incomprehensible, this also left creatures with no communication to the divine. The other cleavage is between the senses and the soul. If the soul is without matter, how can it connect with the body, with the senses, and knowledge which they feed the soul, and the intellect, which is a faculty of the soul (§ 22)? Again there is an abyss between body and soul, matter and form.

Within this framework one can understand Ibn Sina's arguments about the Necessary Existence and the essence/existence distinction. Ibn Sina begins his argument for a Necessary Existence by discussing the question of causation, as mentioned above.[116] There must be one existent from which all others come, one Necessary Existence. It is the One who must be. That said, this is all that can be said about the Necessary Existence. Its quiddity is its existence, it does not have a substance or essence other than its existence.

If one wishes, one may see Ibn Sina as an early existentialist – showing an overwhelming interest in the importance of existence and kinds of existence. The Necessary Existence has no quiddity, only an essence which is its existence. Everything else is created and comes from the Necessary Existence; such things are called possible existents. Each of these creatures has a quiddity, a created essence.[117] This quiddity is different from a thing's existence. This type of quiddity refers only to imperfect beings, that is possible beings. There is one way to bridge the gap between the Necessary Existence and possible existents, and that is mysticism. The imagination may perceive and perhaps even comprehend what the intellect alone is incapable of understanding. Imagination is the territory of mystics and prophets – the philosophical response of faith to an intellectual quandary. This type of deeply felt quandary is not limited to Ibn Sina: Aristotle began the *Metaphysics* by saying that his predecessors only had limited knowledge of the Truth and each of them had made mistakes.[118]

Ibn Sina's inclination toward mysticism is apparent in small clues, such as the reference to love (*ʿishq*) as the highest goal for the human spirit, and works like *Risala fi al-ʿishq* (*The Treatise on Love*). Ibn al-ʿArabi extended his thought and developed the idea of ultimate reality as being the realm of images, perceived by the faculty of the imagination. Throughout his philosophy Ibn Sina demonstrates the limits of reason and intellect in understanding reality.

This brings out a second point of Ibn Sina's metaphysics, his distinction between essence and existence. Ibn Sina became particularly famous for developing this distinction, although it is arguable whether he intended this as an ontological (real-world) distinction, or merely as a mental construct. In other words, did he believe essence and existence really existed separately, or only that they could be thought of as separate concepts in the human mind? His three types of existence are necessary, possible and impossible, although impossible is only a category of things that cannot exist. Ibn Sina maintains that things have no pre-existence. They either exist or do not exist, but they do not have an intermediary state before existence. When a thing comes into existence it becomes whatever it is. For example, in his discussion of souls and the question of when they come into existence in relation to bodies, he states specifically, "it is impossible for them [souls] to exist before the body."[119] Therefore, they are not pre-existing in a never-never land, but come into existence when there is a body suitable for it, for which it has an affinity.[120] Ibn Sina's argument here is that a soul is pure form, it has no matter; and if a soul were to pre-exist the body, it could not be differentiated (from other souls). Pure form has no distinction, thus one soul can not be different from another before its embodiment. Consequently souls and bodies come into existence together. This negates the idea of existence as a kind of supra-added accident, which some scholars have been led to believe as being

Ibn Sina's intention. Ibn Sina distinctly refutes this point of view when he states there is either existence or non-existence, but no middle state.[121]

Another way to understand existence in Sinawiyyan terms is as the relationship of essence to the material world. Although essence cannot exist alone, prior to existence, existence is its condition when it has a relationship with the real world. When he discusses the relative existence of soul and body in terms of their coming into existence and decides they must come into existence simultaneously, this shows he is moving in the direction of considering their relationship as all-important. Otherwise one may be led in a false direction to believe that the body has sensations unconnected to the soul, and that the intellect is capable of reason, without explaining its base in sense perception.

The different perspectives Ibn Sina developed become evident in comparing the points of view in the *Qanun* to those of the *Shifa'*. In the author of the *Qanun* we have a man who is quite capable of seeing the natural world from the point of view of a physician. In the *Qanun* Ibn Sina limits the word *ruh*, often used as a term for soul in religious treatises, to the breath and what its condition indicates for health. In the philosophical works he consistently uses *nafs* for soul, to indicate he is using the philosophical, not the medical term. In Ibn Sina there is a synthesis of many different ideas from divergent backgrounds, including medicine, philosophy, eastern and Hellenic, integrated into a coherent metaphysical scheme.

Question 22 Why shouldn't Ibn Sina be better known in the West?

Response Philosophers are generally remembered for one of two reasons: first, subsequent philosophers comment on their ideas, and in the process keep their names alive; second, some institution becomes the standard bearer for a particular philosopher because his ideas fit the institution's own agenda. In Ibn Sina's case the answer is very complex. Ibn Sina was known in medieval Europe as "Avicenna," both in Latin translations and from mention in Thomas Aquinas's work. But, of course, Thomas Aquinas (d. 1274) did not read Arabic, and thus was familiar with Ibn Sina's work only from the Latin translations. The translators of these works had undertaken the translation of Islamic philosophy from Arabic into Latin, for the purpose of refuting Islam. During this period the reconquest of Muslim Spain by the Christians was already underway, thus such translation was a politically charged undertaking.

These translations were organized by the Church: Raymond, archbishop of Toledo, was particularly famous for arranging the translation from Arabic into Latin in the twelfth century. Among the best known translators of the mid-1100s were Dominic Gundisalvi and Gerard of Cremona. Dominic Gundisalvi (also known as Gundissalinus) worked in tandem with Avendauth (Ibn Daud).[122] It is believed that Avendauth translated the text of Ibn Sina's

Book of the Soul from Arabic into Castilian, probably orally, and then Gundisalvi translated the Castilian into Latin. It is also believed Gundisalvi translated Ibn Sina's *Metaphysics* (*al-Ilahiyyat*).[123] One measure of Gundisalvi's success as a translator, as one commentator has noted, is that "His translations are not always easy to understand, but his vocabulary is more precise and adequate and his style more fluent than that of most of his predecessors and contemporaries."[124] Gerard of Cremona translated Ibn Sina's medical treatise as *Canones medicinae*, as well as part of the encyclopedic *Kitab al-shifa'*.[125]

Thomas Aquinas took over many of Ibn Sina's ideas and incorporated them into his own philosophy. For example, one of Aquinas's early books, *De ente et essentia* (*Essence and Existence*), covers the distinctions of essence and existence, following strongly Ibn Sina's ideas, whether or not "Avicenna" is mentioned in specific passages.

To give an example of Aquinas's misinterpretations of Ibn Sina, perhaps due to inaccurate Latin translations, we must look at a particular instance where Thomas states that Ibn Sina says God has no essence.[126] The original Arabic text actually states, "God's being is his essence." Because the Latin translations flattened Ibn Sina, by using the same Latin word "essentia" for a variety of Arabic words (*mahiyya, dhat*, and *anniyya*) all meaning some variation of "essence," Aquinas missed some of the nuances. While the word *wujud* for existence and *mawjud* for an existing thing both come from the root *wujida*, meaning "to exist," they have different nuances. *Mawjud* also includes the sense of being created, that is, brought into existence. God is *wajib al-wujud* (the Necessary Existence). On the other hand *mawjud* may be used for existing or for a creature. Essentially Ibn Sina needed to separate the unique being of God from the multiple quiddities of creatures. Ibn Sina states in one important passage of *al-Ilahiyyat*, "There is no essence (*mahiyya*) belonging to the Necessary of Existence (*wajib al-wujud*) other than that it is Necessary of Existence *and* this is the *anniyya* (essence)." Here one sees Ibn Sina distinguishing *mahiyya*, a word used only for the essence of created beings, from *anniyya*, used for God's essence alone. Even in terms of *mahiyya* Ibn Sina does not say God has *no* essence, but that his essence is his being in that he is *wajib al-wujud*.[127] Ibn Sina's point here is that God is not a member of a class of existents; He is a uniquely existing being. While in *al-Ilahiyyat* Ibn Sina may say that *wajib al-wujud* does not have a quiddity, this is in a specific, limited sense. The word he uses here for quiddity is a word meaning only created essence (*mahiyya*), and he adds qualifiers. The reader thus understands that Ibn Sina's purpose is not to deny essence to *wajib al-wujud*, but only to emphasize that the essence of the Necessary Existence is uncreated *essence*. The Arabic word *anniyya* is transliterated in Latin, so unless Aquinas knew what the Arabic term meant, it is likely this meaning will not be clear.

Thomas Aquinas knew Ibn Sina solely in his Latin language manifestation. The Latin text of *al-Ilahiyyat* clearly emphasizes the difference between the Necessary Existence and all other existents. But it fails to distinguish among "essences" as the words are used in Arabic. From other writings, Thomas indicates an awareness of the negative description of God[128] so this alone should not mislead him. The main problem appears to be the Latin translations themselves, in this instance. This interpretation leads Aquinas to remark, "Avicenna and Rabbi Moses [say] that God is a certain subsistent existence, and that besides existence there is nothing else in God, hence they say God is an existence without an essence."[129] If Thomas understood Ibn Sina's ideas correctly, he would not have been able to make this mistake.

Aquinas also states that God is pure act, which is his essence. In *al-Ilahiyyat* Ibn Sina stated that (a) God had no essence, *except* his existence; (b) God's essence (*anniyya*) is pure existence; and (c) God did not have an individual essence, such as all other beings have (*mahiyya*). This type of essence belongs only to created beings. As the Necessary Existence, the uncreated being, God cannot have this kind of essence. Thus, Aquinas says the same thing as Ibn Sina – that God is pure act – the only totally self-subsisting being, without any trace of potentiality in him; but he does not give Ibn Sina credit for this remark, apparently because Aquinas did not understand Ibn Sina correctly.[130]

Furthermore, the program for Aquinas's teacher, Albert the Great, and for Aquinas himself was to prove that the coexistence of Aristotle and the dogma of the Roman Catholic Church was acceptable. The success of Aquinas's campaign can be seen in the great reputation both Aristotle and Thomas Aquinas gained throughout the Christian West as a result of Aquinas's labors. There was no such campaign to make Ibn Sina acceptable. On the contrary, philosophy in Islam was viewed by many orthodox scholars as a problem, as philosophers used human reason to discover the nature of God and other issues covered by faith. Philosophers were viewed by the theologians as political enemies.

As mentioned above the primary way philosophers are remembered is when the scholars who follow them comment on their ideas and arguments. Thus, Aristotle is probably the most famous philosopher in western philosophy, because so many subsequent philosophers wrote commentaries on his ideas. Porphyry of Tyre, Alexander of Aphrodisius, Ibn Rushd and Thomas Aquinas are among the commentators. Commentators on Aristotle also include Simplicius and John Philoponus. Commentator is understood to be someone who may criticize and reshape a philosophy as well as explain it. Even when the names of the commentators are forgotten, that of the philosopher who is commented on continues. The second way philosophers are remembered is when a special interest group, like a church or political state, holds the philosopher up for remembrance. Thus Thomas Aquinas holds a high place first, in the Dominican Order, and then in the Roman Catholic Church as a Doctor of the Church, "the Angelic Doctor", one who gave rational guidelines to religious faith. In the case of Thomas, he encouraged the co-existence of religion and philosophy against those who feared that reason might weaken faith.

A few philosophers, such as the astronomer and philosopher Nasir al-Din al-Tusi (d. 672 AH/AD 1274), wrote commentaries on Ibn Sina's works, but they were not able to overcome al-Ghazali's (d. 505 AH/AD 1111) frontal assault on philosophy, *Tahafut al-falasifa* (*On the Incoherence of the Philosophers*).[131] Al-Ghazali found twenty points in which the positions of philosophers were objectionable to Sunni Islam, and three which made them unbelievers. The *Incoherence* is strictly a work of criticism. The three specific ideas al-Ghazali identified as heresy were: the eternity of the world, that God does not know the individual particulars of a person, and the denial of the rising of bodies for the Last Judgement and Resurrection. In al-Ghazali's opinion, to uphold the eternity of the world is to deny the agency of God as Creator. Yet the difference in interest between the theologians and philosophers can be shown easily. The emphasis in the Qur'an is that God is the Creator, not how or why he created the world or the composition of the matter of creation. The philosophers, on the other hand, were interested in how and why God created the world. Aristotle viewed the world as eternally existing matter, which was set in motion by the First Mover. Al-Ghazali's second objection stems from the major question, Does God have knowledge of the particulars about each person or does he only know about people in a general way? The orthodox answer became that God knew each thing individually; while philosophers tended to say God knew things in general, about a class (humans), not an individual. One of the philosophical problems connected with this question is the idea that knowledge of change will change the knower. Since it is unthinkable that God is changeable, he cannot have knowledge of changing things. The other aspect of this problem is temporal: God is eternal, so time in the human sense of past, present, and future cannot have meaning for him. At this point, one would like to point out all humans have a problem with imagining metaphysics and particularly imagining God. Humans are part of the system they are trying to analyze, and this always leads to contradictions. Also a human cannot know beyond her or his limits, an imperfect human cannot imagine a perfect being.

Lastly, al-Ghazali says those who would claim the Resurrection of bodies was metaphorical were also *kafir* (plural, *kuffar*, unbelievers). The Qur'an states that the dead will rise for Judgement. For al-Ghazali this should be understood literally. This question had perplexed both theologians and philosophers. Abu al-Hudhayl, the early theologian mentioned above, took the view that God will recreate the human person again in his same identity and as the same person he was previously.[132] Some thinkers had taken the stand that God recreated bodies anew, some that recreated bodies only resembled their old bodies, and some that they were the actual bodies restored. All of these positions lead to absurdities when they are spun out. Ibn Sina dealt with the question of the Afterlife in two individual treatises on the subject. He takes a rather complicated position in *al-Adhawiyya*. First, he says that the rewards and punishments in the Afterlife are pleasure for the senses and pain in the senses. They have a sensual component according to the Shari‛a. Second, Ibn Sina affirms that pleasures of the senses include a mental, that is, a non-sensual element. The same is true of pain. He emphasizes that the thinking organ (*dimagh*) and the heart are the important parts for actually perceiving pleasure and pain. In this way he emphasizes the importance of mental participation for reward or punishment to be effective.[133]

In the *Secret of Destiny* Ibn Sina states that it is not seemly for God to punish individuals for their deeds, this kind of revenge reflects human desire; the attributes of God make such punishment and revenge unthinkable.[134] God will not put a fornicator in chains and burn him over and over, as the theologians believe; rather the point of these threatened punishments is to make humans behave well. He views the doctrine of reward and punishment as a deterrent for bad actions, rather than important in itself. Thus Ibn Sina has a more complex idea toward the whole of idea of bodily resurrection and what it is supposed to mean, than merely to deny it. In one sense, he is in agreement with the orthodox, that is in stating that individuals are responsible for their actions in this world and those actions will result in the state of the soul in the next world. He emphasizes that the soul's perfection results in its happiness, and is indeed necessary to enjoy paradise.[135]

Al-Ghazali continued the unfortunate tradition of labeling his opponents as believers in heresy (*bida‛*). Essentially, because of the weight of al-Ghazali's reputation, not to mention his training as a jurist, he was able to condemn them for their practice of philosophy. Ibn Rushd (d. 595 AH/AD 1198) tried to overcome this great obstacle with his rebuttal *Tahafut al-tahafut* (*The Incoherence of the Incoherence*). Working against Ibn Rushd was the fact that he was marginalized by being a member of the western Islamic empire, when the center was closer to Baghdad. He also devoted himself most intensely to Aristotelian commentary, which marginalized his writings philosophically for the Islamic world. Consequently his reputation was not strong enough, particularly among the Muslim thinkers, to defeat al-Ghazali. After al-Ghazali's attack, the philosophy that continued was perforce often esoteric and mystical, meaning it was self-protective – so much so that the ordinary person could not understand it. In the end Ibn Sina did not have a major institution to enhance his reputation, the way Aquinas did.

To recapitulate, Thomas Aquinas stole Ibn Sina's thunder. There are points for which Ibn Sina might have been as well known in the West as he was in the Arabic-speaking world, these being: that God's essence is radically different from creatures; his essence is pure existence; and the distinction of essence/existence. Instead these ideas have become associated rather with Aquinas.

APPENDIX

Arabic texts of definitions from the preceding chapters.

CHAPTER 2 AL-KINDI: THE FIRST ARABIC
BOOK OF DEFINITIONS

Substance

الجوهر - هو القائم بنفسه ؛ و هو حامل للأعراض لم تتغير ذاتيَّته، موصوف لا واصف[1] ؛ و يقول : هو غير قابل للتكوين و الفساد وللأشياء التى تزيد لكل واحد من الأشياء التى مثل الكون والفساد ، فى خاص جوهره ، التى إذا عرفت عرفت أيضا بمعرفتها الأشياء العارضة فى كل واحد من الجوهر الجزئى ، من غير أن تكون داخلة فى نفس جوهره الخاصِّى.[2]

The first cause

العلة الأولى -- مبدعة فاعلة متمِّمَّة الكل غير متحركة.[3]

The natural causes

العلل الطبيعية أربع - ما منه كان الشيء ، أعني عنصره ، وصورة الشيء التي بها هو ما هو ، ومبدأ حركة الشيء التي هي علته ، وما من أجله فعلَ الفاعلُ مفعولَه .[4]

Matter

الهيولى - قوة موضوعة لحمل الصور ، منفعلة .[5]

CHAPTER 3 AL-FARABI: THE EMERGENCE OF ARABICIZED GREEK LOGIC

Definitions of definition

والذي تفيده الصناعة الطبيعية في كل جسم طبيعي هو علم جوهره و هو ما يدل عليه حده ويعرف مادته و صورته و فاعله الذي كونه ... و الغاية التي لأجلها كون .[6]

و أيضا فإن حد الشيء قد يُستعمَل بدل الشيء ويُظن أنه لا فرق بين الشيء و ‹بين› حده .[7]

ولمَّا كان الحد الكامل هو لشيء وحده أمكن أن يجاب به في جواب أي شيء هو ، وأن يُستعمَل في الدلالة على تمييز الشيء عن كل ما سواه . والحد يعرِّف من الشيء أمرين اثنين ، أحدهما أنَّه يعرِّف ذات الشيء وجوهره ، والثاني ‹أنه› يعرِّف ما يتميَّز به عن كل ما سواه .[8]

الي كل ما يحتاج اليه في التحديد على الحقيقة ...[9]

APPENDIX

الجوهر :Substance

وقد جرت العادة أن يسمّيَ هذا المشار إليه المحسوس الذى لا يوصف به شيء أصلاً إلاّ بطريق العرض وعلى غير <ال>مجرى الطبيعي ، وما يعرف ما هو هذا المشار إليه ، الجوهر على الإطلاق ، كما يسمونه الذات على الإطلاق . لأنّ معنى جوهر الشيء هو ذات الشيء وماهيّتُه وجزء ماهيّته، فالذى هو ذات فى نفسه وليس هو ذاتا لشيء أصلا هو جوهر على الإطلاق ، كما هو ذات على الإطلاق ، من غير أن يضاف إلى شيء أو يقيّد بشيء. وما يعرّف ما هو هذا المشار إليه هو جوهر هذا المشار إليه.[10]

أسباب :Causes

فأصناف الحروف التى تُطلَب بها أسباب وجود الشيء وعلله على ما يظهر ثلاثة: " لِما " وجوده ، و " بماذا " وجوده ، و " عن ماذا " وجوده .[11]

المادة :Matter

وبيّن أنّ ماهية الشيء الكاملة إنّما هي بصورته إذا كانت في مادة ملائمة معاضدة على الفعل الكائن عنها . فإذن للمادة مدخل لا محالة في ماهيته. فإذن ماهيته بصورته في مادته التي إنّما كوّنت لأجل صورته الكائنة لغاية ما . فإذا كان كذلك ، فإن الفطرة التى كان الناس يعنون بقولهم "الجوهر" إنّما هي ماهية الإنسان ، وهي التى بها الإنسان إنسان بالفعل . فإذن إنّما يعنون بالجوهر ماهية الإنسان، كان ذلك جوهر زيد أو آبائه أو جنس. وأيضا فإنّهم يظنون أن آباءه وأمهاته وجنسه الأقدمين هم مواده التى منها كُونها، ويظنون أن مواد الشيء متى كانت جيدة كان الشيء جيدا ، مثل مواد الحائط ومواد السرير . فإنّهم يظنون <أنّ> الخشب إذا كان جيدا

كان السرير جيدا، إذ تكون جودة الخشب سببا لجودة السرير ، وإذا كان الحجارة واللبن والآجرّ والطين جيدا كان الحائط المبني منها أيضا جيدا، إذ كانت جودة تلك سببا لجودة الحائط. فعلى هذا المثال يرون في آباء الإنسان وأمهاته وأجداده وقبيلته وأمته وأهل بلده ، فإنّ كثيرا من الناس يخيّل إليهم أنّهم مواد الإنسان الكائن عنهم أو فيهم. وموادّ الشيء هي إما ماهيته وإما أجزاء ماهيته ، فهم إذن إنما يعنون بالجوهر ههنا ماهيته أو ما به ماهيته . [12]

و الصورة هي في الجسم الجوهر الجسمانيّ ، مثل شكل السرير في السرير ، والمادة مثل خشب السرير . فالصورة هي التي بها يصير الجوهر المتجسم جوهرا بالفعل ، والمادة هي التي بها يكون جوهرا بالقوة. ...والمادة إنما وجودها لأجل الصور . ... فلذلك متى لم توجد الصور ، كان وجود المادة باطلاً - ... فلذلك لا يمكن أن توجد المادة الأولى خلوا من صورة ما . [13]

CHAPTER 4 IBN SINA: THE SECOND
BOOK OF DEFINITIONS

Definitions of definition

حد الحد ما ذكره الحكيم فى كتاب طوبيقا أنه القول الدال على ماهية الشيء أى على كمال وجوده الذاتى وهو ما يتحصل له من جنسه القريب وفصله . [14]

... بل هو مجموع الصورة والمادة ، فإن هذا هو ما هو المركب ، والماهية هذا التركيب . فالصورة أحد ما يضاف إليه التركيب ، والماهية هي نفس هذا التركيب الجامع للصورة والمادة ، والواحدة الحادثة منهما لهذا الواحد.[15]

الجوهر Substance:

حد الجوهر هو اسم مشترك يقال جوهر لذات كل شيء كان كالإنسان أو كالبياض ويقال جوهر لكل موجود لذاته لا يحتاج فى الوجود إلى ذات أخرى يقارنها حتى يقوم بالفعل وهذا معنى قولهم الجوهر قائم بذاته ||.

ويقال جوهر لما كان بهذه الصفة وكان من شأنها أن يقبل الأضداد بتعاقبها عليه ويقال جوهر لكل ذات وجوده ليس فى محل ويقال جوهر لكل ذات وجوده ليس فى موضوع وعليه اصطلح الفلاسفة القدماء مذ عهد أرسطوطاليس فى استعمالهم لفظة الجوهر وقد فرقنا بين الموضوع والمحل قبل هذا فيكون معنى قولهم الموجود لا فى موضوع الموجود غير مقارن الوجود لمحل قائم بنفسه بالفعل مقوم له ولا بأس بأن يكون فى محل لا يقوم المحل دونه بالفعل فانه وإن كان فى محل فليس فى موضوع .

فكل موجود وإن كان كالبياض والحرارة والحركة فهو جوهر بالمعنى الأول والمبدأ الأول جوهر بالوجه الثانى والرابع والخامس وليس جوهرا بالمعنى الثالث و الهيولى جوهر بالمعنى الرابع والخامس وليس جوهرا بالمعنى الثانى والثالث والصورة جوهر بالمعنى الخامس وليس جوهرا بالمعنى الثانى والثالث والرابع ولا مشاحة فى الأسماء .[16]

APPENDIX

Cause: **العلة**

العلة كل ذات وجود ذات آخر بالفعل من وجود هذا بالفعل ووجود هذا بالفعل ليس من وجود ذلك بالفعل .[17]

The caused: **المعلول**

المعلول كل ذات وجوده بالفعل من وجود غيره ووجود ذلك الغير ليس من وجوده ومعنى قولنا من وجوده غير معنى قولنا مع وجوده فان معنى قولنا من وجوده هو أن تكون الذات باعتبار نفسها ممكنة الوجود وإنما يجب وجودها بالفعل لا من ذاتها بل لان ذاتا أخرى موجودة بالفعل يلزم عنها وجود هذه الذات ويكون لها في نفسها الإمكان فيكون لها في نفسها بلا شرط الإمكان ولها في نفسها بشرط العلة الوجوب ولها في نفسها بشرط لا علة الامتناع ./‏/

وفرق بين قولنا بلا شرط وبين قولنا بشرط لا كالفرق بين قولنا عود أبيض لا وبين قولنا عود لا أبيض . وأما معنى قولنا مع وجوده فهو أن يكون اي واحد من الذاتين فرض موجودا لزم أن يعلم أن الآخر موجود وإذا فرض مرفوعا لزم أن الآخر مرفوع والعلة والمعلول معا بمعنى هذين اللزومين وإن كان وجها اللزومين مختلفين لأن أحدهما و هو المعلول إذا فرض موجودا لزم أن يكون الآخر قد كان بذاته موجوداً حتى وجد هذا وأما الآخر وهو العلة فلما فرض موجودا لزم أن يتبع وجوده وجود المعلول وإذا كان المعلول مرفوعا لزم أن يُحكم أن العلة كانت أولا مرفوعة حتى يصح رفع هذا لا أن رفع المعلول أوجب رفع العلة وأما العلة فاذا رفعناها وجب رفع المعلول بايجاب رفع العلة رفعه.[18]

APPENDIX

Matter₁: **الهيولى**

حد الهيولى أما الهيولى المطلقة فهى جوهر وجوده بالفعل إنما يحصل بقبوله الصورة الجسمية لقوة فيه قابلة للصور وليس له فى ذاته صورة تخصُّه إلا معنى القوة و معنى قولي لها جوهر هو أن وجودها حاصل لها بالفعل لذاتها و يقال هيولى لكل شيء من شأنه أن يقبل كمالا مَّا وأمرا ليس فيه فيكون بالقياس إلى ما ليس فيه هيولى وبالقياس إلى ما فيه موضوعا.[19]

Matter₂: **المادة**

فى المادة المادة قد يقال اسما مرادفا للهيولى ويقال مادة لكل موضوع يقبل الكمال باجتماعه إلى غيره و وروده عليه يسيرا يسيرا مثل المنى والدم لصورة الحيوان فربما كان ما يجامعه من نوعه وربما لم يكن من نوعه.[20]

166

NOTES

INTRODUCTION

1 The author would like to thank Omar Trezise for his perfect pitch in phrasing this idea. (1 July, 1998).
2 Ross Day (16 March, 1998).

1 WHAT IS A DEFINITION?

1 E. R. Dodds, *The Ancient Concept of Progress and other Essays on Greek Literature and Belief* (Oxford: Clarendon, 1973), p. 129.
2 See Christel Hein, *Definition und Einteilung der Philosophie* (Frankfurt: Peter Lang, 1985) and Francis E. Peters, *Aristoteles Arabus: The oriental translations and commentaries of the Aristotelian corpus* (Leiden: Brill, 1968).
3 *Hayula* is a transliterated Greek term, and one would therefore not expect to find it in the Qur'an.
4 Ibn Na^cima's translation of *The Theology of Aristotle* was corrected by al-Kindi, according to the title inscription. See *Plotinus Apud Arabes*, ed. ^cAbdurrahman Badawi (Cairo, 1955), p. 3 [Arabic text], and *Plotini Opera*, ed. Paul Henry and Hans-Rudolf Schwyzer (Paris: Desclée de Brouwer, 1959), v. 2, p. 486.
5 See Chapter 4 for a list comparing the order of al-Kindi's list with that of Ibn Sina.
6 The "Letters" of the title refer to the Greek letters used to number Aristotle's chapters in the *Metaphysics*.
7 Muhsin Mahdi, "Al-Farabi's Imperfect State," *JAOS* 110 (1990): 699 and passim.
8 See Chapter 3, pp. 33–35, for a discussion of the state of received Greek philosophy as it affected al-Farabi; and p. 41 for its relation to al-Farabi's definition of *sabab*.
9 There is a large body of literature covering this problem. See references in notes for Chapter 3.
10 See Chapter 3, pp. 33–35, for a discussion of the known differences between translated texts available to al-Farabi and al-Kindi.
11 For information on the *mihna*, see W. M. Patton, *Ahmed Ibn Hanbal and the Mihna* (Leiden: Brill, 1897). In either 219 AH/AD 834 or 220 AH/AD 835 Ahmed ibn Hanbal was flogged by the khalif al-Mu^ctasim for refusing to declare that the Qur'an was created. Al-Mu^ctasim released Ibn Hanbal because the populace of Baghdad became extremely restive on his behalf. This argues that Ibn Hanbal was a popular leader, with political, as well as religious influence; hence the *mihna* appears to take on political overtones. See *"Mihna"* by M. Hinds, EI^2, v. 7, p. 3, on

Ibn Hanbal. The created Qur'an had less prestige than the uncreated Qur'an and consequently by championing the created Qur'an the khalif could enhance his power. (Hind (p. 5) cites M. Watt on this point.) It also gave the khalif more direct control over the courts since he directed that the *qadi*s were to be tested.

In an analysis of the aims of the *mihna*, Ira Lapidus says:.

> In 833 al-Ma'mun inaugurated a *mihna* or inquisition to force government officials and religious leaders to accept his religious views and his authority in matter of religious ritual and doctrine. Though the *mihna* was part of a general effort to restore the ideological authority of the Caliphate, it was also a response to the political activism of the *ahl-Khurasan* who asserted the priority of *kitab* and *sunna* against the authority of the Caliph.

Ira Lapidus, "Separation of State and Religion in Early Islamic Society," *IJMES*, 6:4 (1975), p. 379.

12 R. Arnaldez, "Ibn Rushd," EI^2, v. 3, p. 919.
13 The focus is particularly on the use of terms in the Arabic language. This may include words transliterated from the Greek and used extensively and deliberately, such as *hayula*; and words adopted from the Persian, such as *jawhar*. Because of the nature of cultural give-and-take between Arabic speakers and Persian speakers, as well as the heritage of many Arabic language authors, words of Persian origin occupy a singular perspective in Arabic language works; they are used without compunction.
14 R. Abelson, "Definition," in *Encyclopedia of Philosophy*, ed. Paul Edwards (New York: Macmillan, 1967), vol. 2, pp. 314–24. See also Richard Robinson, *Definition* (Oxford: Clarendon Press, 1954), for another overview of the problem.
15 Abelson, "Definition," p. 318.
16 *Hippias Major*, 287e4. Quoted by Benson, "Misunderstanding the 'What-is-F-ness?' Question," in *Essays on the Philosophy of Socrates*, ed. H. H. Benson (New York: Oxford University Press, 1992), p. 127. In his commentary to *Hippias Major* (Indianapolis: Hackett, 1982), Paul Woodruff states that fineness applied to the maiden is used "here in the sense of 'beautiful' or 'sexually attractive'." Commentary, p. 47.
17 Benson, "Misunderstanding," pp. 127–8.
18 Benson, "Misunderstanding," p. 133. Other proposed definitions of fineness include: gold makes things fine (289b6–291d5), living a certain kind of life (291d6–293c8), and the beneficial is fine (296d4–297b9). Woodruff lists the definitions in his Commentary to *Hippias Major*, p. 46.
19 Ibn Sina, *Kitab al-hudud*, Arabic text edited and translated by A.-M. Goichon (Cairo: Publications de l'Institut français d'archéologie orientale du Caire, 1963), Arabic text, p. 10, para. 18. Hereafter *Hudud*.
20 *Euthyphro* 6d, trans. by Benjamin Jowett, *Dialogues of Plato* (New York: D. Appleton, 1898), p. 319.
21 *Euthyphro* 11a.
22 Cf. C. C. W. Taylor, "Socratic Ethics," in *Socratic Questions*, ed. B. S. Gower and M. C. Stokes (London: Routledge, 1992), p. 140.
23 *Meno*, 72b.
24 *Meno*, 72c, trans. by R. W. Sharples (Chicago: Bolchazy Carducci, c. 1985), p. 39.
25 H. H. Benson, "The Priority of Definition and the Socratic Elenchus," *Oxford Studies in Ancient Philosophy* 8 (1990), p. 19. Benson provides an extensive survey of the literature in his notes, especially n. 2.

NOTES

26 Taylor, "Socratic Ethics," p. 139.
27 English text, *Topics*, translated by W. A. Pickard-Cambridge, in *The Basic Works of Aristotle*, ed. R. McKeon (New York: Random House, 1941), p. 191. Arabic text in *Mantiq Aristu*, ed. ᶜAbdurrahman Badawi (Cairo: Dar al-kutub al-misriyya, 1948–52), v. 2, p. 474. J. L. Ackrill gives J. Barnes' revision of this translation. The change is to "a phrase in lieu of a name" instead of "a phrase in lieu of a term," in *A New Aristotle Reader* (Princeton: Princeton University Press, 1987), p. 63.
28 Aristotle, *Selected Works*, tran. by H. G. Apostle and L. P. Gerson (Grinnell, Iowa: Peripatetic Press, 1983), p. 146.
29 *A New Aristotle*, p. 66–7.
30 *A New Aristotle*, p. 67.
31 E. Booth, *Aristotelian Aporetic Ontology in Islamic and Christian Thinkers* (Cambridge: Cambridge University Press, 1983), p. 14.
32 Booth, *Aristotelian Aporetic*, pp. 13–14.
33 Muhsin Mahdi gives the title in his *Alfarabi's Philosophy of Plato and Aristotle* (New York: Macmillan, 1962), Introduction, p. 3. See Chapter 3, pp. 44–46 on this treatise.
34 *The Attainment of Happiness*, in *Alfarabi's Philosophy of Plato and Aristotle*, trans. by Muhsin Mahdi, p. 50 (par. 64). For more on the influence of Plato on al-Farabi, see also: Leo Strauss, "Farabi's Plato," in *Louis Ginzberg Jubilee Volume* (New York: American Academy for Jewish Research, 1945), pp. 357–93.

2 AL-KINDI: THE FIRST ARABIC *BOOK OF DEFINITIONS*

1 Al-Kindi died between 252–260 AH/AD 866–873 The standard sources for his life and works are Ibn al-Nadim, *Kitab al-fihrist*, ed. Gustav Flügel (Reprint ed., Beirut: Khayats, 1964), pp. 255–61; and ᶜAli ibn Yusuf al-Qifti, *Ta'rikh al-hukama'*, ed. J. Lippert (Leipzig: Dieterich'sche Verlagsbuchhandlung, 1903), pp. 366–78. Also EI^2, s.v. "al-Kindi," by J. Jolivet and R. Rashed.
2 EI^2, s.v. "Al-Farra'," by R. Blachère; and Carl Brockelmann, *Geschichte der arabischen Literatur* (Leiden: Brill, 1943), v. 1, p. 118, and *Supp.*, v. 1, p. 178. (The title is *The Book of Definitions*; its subject is definitions of grammar.).
3 Henry George Liddell and Robert Scott, *A Greek-English Lexicon* (Reprint ed., Oxford: Clarendon Press, 1966), p. 1848.
4 Liddell and Scott, *A Greek-English Lexicon*, pp. 1847–8. Emphasis in the original.
5 Style here is meant to encompass the distinctive features of al-Kindi's writing including content, arrangement, form, and method in general, but not literary style.
6 Al-Kindi, *Rasa'il al-Kindi al-falsafiyya*, ed. by M. A. Abu Ridah (Cairo: Dar al-fikr al-ᶜarabiyya, 1953). All references are to vol. 1. Hereafter AR.
7 AR, p. 163, editor's introduction to *Fi hudud*. Likewise there is evidently no date on this copy of the treatise.
8 See *al-Munjid*, (Beirut: Dar al-mashreq, 1986) p. 205, *dibajah* entry no. 2 under *d-b-j*. See also K. Kennedy-Day, "Al-Kindi: a New Dibajah?" in *Islamic Quarterly*, 44: 2 (2000), pp. 429–33.
9 Samuel M. Stern, "Notes on al-Kindi's Treatise on Definitions," *Journal of the Royal Asiatic Society* (1959): 32, 36.
10 Felix Klein-Franke, "Al-Kindi's 'On Definitions and Descriptions of Things'," *Le Muséon* 95 (1982): 191–216.
11 George N. Atiyeh, *Al-Kindi: the Philosopher of the Arabs* (Rawalpindi, Pakistan: Islamic Research Institute, 1966).

NOTES

12 Michel Allard, "L'Épître de Kindi sur les définitions et les descriptions." *Bulletin d'études orientales* 25 (1972): 47–83, here p. 56, n. 1. However Allard does not specify the type of copy.
13 Tamar Zahara Frank, "Al-Kindi's Book of Definitions: Its Place in Arabic Definition Literature" (Ph.D. diss., Yale University, 1976).
14 Al-Kindi, *Cinq épîtres*, trans. Daniel Gimaret (Paris: Éditions du Centre national de la recherche scientifique, 1976); see p. 7 of the Introduction for his notes on the text.
15 In addition to the three manuscripts that are generally accepted as authentic there is another recently published by Dr. ᶜAbd al-Amir al-Aᶜsam in *al-Mustalah al-falsafi* (Cairo: 1989, 2nd ed.), which he discovered in a private library in Afghanistan.
16 M.A.S. Abdel Haleem, "Early Islamic Theological and Juristic Terminology: *Kitab al-hudud fi'l-usul*, by Ibn Furak" (with Arabic text), *BSOAS* 54 (1991): 5–41. Ibn Furak died 406 AH/AD 1015, making him late tenth-century or early eleventh-century.
17 *Hadd* is defined in the Lisbon manuscript, p. 215 no. 89 in Klein-Franke's list, but it does not appear in Abu Ridah's or Stern's edition.
18 Ibn al-Nadim, *Fihrist*, p. 251:27–8. For a discussion of Ustath (or Astat, vowelling uncertain) and al-Kindi, see *Notice, Tafsir ma baᶜd at-tabiᶜat*, ed. Maurice Bouyges (Beirut: Dar al-mashreq, 1990), pp. cxviii–cxxi. Bouyges says that translations were often done for patrons, and it is possible al-Kindi served as Ustath's patron in this case.
19 For Aristotle's *Metaphysics*, Book *Dal* (5), see Ibn Rushd, *Tafsir ma baᶜd at-tabiᶜat*, v. 2, pp. 473–696. The printed text is marked with "text" and "commentary". As far as is known, the Arabic translation of Aristotle's *Metaphysics* did not survive separately, but only in conjunction with the commentary of Ibn Rushd.
20 Lacuna in the Arabic text of Aristotle from 1017b 26–1018b 9, *Tafsir ma baᶜd at-tabiᶜat*, v. 2, pp. 564–67.
21 AR, p. 166:7–11. The second half of this definition is not in the text of the London manuscript used by Stern, like the Lisbon manuscript. See also Klein-Franke, "Al-Kindi," p. 210, n. 12. Numbers are inserted in the text for ease of reference.
22 F. Steingass, *A Comprehensive Persian-English Dictionary* (1892. Reprint ed., Beirut: Librarie du Liban, 1970), p. 379.
23 For example, see *Categories*, 1. 5. 2a11–4b20, *Metaphysics* 7. 3. 1028b32–1029b15.
24 For Aristotle's remarks about substance bearing accidents, see *al-Maqulat*, v. 1, *Mantiq Aristu* 1. 5. 3a15–26: p. 10:12–19.
25 The reference to "one says" appears to be vague here, and does not necessarily refer to Aristotle. T. Z. Frank is silent on references to Aristotle in this definition, and she has given all the others she found. Gimaret directs the reader to Aristotle's comments on generation and corruption in *Metaphysics*, 12. 2. There Aristotle discusses two different forms of matter – the matter of things that change and the matter of eternal things which are not generable. See 1069b25. Perhaps this definition is attempting to define two forms of *jawhar* and the text has been conflated.
26 Atiyeh, *Al-Kindi*, p. 88. Atiyeh's footnote (n. 58) refers the reader to AR, p. 166. The technique of the book is to footnote the reference, but not to indicate exact quotes. It is a close paraphrase.
27 Allard, "L'Épître de Kindi," p. 58 (Arabic text, p. 59).
28 Frank, "Al-Kindi's Book of Definitions: Its Place in Arabic Definition Literature," p. 56.
29 Gimaret, *Cinq épîtres*, p. 31, no. 12 (question marks in the original). In his notes on the translation, Gimaret adds: "(B) La seconde définition ne figure ni dans B ni dans M. Le texte est obscur, et la traduction proposée ici se contente de le rendre

autant que possible littéralement. En tout cas, cette seconde définition, selon laquelle la substance n'est pas susceptible de génération et de corruption, ne paraît pas aristotélicienne: pour Aristote, génération et corruption concernent précisément la substance, cf. Gén. et corr., A, 5; Mét., L, 2." p. 43.
30 AR, p. 166, n. 10.
31 AR, p. 166, n. 10.
32 *Metaphysics*, 12. 7. 1073a 5–7, in *A New Aristotle Reader*, pp. 348–9. I am indebted to Majid Fakhry for bringing this passage to my attention (private communication).
33 AR, p. 165:4.
34 AR, p. 169: 12–14, except following Gimaret's substitute of *mabda'* for *mubtada'* (AR's text). "Je lis *mabda'* plutôt que I :*mubtada'*, par rapprochement avec K I 101,4." Gimaret, *Cinq épîtres*, p. 50, commentary on no. 42. This is from *al-Falsafa al-ula* and the same four causes are given here. (Cf. AR, 101:3–4.) Gimaret translates as: "... et ce en vue de quoi celui qui fait fait ce qu'il fait." p. 33, no. 42.
35 See the Qur'an S. 2.117 and 6.101.
36 For examples, see Qur'an, S. 26.166, 27.60, 29.44, 29.61 and 30.8.
37 AR, p. 165:11.
38 Klein-Franke, "'On Definitions'," 210, no. 6.
39 Aristotle, *al-Tabiᶜa*, tran. Ishaq b. Hunayn, ed. A.R. Badawi (Cairo:1964), v. 1, p. 100:4 and 12, for example. Ishaq b. Hunayn died 289 AH/AD 910–1 (EI^2, s.v. "Ishak b. Hunayn," by G. Strohmaier). This places him after al-Kindi.
40 The *mihna*, a type of Inquisition, was rampant from 218 AH/AD 833 to 237 AH/AD 851, for dates see EI^2, s.v. "Mihna," by M. Hinds. See W. M. Patton, *Ahmed Ibn Hanbal and the Mihna*. Al-Kindi lost his library during the *mihna*, showing that the fear of persecution for failure to maintain religious orthodoxy was justified on the part of public figures.
41 AR, p. 166:2.
42 AR, p. 217:16–19.
43 AR, p. 101:3–4.
44 Translating *hayula* as matter, for further discussion see Chapter 4, on Ibn Sina's definitions of *hayula* and *madda*, including the distinction (or lack of it) between them. See also W. Charlton's discussion "Did Aristotle Believe in Prime Matter?" (which he answers negatively), Appendix in *Aristotle's Physics Books I and II* (Oxford: Clarendon Press, 1970), pp. 129–45.
45 AR, p. 166:1.
46 Liddell and Scott, *A Greek-English Lexicon*, p. 1848.
47 Roy Sorenson, "Vagueness and the Desiderata for Definition," in *Definitions and Definability: Philosophical Perspectives*, ed. James H. Fetzer, David Shatz and George N. Schlesinger (Boston: Kluwer Academic Publishers, 1991), p. 71.
48 *The Holy Qur'an*, tran. by A. Yusuf Ali (pub. in the U.S. by The Muslim Students Association of the United States and Canada, 1975), here S.3.49. Other examples are S. 5.110, and S. 23.12. *Tina* is a variation of *tin*. Qur'anic citations are given thus: S. 3.49 where "S." is an abbreviation for *sura* (chapter), the first number is the chapter, the second is the verse.
49 AR, p. 166:3.
50 M. F. ᶜAbd al-Baqi, *al-Muᶜjam al-mufharis li-alfaz al-Qur'an al-karim* (Beirut: Khayyat, n.d.). No entries exist for these words.
51 *Fihrist*, p. 249–52.
52 *Fihrist*, p. 249. See also: Francis E. Peters, *Aristoteles Arabus. The oriental translations and commentaries of the Aristotelian corpus* (Leiden: Brill, 1968).

53 *EI²*, s.v. "Hunayn b. Ishak al-ᶜIbadi," by G. Strohmaier; and *Fihrist*, p. 246:5.
54 See Shukri Abed, *Aristotelian Logic and the Arabic Language in Alfarabi* (Albany: State University of New York Press, 1991), pp. 123–7, for one discussion of the use of the copula in Arabic.
55 *Tahdhib al-akhlaq*, ed. by Qustantin Zurayq (Beirut: American University of Beirut, 1966), pp. 219–21. The treatise is referred to as *Kitab daf ᶜal-ahzan* (p. 219:11). Al-Kindi is also mentioned on p. 190:3 and p. 191:4. It was translated into English as *The Refinement of Character* by Qustantin Zurayq (Beirut: American University of Beirut, 1968), pp. 194–6; references at p. 169 and p. 170.

3 AL-FARABI: THE EMERGENCE OF ARABICIZED GREEK LOGIC

1 Ibn al-Nadim, *Fihrist*, p. 263:10.
2 Al-Farabi, *Kitab al-huruf* (*Book of Letters*), ed. Muhsin Mahdi (Beirut: Dar al-mashreq, 1970), p. 110:9–10 and p. 111:1–3 (par. 80 and 81). Hereafter referred to as *Huruf* in the notes.
3 See F. Steingass, *A Comprehensive Persian-English Dictionary*, p. 1526, *yaft*, "he found; discoverable, to be found; ... *nayaft*, Not to be found, non-existing."
4 Abu Nasr Muhammad b. Muhammad b. Tarkhan Uzlugh al-Farabi died in Damascus in 339 AH/AD 950–951. On al-Farabi's life see: Ibn Khallikan, *Wafayat al-aᶜyan wa anba' abna' al-zaman* [Biographical dictionary] (Beirut: Dar al-thaqafa, n.d.), v. 5, pp. 153–57; *Wafayat* ..., trans. B. MacGukin de Slane (1868. Reprint, New York: Johnson Reprint Corp., 1961), v. 3, pp. 307–11. Ibn Khallikan only entered those men whose death dates he knew, hence the name. See also: Ibn al-Nadim, *Fihrist*, p. 263; al-Qifti, *Ta'rikh al-hukama'*, pp. 277–80; *EI²*, s.v. "Al-Farabi," by Richard Walzer and also his Introduction to *Al-Farabi on the Perfect State* (Oxford: Clarendon, 1985), pp. 2–5; and Ian Netton, *Al-Farabi and his School* (London: Routledge, 1992). For information on al-Farabi in English, see also: "Al-Farabi," by Muhsin Mahdi, *Dictionary of Scientific Biography*, v. 4, pp. 523–25 (bibliography p. 526).
5 Al-Farabi, *Kitab mabadi' ara' ahl al-madina al-fadila* (Beirut: al-Matbaᶜa al-kathulykiyya, 1959). The title translates as: *The Book of the Principles of the Opinions of the People of the Virtuous City*, hereafter referred to as *The Virtuous City*.
6 M. E. Marmura, Review, *JNES* 24 (1965): 122.
7 Henri Hugonnard-Roche, "L'Intermédiaire syriaque dans la transmission de la philosophie grecque à l'arabe: le cas de l'*Organon* d'Aristote," *Arabic Sciences and Philosophy* 1 (1991): 198.
8 J. N. Mattock, "The Early Translations from Greek into Arabic: an Experiment in Comparative Assessment," in *Symposium Graeco-Arabicum II*, ed. Gerhard Endress (Amsterdam: B. R. Grüner, 1989), pp. 73–102.
9 Sebastian Brock, "From Antagonism to Assimilation: Syriac Attitudes to Greek Learning," in *Syriac Perspectives on Late Antiquity*, no. 5 (London: Variorum Reprints, 1984), pp. 17–34, here p. 17, quoting Ephrem from *Hymni de Fide*, II.I, ed. E. Beck, CSCO, CLIV–CLV. Although Brock's primary interest is of the reception of Greek literature into Syriac, many of his conclusions are equally applicable to further translation into Arabic, particularly as Syriac was often a waystation in the translation into Arabic. He mentions information about Arabic translation specifically only in passing.
10 Brock, "Antagonism," p. 21.

NOTES

11 Brock, "Antagonism," p. 18.
12 Brock, "Antagonism," p. 18.
13 Brock, "Antagonism," p. 18.
14 S. Brock, "Aspects of Translation Technique in Antiquity," in *Syriac Perspectives on Late Antiquity*, no. 3, here pp. 73–75. This is the standard view of the development of translation. However it is ex post facto and may not entirely reflect reality, as will be discussed later.
15 *Fihrist*, p. 251:25.
16 *Fihrist*, p. 251:25–26.
17 *Huruf*, M. Mahdi's Introduction, pp. 30–34.
18 *Huruf*, pp. 30–31.
19 *Fihrist*, p. 263:11–12.
20 *Huruf*, M. Mahdi's translation of section titles, Contents (English) pp. xii–xv; Arabic text, pp. 7–20. Literally, "The Particles and the Names of the Categories."
21 *Huruf*, p. 9, Mahdi's translation, p. xiv.
22 *Huruf*, pp. 97–105.
23 *Huruf*, p. 97:20–p. 98:9, par. 62.
24 *Huruf*, beginning p. 100:17 ff., par. 67. See below for this definition.
25 *Topics* 1. 5. 101b39, in *Mantiq Aristu*, v. 2, p. 474:16. See Chapter 1 for a discussion of descriptive vs. prescriptive definitions. "Statement" translates *al-qawl* (*logos*), as long as we understand that it is not thought of as "sentence." For a discussion of the Greek word, *logos*, see *Topica et Sophistici Elenchi*, ed. W. D. Ross (Greek text) (1958. Reprint ed., Oxford: Oxford University Press, 1963), p. 4. *Al-lafz* is usually translated "utterance."
26 *Topics* 1. 8. 103b15, in *Mantiq Aristu*, v. 2, p. 481:14.
27 *Topics* 1.4. 101b23, in *Mantiq Aristu*, v. 2, p. 474:1–2. "Let us call that which signifies what a thing is 'definition'..."
28 *Topics* 1. 5. 101b36, in *Mantiq Aristu*, v. 2, p. 474:2–4.
29 See also Shukri Abed's discussion of al-Farabi on definition in Ch. 2 "Definition and Description," in his *Aristotelian Logic*, especially pp. 35–49.
30 Al-Farabi, "Fi al-radd ᶜala Jalinus," in *Traités philosophiques*, ed. A. R. Badawi (Benghazi, Libya: 1973), p. 39:10–13.
31 *Jalinus*, p. 39:10–13. Note here the use of *madda* for material, in a discussion that otherwise relates to the four causes. Cf., al-Kindi and Ibn Sina, both of whom use ᶜ*unsur* (element) for material cause.
32 Al-Farabi, *al-Alfaz al-mustaᶜmala fi al-mantiq*, ed. Muhsin Mahdi (Beirut: Dar al-mashreq, 1968) p. 78:19–22.
33 *Alfaz*, p. 81:12–13.
34 Al-Farabi, "Kitab al-burhan," in *al-Mantiq ᶜinda al-Farabi*, ed. Majid Fakhry (Beirut: Dar al-mashreq, 1986), p. 45:1–2.
35 *Burhan*, p. 45:6 (Arabic text).
36 For al-Kindi's title, see Chapter 2.
37 *Alfaz*, p. 78:19. See above.
38 *Burhan*, p. 47:6.
39 *Burhan*, p. 52:8.
40 *Burhan*, p. 52:18; literally, the middle limit.
41 *Burhan*, p. 52:13.
42 See the Introduction to *Huruf* (pp. 43–44), for Muhsin Mahdi remarks. However, Mahdi states that this is speculation, as al-Farabi never listed the order in which he wrote his books.
43 *Huruf*, p. 63:6–13.

NOTES

44 For al-Kindi see AR, p. 166:7–11, and Chapter 2; Aristotle, *Metaphysics* 7. 15. 1039b 20ff. Arabic text in *Tafsir ma ba^cd at-tabi^cat*, v. 2, p. 982ff. For the Mutakallimun's view of atomism (*jawhar*) see Alnoor Dhanani, *The Physical Theory of Kalam: Atoms, Space, and Void in Basrian Mu^ctazili Cosmology* (Leiden: Brill, 1994).

45 AR, p. 166:7–11, see Chapter 2 for full definition, translation and discussion.

46 *Huruf*, p. 97:20–p. 98:9, par. 62.

47 For Arabic text see "*Kitab al-maqulat*," in *al-Mantiq ^cinda al-Farabi*, ed. Rafiq al-^cAjam (Beirut: Dar al-mashreq, 1985), v. 1. Page references are to this edition, unless otherwise noted. See also al-Farabi, "Al-Farabi's Paraphrase of the 'Categories' of Aristotle," pt. 1, ed. and trans. D. M. Dunlop, *Islamic Quarterly* 4 (1957–58): 168–197, and pt. 2, *Islamic Quarterly* 5 (1958–59): 21–54. (There is a slight variation in the Arabic text ed. by al-A^cjam and Dunlop's Arabic text.).

48 Dunlop, pt. 1, p. 168. Dunlop considers this text to be al-Farabi's paraphrase of Ishaq ibn Hunayn's version of Aristotle's *Categories*.

49 *Maqulat*, p. 91:14–15.

50 *Categories* 1. 5. 3a8–9, *al-Maqulat*, in *Mantiq Aristu*, p. 10:6–7.

51 *Maqulat*, p. 91:4.

52 *Maqulat*, p. 91:2–3.

53 *Maqulat*, p. 91:11.

54 *Maqulat*, p. 92:3–4.

55 *Huruf*, p. 205: 1–2. See also definition no. 3 below for further discussion. *Asbab* is translated as "reasons" here; see discussion below.

56 Michael E. Marmura, "Ghazalian Causes and Intermediaries," *JAOS* 115 (1995): 97.

57 See *al-Tabi^ca*, v. 1, pp. 100–109 for examples.

58 Cf. Shukri Abed's analysis of this statement in *Aristotelian Logic*, pp. 88–90.

59 Joseph Owens, *A History of Ancient Western Philosophy* (New York: Appleton Century Crofts, 1959), p. 312. Owens classifies matter and form as "the intrinsic causes."

60 Cf. al-Farabi, *The Political Regime (Al-Siyasa al-madaniyya also Known as the Treatise on the Principles of Beings)*, ed. Fauzi M. Najjar (Arabic text) (Beirut: Imprimerie Catholique, 1964), p. 36:6–14. Hereafter, *Siyasa*, and al-Farabi, *Risala fi jawab masa'il su'ila ^canha: Alfarabi's Philosophische Abhandlungen*, ed. Friedrich Dieterici (Leiden: Brill, 1890), p. 99:10–11. See also definition of *al-madda* below.

61 *Physics* 2. 7. 198a25 in *al-Tabi^ca*, v. 1, p. 137:20.

62 Muhsin Mahdi, *Ibn Khaldun's Philosophy of History* (Chicago: University of Chicago Press, 1964), p. 63, n. 2.

63 E.g., *al-Tabi^ca* 2. 3. 194b:18 and 2. 7. 198a:14.

64 *Falsafat Aristutalis*, ed. Muhsin Mahdi, (Beirut, 1961) p. 75:8–9.

65 Here *al-madda* will be translated as "matter." See Chapter 4 for a full discussion of *al-madda* and *al-hayula* and their translation.

66 *Al-qabila* literally means "tribe" in the early Islamic sense, but it is a word so fraught with significance today, indicating a less-highly organized society, that I have chosen only to transliterate it.

67 *Huruf*, p. 99:16–p. 100:8.

68 *Huruf*, p. 99:21–p. 100:1.

69 *Masa'il*, p. 99:10–11. Compare with Aristotle's statement in the *Metaphysics*: "Also identity (*al-huwiyya*) signifies the quiddity of a thing and its reality." *Metaphysics* 5. 7. 1017a30, quoted in Ibn Rushd, *Tafsir ma ba^cd at-tabi^cat*, v. 2, p. 555:8–9.

NOTES

70 Hanna E. Kassis, *A Concordance of the Qur'an* (Berkeley: University of California Press, 1983), s.v. *TYN*, p. 1247. See Qur'an S. 3.49, 5.110, 6.2, and others.
71 *Maqulat*, p. 91:4.
72 Literally "first matter." This means the same as "prime matter."
73 Al-Farabi, *Siyasa*, p. 36:6–8, 11, 31, and 41.
74 See also *Siyasa*, p. 38:10.
75 *Siyasa*, p. 36:14–15.
76 *Siyasa*, p. 38:13–14.
77 The translation of the title is Muhsin Mahdi's. He gives the title of this work in his introduction to *Alfarabi's Philosophy of Plato and Aristotle* (New York: Macmillan, 1962), p. 3. Its Arabic title is *Kitab al-jam^c bayna ra'yay al-hakimayn (Aflatun al-ilahiy wa Aristutalis)* [*The Book of harmonization of the opinions of the two wise men: Plato the Divine and Aristotle*], ed. Albert Nadir (Beirut: Dar al-mashreq, fourth printing, copyright 1968). (The full title is from p. 79 at the head of Nadir's text.).
78 For a discussion of al-Farabi's theory of emanation in different works, see Thérèse-Anne Druart, "Al-Farabi and Emanationism," in *Studies in Medieval Philosophy*, ed. John F. Wippel (Washington: Catholic University Press, 1987), pp. 23–43.
79 *Fihrist*, p. 263:10.
80 F. W. Zimmerman, *Al-Farabi's Commentary and Short Treatise on Aristotle's De Interpretatione* (Oxford: Oxford University Press, 1981), p. xxxv.
81 See above section on *jawhar* from *Maqulat*, given above under definition of *jawhar*. It is compared with the Aristotle text at that place.
82 *Categories* 1. 5. 3a8–9, also given above.
83 Richard Walzer, *Al-Farabi on the Perfect State*, Introduction, p. 9. *Ara'* is Walzer's short reference to *The Virtuous City*.
84 Walzer, "Al-Farabi," *EI^2*, v. 2, p. 780.
85 Al-Farabi, *Risala Zaynun* (Hyderabad: 1346 AH), p. 3–4; and *Kitab al-ta^{c}liqat* (Hyderabad: 1346 AH), p. 6.

4 IBN SINA: THE SECOND *BOOK OF DEFINITIONS*

1 Ibn Sina was born in Bukhara about 370 AH/AD 980 died in 428 AH/AD 1037. For Ibn Sina's life see: *EI^2*, s.v. "Ibn Sina," by A.-M. Goichon; Dimitri Gutas, "Avicenna. ii, Biography," in *The Encyclopaedia Iranica*, ed. Ehsan Yarshater (New York: Routledge, 1987); and Ibn Sina, *The Life of Ibn Sina*, Arabic text and English trans. W. E. Gohlman (Albany: SUNY, 1974). (Hereafter referred to as *Life*; Arabic and English texts are on facing pages.) For Ibn Sina's life see also: Ibn Abi Usaybi^{c}ah, *Kitab ^{c}uyun al-anba' fi tabaqat al-atibba'*, ed. August Müller (Göttingen: 1884), v. 2, pp. 2–20; and al-Qifti, *Ta'rikh al-hukama'*, pp. 413–26.
2 See *al-Munjid*, *d-b-j*, p. 205.
3 Ibn Sina, *Hudud*, p. 1:3–4. Page numbers refer to Arabic text, unless otherwise noted.
4 Al-Kindi's order taken from AR, pp. 165–66; Ibn Sina's from *Hudud*, pp. 11–23.
5 In this instance { } indicates taken out of order; ... indicates omitted words.
6 E.g., al-Ash^{c}ari gives a Mu^{c}tazili description of God his *Kitab al-maqalat al-islamiyyn*, p. 155. Among other attributes, Ibn Sina states that God has no definition, no description, no genus, no differentia, etc. *Hudud*, p. 11:1–2.
7 The definitions of form are dissimilar as given in the two Books of Definition. However, in the *K. al-Najat* Ibn Sina uses a definition of *sura* (form) that is very similar to al-Kindi's, as will be shown in Chapter 5.

NOTES

8 Some manuscript traditions add a pronoun between the defiendum and the defiendens, e.g., *Hudud*, p. 10:8 (*hadd*), p. 11:8 (*ᶜaql*) and p. 22:5 (*jism*). Goichon often prefers the mss. without the copula.

9 Goichon gives mss. variants of *hadd al-x al-x*, which occur at the beginning of many definitions in the footnotes, but she often prefers the version which does not have the formula *hadd al-x* in it. For example, *hadd* is omitted from her text (*Hudud*) while found in some mss.: see p. 10:11 (*rasm*), p. 18:7 (*madda*) and p. 19:1 (*ᶜunsur*).

10 *Hudud*, e.g., *ᶜaql*, p. 11:8.

11 *Hudud*, p. 24:9–12. See definition of *jawhar* below, for full text.

12 *Hudud*, p. 3: 6ff.

13 Al-Farabi, *Burhan*, p. 52:13, and Ibn Sina, *Hudud*, p. 3:6.

14 *Hudud*, p. 3:7.

15 Al-Farabi, *Alfaz*, p. 78:20.

16 *Alfaz*, p. 81:12–13.

17 *Hudud*, p. 3:11–12.

18 *Hudud*, p. 10:8–10. From "*al-qawl ... al-shay'*" lines 8–9, the Arabic exactly replicates the Arabic text of Aristotle's *Topics* 1. 5. 101b37, *Mantiq Aristu*, v. 2, p. 474. Cf. Chapter 3, pp. 36–38 for al-Farabi's views.

19 *Eisagoge*, in *Mantiq Aristu*, v. 3, p. 1038:6–7.

20 *Hudud*, p. 10: 11–13.

21 Ibn Sina, *al-Shifa': al-Ilahiyyat*, ed. M.Y. Moussa, S. Dunya and S. Zayed. (Cairo: Organisation générale des imprimeries gouvernementales, 1960), v. 1, p. 245:10–13. Reading *mahiyya*, ending in *ta marbuta*, not the *h* as found in the text.

22 Abdel Haleem, "Early Islamic Theology ..." p. 23 (p. 2, no.5 Arabic text of Ibn Furak's *Kitab al-hudud fi al-usul*).

23 Cf. "associatum" in Latin translation "Tractatus de diffinitionibus," in *Avicennae Philosophi praeclarissimi*, tran. Andrea Alpago (1546. Reprint ed., Farnborough: Gregg International, 1969), p. 130v.

24 *Hudud*, p. 23:8–24:13. Cf. *al-Ilahiyyat*, p. 10:8 and p. 54:9–10. For a discussion of *jawhar* in Persian, see Ibn Sina's *Danashnamah-i ᶜAla'i, Ilahiyyat*, Anjuman-i athar-i milli silsilah-i intisharat, ed. Muhammad Muᶜin (Tehran, 1371/AD 1952), pp. 9–11 and pp. 36–39. See also *Encyclopaedia Iranica*, Michael Marmura s.v. "Avicenna. xi, Persian Works," on the *Danashnamah*. Dozy, *Supplément aux dictionnaires arabes*, vol. 1, p. 731. Dozy quotes de Slane on *mushahha*: III "chicaner ... on ne doit pas chicaner sur les termes," for the same expression. For another definition of *jawhar* cf. *Al-Ilahiyyat*, p. 54:9–15.

25 See also J.R.T.M. Peters, *God's Created Speech* (Leiden: Brill, 1976), pp. 148–49 for a discussion of *li-dhatihi*. See also M. S. Saeed Sheikh, *A Dictionary of Muslim Philosophy* (Lahore: Institute of Islamic Culture, 1970), p. 55 for a definition of *dhat*.

26 AR, p. 166:7.

27 Ibn Sina does not define these terms per se, in the *Hudud*; however, he discusses them in *al-Ilahiyyat*, Chapter 4, pt. 2, v. 1, pp. 180–85.

28 *al-Ilahiyyat*, p. 10:6–8.

29 *Hudud*, p. 41:1–2. Cf. the Latin in Ibn Sina, "Tractatus de diffinitionibus," f.136v. Cf. *al-Ilahiyyat*, p. 8:12 (note use of *sabab* vs. *ᶜilla*) and p. 29:12, also, v. 2, p. 267:11.

30 *Dhat*, here it means "entity, thing, being." A further discussion of the translation can be found in Part 2 with the complete translation.

31 *Hudud*, p. 41:3–42:10.

32 E.g., *faᶜil*, used to describe the efficient cause, see *al-Ilahiyyat*, v. 2, p. 257:7 and below.

NOTES

33 *Al-Ilahiyyat*, v. 2, p. 257:7. Discussion continues through line 17.
34 AR, p. 101:3–4 and Chapter 2, pp. 26–28.
35 *Hudud*, p. 19:3 (definition, p. 19:1–4).
36 His examples are also given in abbreviated form. They are easier to understand if we add a phrase, such as "is thrown on the fire," to flesh out his examples. Then we have either (a) "a stick without condition is thrown on the fire," or (b) "a stick with the condition of not being white is thrown on the fire." Further interpretation gives us (a) "any stick is thrown on the fire," or (b) "no white stick is thrown on the fire." Thus we see one (a) is a universal statement and affirmation; while (b) is a specific denial of the particular. Furthermore, this indicates that for Ibn Sina *bi-la shart* equals *mutlaq*.
37 *al-Ilahiyyat*, (ᶜ*ilal*) v. 2, p. 257:7–17.
38 *al-Ilahiyyat*, p. 8:12. *Al-ᶜilal* and *al-asbab* are the plural forms, both mean "causes."
39 *Metaphysics* 5. 4. 1015a6. Arabic text in *Tafsir ma baᶜd at-tabiᶜat*, v. 2, p. 507:5–6. Soheil M. Afnan attributes this translation to Ustath (Afnan, *Philosophical Lexicon in Persian and Arabic* (Reprint ed., Beirut: Dar el-mashreq,1964), p. 326).
40 *Metaphysics* 5. 4. 1015a14–15; Arabic text in *Tafsir ma baᶜd at-tabiᶜat*, v. 2, p. 507:12–13. Maurice Bouyges, the editor, states that Ustath (nineth century AD) was the primary translator. *Notice*, p. cxxi.
41 *Metaphysics*. 5. 4. 1014b31–32, in *Tafsir ma baᶜd at-tabiᶜat*, v. 2, p. 506:9–10. Ustath may have been the translator.
42 *Metaphysics* 12. 2. 1069b12, in *Tafsir ma baᶜd at-tabiᶜat*, v. 3, p. 1437:1–2 and variation (b) given p. 1437, line notes 1–2 (below text). Afnan gives the translator (of the first version) as Abu Bishr Matta. (*Philosophical Lexicon*, p. 273).
43 In the second version the translator used *al-ᶜunsur* for matter.
44 *Metaphysics* 12. 2. 1069b24–25, in *Tafsir ma baᶜd at-tabiᶜat*, v. 3, p. 1446:12–1447:2. Afnan gives the translator as Abu Bishr Matta. (*Philosophical Lexicon*, p. 273.).
45 *Metaphysics* 8. 4. 1044a15, *Tafsir ma baᶜd at-tabiᶜat*, v. 2, p. 1068:15–1069:1. Afnan gives Ustath as the translator. (*Philosophical Lexicon*, p. 57.).
46 Charlton, "Appendix: Did Aristotle Believe in Prime Matter?" pp. 129–45.
47 Charlton, "Appendix," p. 130.
48 Charlton, "Appendix," p. 142.
49 Edward William Lane considers *al-madda* to be "matter" and gives *tina* as another term for it. He states that "it [*madda*] is especially termed *hayula* as that from which composition commences." Lane, *An Arabic-English Lexicon* (1863. Reprint ed., Beirut: Librarie du Liban, 1980), pt. 7, pp. 2697–98.
50 Cf. *Ilahiyyat*, p. 10:8 and p. 23:17. I prefer to translate *hayula* as "matter$_1$" and *madda* as "matter$_2$."
51 Dozy, *Supplément aux dictionnaires arabes*, v. 1, p. 716. See Commentary for a discussion of matter and form.
52 *Hudud*, pp. 17:9–18:2. This term will be further discussed in Chapter 5.
53 *Hudud*, p. 18:7–10.
54 I would like to thank Prof. John Richardson (New York University) for this suggestion.
55 *Fihrist*, p. 251:25–26, and p. 251:27–28.
56 See J. N. Mattock, "The Early Translations from Greek into Arabic," pp. 73–102, for an analysis of one of the few surviving parallel passages translated by both Ustath and Ishaq.
57 Ibn Sina's definition of matter, given in *hayula*, can be read as two separate meanings, with "one says" indicating the break. See A.-M. Goichon, *Lexique*

de la langue philosophique d'Ibn Sina (Paris: de Brouwer, 1938), p. 379, no. 662.2, where she says: "Dans l'Épître sur les définitions, on trouve ces deux sens: '*Madda* est parfois synonyme de *hayula* (matière première). Et l'on appelle aussi *madda* (sorte de *matière seconde*) tout sujet qui reçoit la perfection ...'."

58 Ibn Sina, *Kitab al-najat*, ed. by Majid Fakhry (Beirut: Dar al-Afaq al-jadida, 1985), p. 239:21–22. Hereafter, *Najat*. This text is Ibn Sina's own abridgement of *al-Ilahiyyat*. See below for exact quote.
59 Goichon chose the following selections to illustrate her *Lexique*.
60 *Najat*, p. 237:4–6.
61 *Najat*, p. 237:14–15.
62 *Najat*, p. 239:21–22.
63 *al-Ilahiyyat*, v. 2, p. 257:11.
64 Goichon, *Lexique*, p. 207; *Shifa'*, v. 1, pt. 6 (*al-Jadal*), p. 193:13 and p. 273:4. See also *al-Tabi^{c}yyat*, pt. 1: *al-Sama^c al-tabi^{c}i* p. 15:1, for another example.
65 According to Lane, *tin* means "clay, earth, mould, soil, or mud" while *tina* "a piece or portion thereof." The *ta marbuta* appears to indicate a partitive sense. See Lane, *An Arabic-English Lexicon*, pt. 5, p. 1906.

5 COMPARISON OF VOCABULARY

1 See AR, p. 165, for these examples.
2 *Huruf*, beginning at p. 110:9 (par. 80).
3 *Huruf*, p. 111:1–3.
4 See Chapter 4, pp. 50–51.
5 Afnan, *Philosophical Lexicon*, p. 57.
6 Dozy, v. 1, p. 237, "le *jawhar* d'une chose est son essence." In the Arabic translation of Aristotle's *Categories*, *jawhar* is used, see *al-Maqulat*, in *Mantiq Aristu*, p. 7 (chapter title) and passim.
7 These texts are repeated from the earlier chapters. Any part which does not directly bear on the comparison is omitted here.
8 AR, p. 166:7–11.
9 *Huruf*, p. 63:6–13.
10 *Hudud*, p. 23:8–24:8.
11 *Huruf*, pp. 97–105. Accident is discussed in the section before *jawhar, al-^{c}arad*, pp. 95–97.
12 *Al-Maqulat* 4a 10–22, in *Mantiq Aristu*, p. 13.
13 See Chapter 2, pp. 23–26.
14 *Huruf*, pp. 97–98, para. 62. See the discussion of *jawhar*'s foreign origin in Chapter 2, pp. 23–26.
15 In *al-Maqulat*, 2a 14, Aristotle's example is human being or horse (in *Mantiq Aristu*, v. 1, p. 7).
16 *Mantiq Aristu*, v. 3, p. 1050:7 (*Eisagoge*, nos. in the margin, 13:1).
17 *Hudud*, p. 24:9–10.
18 *Hudud*, p. 24:13.
19 Al-Farabi also states *jawhar* is not in a subject, *Huruf*, p. 100:17–18.
20 Cf. *al-Maqulat*, 2a 13, in *Mantiq Aristu*, v. 1, p. 7:2–3.
21 *Hudud*, p. 24:9–13; see Chapter 4, p. 52 for the full text and translation.
22 Richard Frank, *Al-Ghazali and the Ash^{c}arite School* (Durham: Duke University Press, 1994), pp. 36–39, for section on Creation and Secondary Causes. God is the initial cause and causes on earth are all secondary causes.
23 Afnan, *Philosophical Lexicon*, p. 186.

NOTES

24 Liddell and Scott, *A Greek-English Lexicon*, p. 44.
25 AR, p. 165:4.
26 AR, p. 169:12–14.
27 *Huruf*, p. 205:1–2.
28 *Hudud*, p. 41:1–2.
29 *Hudud*, p. 41:3–42:10.
30 Al-Farabi appears to integrate the idea of *mabda'* (pl. *mabadi'*) into his scheme of causation. In the opening lines of *al-Siyasa al-madiniyya*, he says there are six kinds of principles (*mabadi'*) which are ranked. Then he says the first cause is in the first rank. This indicates he is equating the first cause with the first principle. (*Siyasa*, p. 31:2–4.) Similarly in Ishaq ibn Hunayn's translation of the *Physics*, Ishaq uses *mabadi'aha* for the principles searched for in our study of things. (*al-Tabi^{c}a*, v. 1, p. 100:9–11.) "It is suitable for us also that we do this in the matter of generation, corruption, and natural change – all of them – so that we will, when we know the principles connected, refer back to them for each thing, of which we are investigating." (194b 21–23) These principles are the causes of change in a thing. Thus al-Farabi's use of *mabda'* in this sense of cause is very Aristotelian.
31 *Mutammimat al-kull* may be interpreted as referring to the formal cause if we consider form as completing matter. Ibn Sina says in his definition of *hayula* that matter only becomes complete when it receives form. *Hudud*, p. 17:9–18:2. Thus a cause that completes everything may be interpreted as necessarily including the formal cause.
32 Cf. Gimaret, *Cinq épîtres*, p. 40, no. 1 (Notes), says *fa^{c}ilah* and *mutammimat al-kull* can be translated as efficient and final. The question of overlap or inclusion will be discussed more fully in the analysis of al-Farabi's definition.
33 See Chapter 2 for Qur'anic references and a theological discussion of the root (*b-d-^{c}*) of this word.
34 Reading *mabda'* for *mubtada'* with Gimaret. See Chapter 2 for a discussion of this point.
35 Abed, *Aristotelian Logic*, p. 88–90. See also Chapter 3.
36 Abed, *Aristotelian Logic*, p. 101, n. 10. Abed reaches this conclusion because the particle ^{c}*an* can have the sense of *min* (from).
37 *Al-Tabi^{c}a*, v. 1, p. 137:4–6 (in Aristotle's text). "Thus a question about 'Why?' refers to all of them, so the answer is completed for the natural philosophers, that is the material [cause], the formal, the efficient and 'What it is for the sake of?' ..." The answer given is to the question what cause is. ("What it is for the sake of?" refers to the final cause.).
38 *Fihrist*, pp. 255–56.
39 *al-Tabi^{c}a*, Badawi's "Introduction," v.1, p. 9.
40 *al-Tabi^{c}a*, Badawi's "Introduction," p. 17.
41 Mahdi, SSIPS Conference lecture, Oct. 15, 1994 (SUNY Binghamton, NY).
42 See Chapter 3.
43 For some examples of Ibn Sina's terminology see: *Hudud*, p. 11:3; *al-Ilahiyyat*, Book 1, Chapter 6, pp. 37–42 (for a whole chapter's discussion of these two terms); and *al-Risala al-^{c}arshiyya* (ed. Ibrahim Hilal, Cairo: n.d., c. 1981), pp. 15–16.
44 Charlton, "Appendix: Did Aristotle Believe in Prime Matter?" p. 140. See also Chapter 4 for a fuller discussion of this issue.
45 See Chapter 4, p. 57, for an earlier discussion of this issue.
46 AR, p. 166:1.
47 *Huruf*, p. 99:16–p. 100:8.
48 *Siyasa*, p. 36:6–8, 11, 13, and 14.

NOTES

49 *Hudud*, pp. 17:9–18:2.
50 *Hudud*, p. 18:7–10.
51 *Masa'il*, p. 99: 10–11. See Chapter 3 for quotation and translation.
52 Frank, pp. 50–52. She concludes that al-Kindi's different terms for matter are generally not well differentiated. She says that *tina* and *hayula* refer to "undifferentiated matter" and *ᶜunsur* and *usutqas* refer "to the four elements," p. 52. See for the definitions of *tina*: AR, p. 166:3; *ᶜunsur*: AR, pp. 166:3, 168:11, 169:12, and 169:15; see also *Fi al-falsafa al-ula*, AR, p. 101: 12–13; *ustuqas* (definition), AR, p. 168:10–11; and *hayula* in *Fi al-falsafa*, AR, p. 108:11.
53 See Chapter 2.
54 AR, p. 166:3.
55 AR, p. 168:11–12.
56 See Chapter 2.
57 AR, p. 166:2.
58 Ibn Sina, *al-Tabiᶜyyat: al-Samaᶜ al-Tabiᶜi* (Cairo: 1983), pt. 1, p. 34:9.
59 AR, p. 166:1.
60 AR, p. 166, n. 10.
61 See Chapter 3, p. 43 and n. 69 for quote.
62 Ibn Sina has also defined *ᶜunsur* in *The Book of Definitions*, p. 19:1–4; and *ustuqas*, p. 19: 5–8.
63 Andrea Alpago, *Tractatus de diffinitionibus*, 127V–128R. "Matter (*materia*) is said at some time, etc. From the account of Ibn Sina it is clear that matter (*materia*) is said synonymously with *hyle* and with all subject (substrate) because together with another thing [it forms] the same species or another species, when it receives some perfection or form."
64 AR, p. 169:13.
65 *Al-Ilahiyyat*, v. 2, p. 257:13–16.

6 THE SOCIO-POLITICAL MILIEU OF IBN SINA

1 "*Faqha al-dunya bukhara*," Abu Ahmad b. Abi Bakr al-Katib quoted in Yaqut's *Kitab muᶜjam al-buldan* (Leipzig: 1866), v. 1, p. 519.
2 See "Ghazna" by C.E. Bosworth, *EI²*, v. 2, p. 1048–49.
3 Ibn Sina, *al-Ilahiyyat*, Bk. 10, ch. 4, (v. 2) pp. 447–451.
4 Al-Bayhaqi, *Tarikh hukama' al-Islam* (Damascus, 1946), p. 55.
5 See "Kakuyids" by C. E. Bosworth, *EI²*, v. 4, p. 465 for more information on ᶜAla' al-Dawla.
6 Ibn Sina, *al-Qanun fi al-tibb*, ed. by Idwar al-Qashsh (Beirut: Muᶜassassat ᶜIzz al-din, 1987), v. 1, p. 16.
7 *Qanun*, v. 1, p. 34.
8 Here the term Arab is being used loosely to refer to Arabic speakers, regardless of ethnicity.
9 See commentary Chapter 8 for more on these subjects.
10 There are many introductory books on Islam for readers who want more information, e.g., Fazlur Rahman, *Islam* (New York: Anchor, 1968), and Marshall Hodgson, *The Venture of Islam: The Classical Age of Islam* (Chicago: University of Chicago Press, 1977), v. 1.
11 Al-Tabari, *The History of al-Tabari: General Introduction and From Creation to the Flood*, trans. by Franz Rosenthal (Albany: SUNY Press, 1989), v. 1, p. 199.
12 *The Qur'an A Modern English Version*, trans. by M. Fakhry (Reading, U.K.: Garnet Publishing, 1997), S. 2. 114/115, p. 15.

NOTES

13 Ibn Sina dealt with the concerns of the Muʿtazilite and Shiʿite theologians, who formed the prevalent schools in Persia in his day. The Ashʿarites had a later influence in this area, according to George Hourani, see "Ibn Sina's 'Essay on the Secret of Destiny'," *BSOAS*, v. 29 (1966), p. 39 (Arabic title: *Risala fi sirr al-qadar*). The question of God's hand and face is mentioned here to give readers an idea of the subjects of theological debates. Muʿtazilite views of God are discussed in the Commentary (Question six).
14 *The Life of Ibn Sina*, pp. 29–31. (Facing pages Arabic text and translation.).
15 Abel Remusat, "Essai sur la langue et la littérature chinoises," in *Academie des Inscriptions et Belles-Lettres, Institut de France. Histoire et Memoirs*. v. 8 (1827), pp. 60–130, quoted, pp. 129–30.
16 M. Hartmann- [C.E. Bosworth], "al-Sin" in EI^2, v. 9, p. 618.
17 J. A. Boyle, "Cinghiz-Khan" in EI^2, v. 2, p. 43.
18 The invasions took place from 616 AH/AD 1219 to 620 AH/AD 1223 according to D. O. Morgan, "Mongols" in EI^2, v. 7, p. 231; and *The Mongols* (New York: Blackwell, 1986), p. 74.
19 Gohlman, *Life*, p. 17. Gohlman follows Arberry's translation here.
20 Translating *ahl* as "folk." See W. Chittick, *The Sufi Path of Knowledge* (Albany: SUNY Press, 1989), Glossary, and p. 388, n. 20. The term *walid* for the male parent is more impersonal than *abu* (father).
21 See Part 1, Chapter 3, for basic information on Al-Farabi's *Book of Letters*.
22 H. Corbin, *Creative Imagination in the Sufism of Ibn ʿArabi*, trans. by R. Manheim (Princeton: Princeton University Press, 1969), pp. 53–67.
23 Gohlman, *Life*, pp. 55–57.

7 TRANSLATION: *THE BOOK OF DEFINITIONS*

1 There are two published editions of *Kitab al-hudud* (*The Book of Definitions*). The first is in *Tisʿ rasa'il* (*Nine Treatises*), (Constantinople: al-Jawa'ib, 1881), and the second is *Kitab al-hudud, Livre des définitions*, Arabic text edited and translated by A.-M. Goichon (Cairo: Publications de l'Institut francais d'archéologie orientale du Caire, 1963). Although the Constantinople ed. gives no information as to the manuscript consulted, a comparison of the text with the Goichon ed. demonstrates that the anonymous editor of the Constantinople ed. used the same manuscript as a base that Goichon used. The Latin translation by Andrea Alpago appears as *Tractatus de diffinitionibus*.
2 Following George F. Hourani in translating *al-Shaykh al-ra'is* as "the eminent shaykh" as found in "Ibn Sina's 'Essay on the Secret of Destiny'," in *BSOAS*, v. 29 (1966), p. 31.
3 It appears that § 3–4 may represent a corrupt text. These paragraphs appear in *Tisʿ Rasa'il*, Goichon's edition and the Tashkent manuscript no. 2385, which I have seen, but not in Alpago's Latin translation, which begins with § 18. Although they express a formulaic modesty, this is very unusual for Ibn Sina, leading the reader to wonder if it may be a later addition. While the basic ideas come through, it is very difficult to translate literally. Goichon did not translate these paragraphs in an entirely literal manner. The rest of the text (the definitions themselves) are much clearer.
4 Perhaps this refers to Ibn Sina's fear of Mahmud of Ghazna, from whom he fled.
5 This statement refers to the essence/existence distinction. See the Commentary for further remarks. This passage also appears to indicate Ibn Sina includes existence with the thing, not as a super-accident.

NOTES

6 Goichon states in her note to the French translation (*Kitab al-hudud*, p. 6, n. 1) that Aristotle did not discuss the descriptive definition. Goichon remarks that I. Madkour had proposed Galen as the philosopher Ibn Sina was thinking of. (See his *L'Organon d'Aristote dans le monde arabe* [Paris: Vrin, 1969, 2nd ed., *Études musulmanes*. 10], p. 119.) The two places in the *Topics* that Goichon mentions are: 4.4 (141b 36–142a 6) where Aristotle objects to definitions when they are the definitions of individuals, not groups; and 1.15 (107b 10) where he discusses the problem of differentiae that are synonymous terms, such as the Greek terms for sharp and white. But Aristotle does not really discuss the objection Ibn Sina says he does.

7 Ibn Sina quotes al-Kindi here from the treatise *On the Definitions*. Al-Kindi says, "Love (*mahabba*) is the cause of the coming together of things," (AR: 168:8) and "Yearning love (*cishq*) is the excess of love." (AR: 176:1) See commentary for further discussion.

One problem here is that *cishq* and *mahabba* cannot both be translated as "love," or the contradiction is lost. While *cishq* may include the idea of passion and physicality; it also includes the idea of yearning or longing for the object of love. Furthermore, two words from the same root, *ifrat* (excess) and *mufrita* (overflowing, excessive) are translated here with unrelated English words, to try to keep Ibn Sina's sense. For Ibn Sina in general *cishq* is an acceptable love. However, Ibn Sina's main point seems to be that this statement demonstrates the reversal of word order of the differentia and genus. Let *a* stand for the genus and *b* for the differentia, and then al-Kindi defines the term: *cishq* is *b a*; and Ibn Sina states that the proper order is: *cishq* is *a b*. Since in English the adjective normally precedes the noun, this point is not readily apparent in translation.

8 These are the failed definitions, and Ibn Sina is referring to the obscurity in meaning due to a bad definition.

9 That is, to take what is not his.

10 These are category mistakes, since agreeable cannot be predicated of the faculty of understanding, nor number of the soul. See Aristotle, *Topics* 6.3 (123a 33) where he says the soul cannot be a species of number. Pythagoras considered numbers held the key to the universe, as a form of mystical knowledge. Not only physical objects, but non-physical ideas and entities equaled numbers. Justice equaled the number 4. Thus souls were also related to numbers. See "Pythagoras and Pythagorism" by W. K. C. Guthrie, in *The Encyclopedia of Philosophy*, v. 7, pp. 37–39, for more information and further readings.

11 Passion refers to a passive quality. It is one of Aristotle's *Categories*. Passion happens to an agent, and it is opposed to action.

12 Goichon translates this as the reverse, roughly: "When the passions intensify, the thing is reduced to nothing." (French, p. 9) However, the Arabic text does not support this translation. Since Ibn Sina is giving a long and varied list of mistakes in definition there is not really a problem here. The meaning is that it is a mistake to think intensifying the passions will make a thing established and strong.

13 Porphyry of Tyre, a third century AD Greek philosopher, wrote the *Eisagoge*, an introduction to Aristotle's logical works, which became part of the classical curriculum. His work was translated into Arabic and many Arab philosophers wrote commentaries on it in their turn.

14 The reference is to obscurity in the definition, that is the definition is not clear because a thing is defined in terms of itself. Cf. Aristotle, *Topics*, 131b:13–15.

15 The definition exactly replicates the Arabic text of Aristotle's *Topics* 101b37, in *Mantiq Aristu* (Cairo: 1949), v. 2, p. 474. The word used for quiddity here is

mahiyya. Aristotle is referred to as the philosopher (*al-hakim*), he is almost never mentioned by name.

16 Omitting the word *fasl* (found in the 1881 Constantinople and Goichon editions); in viewing the microfilm of the Biruni Institute in Tashkent, Ms. 2385 fol. 120B "*fasl*" appears a few lines earlier at the end of § 18 and perhaps it was repeated by accident. It does not fit here. The definition of the Creator which follows is similar to the Mu'tazili statement about God given by al-Ash'ari, in *Kitab maqalat al-Islamiyin*, pp. 155–56.

17 Translating ^{c}*aql* as "intellect." The Arabic word ^{c}*aql* refers to the faculty that processes both intuitive and learned kinds of knowledge. Unlike Latin and Greek there are not separate words in Arabic for these two functions. See the commentary for further remarks.

18 Translating *ism mushtarak* as common term. Literally, it could be translated as "common name" to refer to Aristotle's use of the term "common name" in the *Categories*. *Ism* means noun as well as name, *mushtarak* means common in the sense of participating in. Aristotle begins the *Categories* saying "When things have only a name in common and the definition of being which corresponds to the name is different, they are called homonymous." (1 a1, tran. by J. L. Ackrill, Oxford: Clarendon Press) A literal translation would be "a homonymous name (or noun)," but this is a rather infelicitous expression in English.

19 The Arabic title is *Kitab al-burhan*.

20 That is, intuition.

21 Literally *kull* means "the all," here it refers to the universe. I have translated it as "the universe," to fill in the ellipsis. See also Majid Fakhry's translation of *Risala fi'l-nafs* in *Ethical Theories in Islam* (Leiden: Brill, 1991), p. 216.

22 World, while actually specifically mentioned here, is to be understood in the large sense of the whole cosmos.

23 *Al-jirm*, considering "body" in its vaguest sense, as an entity, not as a material thing specifically.

24 Sufi tendencies appear in this sentiment. This sentence finds echoes later in Ibn al-^{c}Arabi, "I was a hidden treasure, longing to be known." See commentary.

25 Following the Constantinople text here.

26 Following Constantinople text.

27 Following Goichon's text here.

28 That is, all individuals have form. For example, all humans represent the form of human. But form alone does not give humans their individuality.

29 Cf. *Ilahiyyat*, p. 10:8 and p. 23:17. I prefer to translate *hayula* as "matter$_1$" and *madda* as "matter$_2$." Translating *hayula* as "prime matter" says too much. See the Appendix in *Aristotle's Physics*, translated by W. Charlton, for a discussion of Aristotle's views on prime matter.

30 R. Dozy, *Supplément aux dictionnaires arabes*, 3rd edn (Leiden: Brill, 1967), v. 1, p. 716. See commentary for a discussion of matter and form.

31 The word *mahall* is translated here as "substratum," because it is used as a technical term, otherwise it means "place."

32 Since both ^{c}*unsur* and *ustuqas* can be translated as "element," I have chosen to translate ^{c}*unsur* as element$_2$ and *ustuqas* as element$_1$, rather than trying to find an artificially distinctive word.

33 Following the Constantinople edition.

34 Preferring *rukn* from Ms. O, given in line notes. Translating *rukn*, meaning first principle or chief element, as building block, following Alnoor Dhanani, *The*

Physical Theory of Kalam (Leiden: Brill, 1994), p. 97. Considered metaphorically atoms are the building blocks of the universe.

35 Here Ibn Sina is using form not in the idealistic Platonic sense, but its opposite – the immediate object before our eyes.
36 Cf. "associatum" in Ibn Sina, "Tractatus de diffinitio," in *Avicennae Philosophi praeclarissimi*, tran. Alpago, p. 130v.
37 Dozy, *Supplément aux dictionnaires arabes*, vol. 1, p. 731. Dozy quotes de Slane: III "chicaner ... on ne doit pas chicaner sur les termes," for the same expression.
38 This is the only definition that is pointedly given as a verbal definition, he does not claim any existence for *jinn* here. See commentary.
39 "Under the sphere of the moon" should be understood as being under the moon's influence.
40 Sphere is used in the sense of "sphere of influence."
41 Following Goichon's text, the first part is missing in the Constantinople ms.
42 As preceding definition, omitting the opening phrase.
43 Lit., what has no end.
44 That is, other end points of the same kind as these two.
45 Ibn Sina is talking about space or the stretch between two points, but it appears that to indicate linear space between two points, in the sense of distance.
46 That is, it does not exist in the natural world, it is only a mental construct. Perhaps he is talking about a place in terms of its potentiality.
47 *Dhat*.
48 For "two instants" is the term used for duration. See commentary.
49 That is, light objects tend to move up or away from the center, they may even float.
50 A.-M. Goichon says that the next sentence is an added gloss. It is found in the Constantinople edition. "I say that it is necessary to eliminate these two definitions which I do not want in order to understand the common expression and to use the rest." It reads like an addition. See Goichon, *Livre des définitions*, (French translation) p. 50, n. 2.
51 Reading "slow" (*bati'*) for "fast" (*sari^c*) for sense – since items that are supple are pliable and do not come apart or break easily. While *rakhw* can mean brittle as well as supple, the addition of the description of soft (*layyin*) would argue against the idea that it breaks easily. Since Ibn Sina distinguishes *hashsh* (next definition) as being a brittle (*sulb*) mass, he does not think the two words have the same meaning. See E. Lane's *Arabic-English Lexicon*, pt. 3, p. 1061 for *rakhw*.
52 Literally separate.
53 Rarefaction is "The action of rarefying or the process of being rarefied; diminution of density. (Now chiefly of the air or gases, or *Path.* of bones.)" To rarefy means "To make thin, esp. by expansion," quoted from the *Oxford English Dictionary* (Oxford: Clarendon Press, 2nd edn.), v. 13, p. 195.
54 This is according to Goichon's text. The translation of the Constantinople text for this paragraph reads: One knows that rarefaction is a common expression, occurring in four senses opposite to this meaning. The senses are: one meaning is movement in terms of quantity; second is in the quality of movement; the third is movement while in its position; and the fourth is position.

Thus the textual difference is whether he is continuing the definition of rarefaction or of its opposite condensation. All four senses apply to both terms.
55 The emphasis is on things coming together as a mental construct, rather than in the real world, for example, fifty states in North America form one country, the United States of America.

NOTES

56 Goichon has *mutadakhil* (p. 38), and the Constantinople edition has *mudakhil* (p. 67). See commentary, Question twelve for a discussion of this term. In the past *mudakhil* has frequently been translated as "interpenetrant," a term that is awkward in contemporary English, and which has sexual connotations.
57 The Constantinople edition has "soul" for "phoenix." (*Nafs*, instead of *qaqnus*, p. 67.) *Qaqnus* is a Persian word, see commentary for a discussion of the phoenix.
58 That is, it is not from any other.
59 *Dhat*, here it means "entity, thing, being." Ibn Sina uses it to refer to the quiddity and essence of a thing in terms of its existing qua that thing. Thus it almost means "existing thing," and I have used "being." In this definition Ibn Sina is at his most telegraphic, so I have added words to smooth it out.
60 Lit., not in regard to a time-without-time.
61 Are angels an example of generation outside of time?.
62 In the sense of cause.
63 S. 17.43. Goichon's reference. "Glory be to Him, and may He be greatly exalted above what they say." *The Qur'an*, tran. by M. Fakhry, p. 173.

8 COMMENTARY

1 Some manuscript traditions have "the definition of x" before many terms, some only give the term to be defined.
2 Ibn Sina, *Ilahiyyat*, v. 2, pp. 343–49.
3 See "al-Ma'mun b. Harun al-Rashid" by M. Rekaya, EI^2, v. 6, p. 336.
4 Thanks to John Richardson for calling my attention to this point.
5 Liddell and Scott, *A Greek-English Lexicon*, hyle, p. 1847–48.
6 E.g., see *Ilahiyyat*, p. 10:8 and p. 23:17 for examples of *hayula*.
7 *Ilahiyyat*, Bk. 8, ch. 4, pp. 343–349.
8 *Najat*, Pt. III, ch. 2, pp. 261–76.
9 See Chapter 2.
10 Aristotle, *Topics* 101b37.
11 See Chapter 4 for a comparison chart of al-Kindi's and Ibn Sina's definitions.
12 Ibn Sina, *al-Tabiʿyyat: al-Samaʿ al-Tabiʿi* (Cairo: al-Matbaʿa al-amiriyya, 1983), pt. 1, p. 34:9 and al-Kindi, AR, p. 166: 2.
13 AR, p. 176:1.
14 E.g., L. Massignon quoted in S. H. Nasr, *An Introduction to Islamic Cosmological Doctrines* (Albany: SUNY Press, c. 1993), p. 189 (in English); Anwar Fuad Abi Khuzam *Muʿjam al-mustalahat al-Sufiyah* (Beirut: Maktabat Lubnan, 1993), p. 127; and ʿAbd al-Munʿim Hifni, *Muʿjam mustalahat al-Sufiyah* (Cairo: Maktabat Madbuli, 1980), p. 184.
15 Ibn Sina, *Kitab al-qanun*, v. 1, p. 17.
16 *Arkan* (§ 35) was translated philosophically as "building blocks," in the sense of "elements" or what a thing is made of.
17 See O. Cameron Gruner, *A Treatise on the Canon of Medicine of Avicenna* (London: Luzac, 1930), which includes a translation of the first book of the *Qanun*, although mixed with notes from the Latin edition. Here, p. 297 ff. Ibn Sina has 19 chapters on taking the pulse and describing the different types of pulse.
18 *Metaphysics* (Bk. I. 1), tran. by W. D. Ross, 980 a 23.
19 Sinawiyyan is the adjectival form of Ibn Sina's name, transliterated from the Arabic.
20 *Ilahiyyat*, v. 1, p. 29.
21 See Michael E. Marmura, "Avicenna on Primary Concepts," in *Logos Islamikos: Studia Islamica in honorem Georgii Michaelis Wickens*, ed. by R. M. Sabory

and D. A. Agius (Toronto: Pontifical Institute of Medieval Studies, 1984), pp. 219–39.
22 *Ilahiyyat*, v. 1, p. 30.
23 *mahiyya*.
24 *Najat*, p. 223: 7; *Avicenna's Psychology*, tran. by F. Rahman (Oxford University Press: 1952), p. 58.
25 For example see the Qur'an S. 24. 2 for flogging as a punishment for adultery and S. 5. 41 for the punishment for theft.
26 Lane, *Lexicon*, ^c*aql* pt. 5, p. 2114, and as a verb, no. 1, p. 2113.
27 The titles were not necessarily given by the author, but may be a later addition.
28 Ibn Sina, *al-Adhawiyya fi al-ma^cad*, ed. by H. ^cAsi (Beirut: al-Mu'assassa al-jami^ciyya lil-dirasat, 1984), p. 129: 1–2.
29 In his discussion of the material intellect, Ibn Sina refers to the intellect as receiving "the essences of things, stripped of matter." (§ 23) Since he often refers to essences stripped of matter, Ibn Sina must believe that finally an essence is non-material and therefore it cannot be seen.
30 I. Madkur, *L'Organon d'Aristote*, pp. 119–20.
31 Madkur, p. 120, n. 1.
32 Called *Mutakallimun* in early Islamic times. Although they had a variety of views, I am presenting a commonly held position, which became the orthodox view.
33 *juththa*.
34 *lahm*.
35 Hourani, "Ibn Sina's 'Essay ...'," p. 39. Hourani states that evidence shows Ibn Sina was responding to Mu^ctazili concerns, not Ash^carite.
36 Al-Ash^cari, *Kitab Maqalat al-Islamiyin*, p. 155.
37 Ibn Sina, *Ilahiyyat*, v. 2, pp. 343–49.
38 See William Chittick, *The Sufi Path of Knowledge* (Albany: SUNY Press, 1989), p. 80, for example, and the texts referred to.
39 Some mss. give this expression as *wajib al-wujud*, and George Hourani has translated it as "Necessary of Existence" for emphasis on the literal Arabic. Both "the Necessary, the Existence" (two words as an appositive) and the "Necessary of Existence" (genitive construction) are found in the manuscript tradition. Changing the wording to "the Necessary Existence" is a compromise to aid understanding, as long as readers remember that all things except God are existents (*mawjud*), and have existence (*wujud*); only God is the existence (*al-wujud*); this emphasizes his ontological difference from creation. See George F. Hourani, "Ibn Sina on Necessary and Possible Existence" in *The Philosophical Forum* 4, no. 1 (1972): 74–86.
40 *Ilahiyyat*, v. 2, pp. 343–49, especially p. 346.
41 Al-Farabi, *Kitab al-ta^cliqat* in *Rasa'il al-Farabi*, attributed to al-Farabi (Hyderabad edition: 1346 AH), *wajib al-wujud*, e.g., pp. 2 and 8.
42 *Ilahiyyat*, v. 2, p. 344:10.
43 Al-Ash^cari, *Maqalat*, p. 155: 2.
44 Aristotle, *Metaphysics* 982a 1–5 for the causes.
45 *Najat*, Book 2, ch. 6, p. 222–3; *Avicenna's Psychology*, p. 56–58.
46 *Najat*, p. 223: 7.
47 Hourani, "Ibn Sina's 'Essay ...'," p. 33 [d].
48 See Chapter 4 for full reference to W. Charlton's "Appendix: Did Aristotle Believe in Prime Matter?" in *Aristotle's Physics*.
49 *Madda*, § 32.
50 ^cAbd al-Razzaq al-Qashani, *Istilahat al-Sufiyah*, ed. by M. K. I. Ja^cfar (Cairo: al-Haya al-misriya al-amma lil-kitab, 1981), p. 46. He does not list or define *madda*,

NOTES

Ibn Sina's other term for matter defined in *The Book of Definitions*. An English translation is available in *A Glossary of Sufi Technical Terms*, tran. by N. Safwat (London: Octagon, 1991), p. 18, no. 79.

51 *Izhar al-shay' ᶜan laysa*. AR, p. 165: 11. Al-Kindi uses *ibdaᶜ*, which is usually translated as creation. Since Ibn Sina gives three words that may be translated as creation, this may increase the confusion.
52 *La ᶜan shay'*.
53 See H.A. Wolfson, *The Philosophy of the Kalam* (Cambridge, Mass.: Harvard University Press, 1976), Ch. 5, Sec. I, pp. 355–72.
54 W. Wright, *A Grammar of the Arabic Language* (New York: Cambridge University Press, 3rd edn), 1971, v. 1, p. 51 (§ 77 B–C).
55 See Aristotle, *al-Tabiᶜa* (Physics) tran. by Ishaq b. Hunayn, 2 vols., ed. by A. R. Badawi (Cairo: al-Maktaba al-ᶜarabiyya, 1964–65), 201 a 9–15, Arabic text, v. 1, pp. 170–171, for evidence.
56 See Richard M. Frank, *The Metaphysics of Created Being According to Abu l-Hudhayl al-ᶜAllaf* (Istanbul: Nederlands Historisch-Archaeologisch Instituut in het Nabije Oosten, 1966), pp. 45–46 and pp. 49–51.
57 *Ilahiyyat*, v. 1, p. 38.
58 Al-Ashᶜari, *Maqalat*, pp. 302:16–303:2 and M. Fakhry, *Islamic Occasionalism*, p. 36.
59 Al-Ashᶜari, *Maqalat*, p. 315 and M. Fakhry, *Islamic Occasionalism*, p. 35.
60 Al-Ashᶜari, *Maqalat*, p. 303:9–14 and "Muᶜammar b. Abbad" by H. Daiber, *EI²*, v. 7, p. 259.
61 G. S. Kirk and J. E. Raven, *The Presocatic Philosophers* (Cambridge: Cambridge University Press, 1962), p. 409, no. 560, "there are some atoms that are very large."
62 Kirk and Raven, explanatory remarks, p. 409.
63 Al-Ashᶜari, quoting al-Nazzam, *Maqalat*, p. 327: 11–12.
64 Hourani, "Ibn Sina's 'Essay ...'," p. 39.
65 Hourani, "Ibn Sina's 'Essay ...'," p. 35.
66 See Question sixteen.
67 See Frank, *The Metaphysics of Created Being*, especially pp. 13–15. This monograph gives an analysis of an early theologian's opinions, through reconstruction.
68 Al-Ashᶜari, *Maqalat*, p. 327:23.
69 Goichon gives full references to what she believes are Aristotle's influences on Ibn Sina in her footnotes to the French translation to *Kitab al-hudud*.
70 Aristotle, *Metaphysics* 11.9. 1065 b 15–16; Ibn Sina, "not in one time," § 57.
71 Aristotle, *Physics* 5.2. 226 b 15.
72 For a parallel discussion of Buddhist influence on theology, see Shlomo Pines, "A Study of the Impact of Indian, Mainly Buddhist, Thought on Some Aspects of Kalam Doctrines," in *Jerusalem Studies in Arabic and Islam*, v. 17 (1994), pp. 182–203.
73 Baij Nath Puri, *Buddhism in Central Asia* (Delhi: Motilal Banarsidas, 1987), p. 24.
74 See Charles Eliot, *Hinduism and Buddhism* (London: Routledge, 1921, reprinted 1962), v. 3, p. 190. Buddhism originated in India, although it had its greatest success further east in China and Japan.
75 Puri, p. 26.
76 Eliot, v. 3, p. 199.
77 Puri, p. 89; and W. Barthold and R. N. Frye, "Bukhara," *EI²*, v. 1, p. 1293.
78 Puri, p. 24–25. Brahmi is a script used for recording Sanskrit rather than being a language itself.
79 G. M. Bongard-Levin and Shin'ichiro Hori "A Fragment of the Larger Prajñâpâramitâ from Central Asia," *Journal of the International Association of Buddhist Studies*, v. 19:1 (1996), pp. 19–60, here pp. 19–21.

80 *The Life of Ibn Sina*, p. 17.
81 *Life*, Gohlman, p. 37. While the text gives Nuh II's title as Sultan, the Samanids were always referred to as Amirs. Nuh II ruled from AD976 to 997, and must have died shortly after he met Ibn Sina. The end of the Samanids was only two years away. See also Gohlman, p. 119, n. 3 and p. 123, n. 32; and C. E. Bosworth "Samanids," EI^2, v. 8, p. 1028.
82 Translated by S.H. Nasr, in *An Introduction to Islamic Cosmological Doctrines* (1993, Albany: SUNY Press), p. 187. *Mantiq al-mashriqiyin*, Arabic text (Cairo: al-Maktaba al-Salafiyya, 1910), p. 3: 6–7.
83 Nasr, *Cosmology*, p. 187.
84 *Life*, p. 21.
85 See Gruner, *A Treatise on the Canon*, chart, p. 289. An abridged version is given in *The Traditional Healer's Handbook A Classic Guide to the Medicine of Avicenna* ((Rochester, Vt: Healing Arts Press, 1991), pp. 80–87.
86 *Huang Ti Nei Ching Su Wen*, The Nei Ching attributed to the Yellow Emperor, tran. by Ilza Veith (Berkley, U. of Calif. Press, 1949, 1972 reprint), pp. 159, 161–2, 195.
87 Ibn Sina, *al-Adhawiyya*, Ch. 2, pp. 91–96.
88 *Tanasukh*.
89 Asanga, *Ornament of Mahayana Sutras*, quoted in *The Buddhist Tradition in India, China and Japan*, ed. by Wm. Theodore de Bary (New York: Vintage, 1972), pp. 94–95. The editor notes that "bliss" in some uses may mean "experience." (p. 94, n. 1.).
90 *Najat*, pp. 280–81.
91 *Najat*, p. 302.
92 Heath, *Allegory*, p. 50, n. 14 and 17.
93 *Najat*, p. 299 ff.
94 The Goichon text has *qaqnus*, but the Constantinople text substitutes *nafs*. Alpago uses the Latin transliteration *alcachones* for *al-qaqnus*, in his translation (1969 reprint, p. 136r).
95 In her first translation published in 1933, A.-M. Goichon keeps "soul" (âme) and "snow," following the Constantinople edition in *Introduction à Avicenne* (Paris: Desclée, 1933), p. 180. When she edits the text herself, she uses *qaqnus* (Arabic text, p. 39, *Kitab al-hudud*, 1963). However, she translates the word not as phoenix, but as swan (*cyne*, French, p. 56). Alpago gives "*alcachones*" in the Latin text, a transliteration of *al-qaqnus*. (*Avicennae Philosophi Praeclarissimi*, Westmead, England: Gregg, reprint, 1969, p. 135.).
96 *The Medieval Book of Birds, Hugh of Fouilloy's Aviarum*, edition, translation and commentary by Willene B. Clark (Binghamton, NY: Medieval and Renaissance Texts and Studies, 1992), pp. 231–32.
97 Priscilla Soucek, "Islamic Art and Architecture" in *Dictionary of the Middle Ages* (New York: Charles Scribner's Sons, 1982), v. 6, p. 603.
98 F. Steingass, *A Comprehensive Persian-English Dictionary*, p. 982. Also found in Ioannis Augusti Vullers, *Lexicon Persico-Latinum* (Graz, Austria: Akademische Druck- U. Verlagsanstalt, 1962 reprint of 1864), v. 2, p. 732 "phoenix, avis fabulosa."
99 "*Simurgh* phoenix. fabulous bird. sphinx." by Abbas and Manoochehr Aryanpur-Kashani, *The Concise Persian-English Dictionary* (Tehran: 1976), p. 693. The Aryanpur-Kashani entry for *qaqnus* is: "*qaqnus, simurgh, ʿanq*, phoenix." p. 912.
100 Translated from the French edition *Le livre des rois* tran. into French by Jules Mohl (Paris: 1876), v. 1, p. 168.
101 However, she translates *qaqnus* as "*cygnet*" – swan. *Le livre des définitions*, p. 56.

NOTES

102 The title is *Mantiq al-tayr*, which is variously translated as "Speech of the birds," "Parliament of the birds," and "Language of the birds." Although the title is Arabic, the poem was written in Persian.
103 Translation by Edward G. Browne in *The Literary History of Persia* (reprint of 1906, London: Cambridge University Press, 1977), v. 2, p. 514–15.
104 Steingass, *sim* p. 717 and *simurgh* p. 718.
105 Lecture on Ibn al-ʿArabi and Jesus, Nov. 14, 1997 at Sufi Books, New York by William Chittick. See *Bezels of Wisdom* by Ibn al-ʿArabi, trans. by R. W. J. Austen (Mahwah, N.J: Paulist Press, 1980), Ch. 15, on Jesus, pp. 172–186.
106 L. Massignon, *La Passion de Husayn Ibn Mansur Hallaj*, v. 1, *La Vie de Hallaj*, (Paris: Gallimard, 1975), p. 24.
107 Massignon, *Vie*, v. 1, p. 570, n. 5.
108 M. Fakhry, "Three Varieties of Mysticism in Islam" in *International Journal for Philosophy of Religion*, v. 2:4 (1971), pp. 193–207.
109 A "hadith" is a report of a saying or action of the Prophet Muhammad, or one of his companions. It provides a pattern of right practice for the believers to follow. Although orthodox hadiths have attested chains of transmission from the date of their collection back to the early days of Islam, this type of hadith is attested by unveiling, Ibn al-ʿArabi's term for his direct intuition of hadiths.
110 William C. Chittick, *The Sufi Path of Knowledge*, p. 128, 131. Also Ibn al-ʿArabi, *Futuhat al-Makiyya* (Beirut: Dar Sadr, n.d., same pagination as Bulaq ed.), v. 2, p. 310: 20–21.
111 Chittick, *Sufi Path*, pp. 168–70, p. 203.
112 Al-Qashani, *Istilahat*, p. 97, and English *A Glossary of Sufi*, p. 57, no. 249.
113 Al-Baydawi, *Anwar al-tanzil wa asrar al-tawil*, ed. by H. O. Fleischer (Leipzig: 1846–48), v. 1, pp. 51–52.
114 See Question 15.
115 Angelicity is a necessary neologism for the condition of being an angel. The definition is quoted from al-Kindi AR, p. 179:19.
116 See Question 13.
117 Quiddity means "whatness," the what-it-is of a thing, from the Latin *quid*, "what." It closely translates the Arabic *mahiyya*, also meaning "whatness."
118 Aristotle *Metaphysics*, 988a32–993b1, especially Bk. II. 1, 993a3 foll.
119 *Najat*, p. 222: 6–7; *Avicenna's Psychology*, p. 56.
120 *Najat*, p. 222: 24–223: 3; *Avicenna's Psychology*, p. 57.
121 *Ilahiyyat*, v. 1, p. 38: 11–16.
122 Many scholars known in medieval Spain are known by two names, that is an Arabic or Hebrew version and a Latin version. For example, Ibn Sina was Latinized as Avicenna, because the Latin *c* is a soft *c* pronounced like *s* in English. The *b* typically becomes a *v* in Latin. Some words in the translations also show the effects of the oral to written method.
123 "Dominic Gundisalvi" by M. T. D'Alverny in *New Catholic Encyclopedia* (Washington, DC: Catholic University of America, 1967), v. 4, pp. 966–67.
124 D'Alverny, "Dominci Gundisalvi," v. 4, p. 966.
125 "Gerard of Cremona" by p. Glorieux in *New Catholic Encyclopedia*, v. 6, p. 377.
126 *Sententiarum*, in *S. Thomae Aquinatis Opera Omnia* (Stuttgard-Bad Cannstatt: Fromman Holzboog, 1980), v. 1, p. 8; ds2 qu1 ar3 co "deus est esse sine essentia."
127 *Ilahiyyat*, p. 346: 11–12.
128 *Summa Theologiae* (New York: Blackfriars and McGraw-Hill, 1964) Latin text and English translation by the Order of Preachers, Ia.12.1. "The unlimited is, as such, unknowable. But we have already shown that God is unlimited, so he must be in himself unknown." (v. 3, p. 3).

129 Flynn, "St. Thomas and Avicenna on the Nature of God," *Abr-nahrain*, v. 14 (1974), pp. 53–65; here, J.G. Flynn's translation, p. 59. Rabbi Moses refers to Maimonides.
130 John F. Wippel, "The Latin Avicenna as a Source for Thomas Aquinas's Metaphysics," *Freiburger Zeitshcrift für Philosophie und Theologie* (Freiburg, 1990, v. 37, pp. 51–89).
131 The Arabic title is: *Tahafut al-falasifa*, ed. by M. Bouyges and Majid Fakhry (Beirut: Dar al-Mashreq, 1986, 4th edn). For a new English translation see: *The Incoherence of the Philosophers*, tran. by Michael E. Marmura (Provo, Utah: Brigham Young University Press, 1997).
132 Frank, *The Metaphysics of Created Being*, p. 37.
133 *Al-Adhawiyya*, Ch. 4, p. 130, Ch. 6, p. 145ff. Shari‛a is Islamic law.
134 Hourani, "Ibn Sina's 'Essay ...'," p. 33.
135 Hourani, "Ibn Sina's 'Essay ...'," p. 32.

APPENDIX

1 The Lisbon manuscript ends here. The text reads:.

الجوهر - قائم بنفسه ، حامل للأعراض ، لا يتغير ، ذاته موصوف ، لا واصف.

Klein Franke, "Al-Kindi," p. 210, no. 12.
2 AR, p. 166:7–11.
3 AR, p. 165:4.
4 AR, p. 169:12–4, except following Gimaret's substitute of *mabda'* for *mubtada'* (AR's text). "Je lis *mabda'* Plutôt que I: *mubtada'*, par rapprochement avec K I 101,4." Gimaret, *Cinq épîtres*, p. 50, commentary on no. 42 مبدأ الحركة. This is from *al-Falsafa al-ula* and the same four causes are given here. (Cf. AR, 101:3–4).
5 AR, p. 166:1.
6 Al-Farabi, *Jalinus*, p. 39:10–13.
7 *Alfaz*, p. 81:12–13.
8 *al-Alfaz al-musta‛mala fi al-mantiq*, p. 78:19–22.
9 *Burhan*, p. 52:8.
10 *Huruf*, p. 63:6–13.
11 *Huruf*, p. 205:1–2.
12 *Huruf*, p. 99:16–p. 100:8.
13 *Siyasa*, p. 36:6–8, 11, 13, and 14.
14 Ibn Sina, *Hudud*, p. 10:8–10.
15 *al-Shifa': al-Ilahiyyat*, v. 1, p. 245:10–13.
16 *Hudud*, p. 23:8–24:13. // indicates page break. Cf. *al-Ilahiyyat*, p. 10:8 and p. 54:9–10. For a discussion of *jawhar* in Persian, see Ibn Sina's *Danashnamah-i ‛Ala'i, Ilahiyyat*, Anjuman-i athar-i milli silsilah-i intisharat, ed. Muhammad Mu‛in (Tehran, 1371/AD 1952), pp. 9–11 and pp. 36–39. See also *Encyclopaedia Iranica*, Michael Marmura s.v. "Avicenna. xi, Persian Works," on the *Danashnamah*.
17 *Hudud*, p. 41:1–2 Cf. the Latin in Ibn Sina, "Tractatus de diffinitio," f. 136v.
18 *Hudud*, p. 41:3–42:10. // indicates page break.
19 *Hudud*, pp. 17:9–18:2.
20 *Hudud*, p. 18:7–10.

BIBLIOGRAPHY

PRIMARY SOURCES IN ARABIC

Aristotle. *Aristu ᶜinda al-ᶜArab*. Edited by ᶜAbdurrahman Badawi. Kuwait: Wakala al-matbuᶜat, 1978, 2nd printing.
—— *Mantiq Aristu*. 3 vols Cairo: Dar al-kutub al-misriyya, 1948–52.
—— *Al-Tabiᶜa*. Translated by Ishaq b. Hunayn. Edited by ᶜAbdurrahman Badawi. 2 vols Cairo: Dar al-qawmiya al-tibaᶜa al-nashr, 1964.
Al-Ashᶜari, ᶜAli ibn Ismaᶜil. *Kitab al-maqalat al-islamiyyin wa ikhtilaf al-musalliyn*. Edited by Hellmut Ritter. Wiesbaden: F. Steiner, 1963.
Al-Farabi. "Al-Farabi's Paraphrase of the 'Categories' of Aristotle." Edited and translated by D. M. Dunlop. *Islamic Quarterly* 4 (1957–58): 168–97; 5 (1958–59): 21–54 (Arabic and English).
—— *Alfarabius de Platonis Philosophia*. Edited by Franz Rosenthal and Richard Walzer. London: Warburg Institute, 1943.
—— *Al-Alfaz al-mustaᶜmala fi al-mantiq*. Edited by Muhsin Mahdi. Beirut: Dar al-mashreq, 1968.
—— *Falsafat Aristutalis*. Edited by Muhsin Mahdi. Beirut: Dar majalla shiᶜr, 1961.
—— *Fi al-radd ᶜala Jalinus. Traités philosophiques*. Edited by ᶜAbdurrahman Badawi. Benghazi: Publications de l'Université de Libye, 1973.
—— *Ihsa' al-ᶜulum*. Edited by ᶜOthman Amin. Cairo: Dar al-fikr al-ᶜarabi, 1949, 2nd printing.
—— *Kitab al-burhan*. Edited by Majid Fakhry. Beirut: Dar al-mashreq, 1987.
—— *Kitab al-huruf*. Edited by Muhsin Mahdi, first edition. (A new edition is forthcoming). Beirut: Dar al-mashreq, 1969.
—— *Kitab al-jamᶜ bayna ra'yay al-hakimayn*. Edited by Albert Nadir. Beirut: Dar al-mashreq, 4th printing 1968.
—— "Kitab al-maqulat." In *Al-Mantiq ᶜinda al-Farabi*. Edited by Rafiq al-ᶜAjam, vol. 1. Beirut: Dar al-mashreq, 1985.
—— *Kitab al-taᶜliqat. Rasa'il al-Farabi*. Hyderabad: Matbaᶜat majlis da'irat al-maᶜarif al-Uthmaniya, 1346 AH.
—— *Kitab mabadi' ara' ahl al-madina al-fadila*. Edited by Albert Nader. Beirut: Dar al-mashreq, 1959.
—— *Kitab tahsil al-saᶜada*. Edited by Jafar Al-Yasin. Beirut: al-Andalus, 1981.
—— *Al-Mantiq ᶜinda al-Farabi*. Edited by Rafiq al-ᶜAjam. Beirut: Dar al-mashreq, 1985, vol. 1.
—— *Risala fi al-ᶜaql*. Edited by Maurice Bouyges. Beirut: Imprimerie Catholique, 1938.

—— *Risala fi jawab masa'il su'ila ᶜanha*. *Alfarabi's Philosophische Abhandlungen*. Edited by Friedrich Dieterici. Leiden: Brill, 1890.

—— *Risala Zaynun*. *Rasa'il al-Farabi*. Hyderabad: Matbaᶜat majlis da'irat al-maᶜarif al-Uthmaniya, 1346 AH.

—— *The Political Regime (al-siyasah al-madaniyyah), also known as the Treatise on the Principles of Beings*. Edited by Fauzi M. Najjar. Beirut: Imprimerie Catholique, 1964.

—— *ᶜUyun al-masa'il*. *Alfarabi's Philosophische Abhandlungen*. Edited by Friedrich Dieterici. Leiden: Brill, 1890.

Ibn Abi Usaybiᶜah. *Kitab ᶜuyun al-anba' fi tabaqat al-atibba'*. Edited by August Müller. 2 vols in 1. Göttingen: Druck der dieterichschen Univ.–Buchdruckerei, 1884.

Ibn al-Nadim. *Kitab al-fihrist*. Edited by Gustav Flügel. Reprint. Beirut: Khayyat, 1964.

Ibn Khallikan. *Kitab wafayat al-aᶜyan wa anba' abna' al-zaman*. Edited by Ihsan ᶜAbbas. 8 vols Beirut: Dar al-thaqafah, pref. 1968.

Ibn Rushd. *Tafsir ma baᶜd at-tabiᶜat ("Grand commentaire" de la Métaphysique)*. Edited by Maurice Bouyges. 3rd edn. 3 vols Beirut: Dar al-mashreq, 1990.

Ibn Sina. *Danashnamah-i ᶜAla'i, Ilahiyyat*. Anjuman-i athar-i milli silsilah-i intisharat. Edited by Muhammad Muᶜin. Tehran, 1371/AD 1952.

—— *Kitab al-hudud*. Arabic text edited and translated by A.-M. Goichon. Cairo: Publications de l'Institut français d'archéologie orientale du Caire, 1963.

—— *Kitab al-hudud*. *Tisᶜ rasa'il (Nine Treatises)*. Constantinople: al-Jawa'ib, 1881.

—— *Kitab al-najat*. Edited by Majid Fakhry. Beirut: Dar al-afaq al-jadida, 1985.

—— *Kitab al-najat*. Edited by ᶜAbd al-Rahman ᶜAmayrah. Beirut: Dar al-jil, 1992.

—— *Al-Mustalah al-falsafi ᶜinda al-ᶜArab*. 2nd edn. Edited by ᶜAbd al-Amir al-ᶜAsam. Cairo: al-Haya al-Misriya al-ᶜamma lil-kitab, 1989.

—— *Al-Qanun fi al-tibb*. Edited by Idwar al-Qashsh. 3 vols Beirut: Muᶜassasat ᶜIzz al-din, 1987.

—— *Al-Risala al-ᶜarshiyya*. Edited by Ibrahim Hilal. Cairo: s.n., pref. 1981.

—— *Al-Shifa': al-Ilahiyyat*. Edited by M. Y. Moussa, S. Dunya and S. Zayed. 2 vols Cairo: Organisme général des imprimeries gouvernementales, 1960.

—— *Al-Shifa': al-Mantiq: al-Jadal*. (pt. 6.) Edited by Ahmad Fu'ad El Ehwany. Cairo: Organisme général des imprimeries gouvernementales, 1485 AH/AD 1965.

—— *Al-Shifa': al-Tabiᶜyyat: al-Samaᶜ al-Tabiᶜi*. Cairo: Organisme général des imprimeries gouvernementales, 1983.

Al-Kindi. *Rasa'il al-Kindi al-falsafiyya*. Edited by Muhammad ᶜAbd al-Hadi Abu Ridah. 2 vols in 1. Cairo: Dar al-fikr al-ᶜarabi, 1953.

Plotinus. *Iflutin ᶜinda al-ᶜArab*. 2nd edn. Edited by ᶜAbdurrahman Badawi. Cairo: Dar al-nahdah al-ᶜarabiyyah, 1966.

Al-Qifti, ᶜAli ibn Yusuf. *Ta'rikh al-hukama'*. Edited by J. Lippert. Leipzig: Dieterich'sche Verlagsbuchhandlung, 1903.

PRIMARY SOURCES IN TRANSLATION

Aristotle. *Aristotle's Physics*. Translated by W. Charlton. Oxford: Clarendon Press, 1970.

—— *Aristotle's Categories and De Interpretatione*. Translated by J. L. Ackrill. Oxford: Clarendon, 1963.

—— *A New Aristotle Reader*. Edited by J. L. Ackrill. Princeton: Princeton University Press, 1987.

BIBLIOGRAPHY

—— *Selected Works*. Translated by H. G. Apostle and L. P. Gerson. Grinnell, Iowa: Peripatetic Press, 1983.

—— "Topics," translated by W. A. Pickard-Cambridge. In *The Basic Works of Aristotle*, edited by R. McKeon. New York: Random House, 1941.

Al-Farabi. *Alfarabi's Philosophy of Plato and Aristotle*. Translated by Muhsin Mahdi. New York: Free Press of Glencoe, 1962.

—— "The Political Regime (*Al-Siyasah al-Madaniyyah*, also known as the *Treatise on the Principles of Beings*)." Translated by Thérèse-Anne Druart, photocopied. Washington, DC: Department of Philosophy, Georgetown University, 1981.

Al-Ghazali. *The Incoherence of the Philosophers*. Translated by Michael E. Marmura. Provo, Utah: Brigham Young University Press, 1997.

Ibn Khallikan. *Kitab wafayat al-aᶜyan wa anba' abna' al-zaman*. Translated by B. MacGukin de Slade. 1868. Reprint. New York: Johnson Reprint Corp., 1961.

Ibn Sina. *Avicenna's Psychology*. Translated by F. Rahman. Oxford University Press: 1952.

—— *The Life of Ibn Sina*. Translated by W. E. Gohlman. Albany: SUNY, 1974. (Arabic and English texts.)

—— *The Metaphysica of Avicenna (ibn Sina)*. Translated by Parviz Morewedge. New York: Columbia University Press, 1973.

—— *Remarks and Admonitions Part One: Logic*. Translated by Shams Constantine Inati. Toronto: Pontifical Institute of Mediaeval Studies, 1984.

—— "Tractatus de diffinitionibus." in *Avicennae Philosophi praeclarissimi*. Translated by Andrea Alpago (Latin trans.) 1546. Reprint. Farnborough: Gregg International, 1969.

Al-Kindi. *Cinq épîtres*. Edited by D. Gimaret. Paris: Editions du Centre national de la recherche scientifique, 1976.

—— "L'Épître de Kindi sur les définitions et les descriptions." Translated by Michel Allard. *Bulletin d'études orientales* 25 (1972): 47–83.

—— "Al-Kindi's Book of Definitions: Its Place in Arabic Definition Literature." Translated by Tamar Zahava Frank. PhD dissertation, Yale University, 1975.

—— *Al-Kindi's Metaphysics: A Translation of Yaᶜqub ibn Ishaq al-Kindi's Treatise "On first philosophy."* Translated by Alfred L. Ivry. Albany: State University of New York Press, 1974.

Plato. *Dialogues of Plato*. Translated by Benjamin Jowell. New York: Appleton, 1898.

—— *Meno*. Translated by R. W. Sharples. Chicago: Bolchazy-Carducci, 1985.

Qur'an. *The Holy Qur'an*. Translated by A. Yusuf Ali. Pub. in the US by The Muslim Students Association of the United States and Canada, 1975.

—— *The Qur'an: a Modern English Version*. Translated by Majid Fakhry. Reading, UK: Garnet, 1997.

SECONDARY SOURCES

ᶜAbd al-Baqi, Muhammad Fuᶜad. *al-Muᶜjam al-mufharis li-alfaz al-Qur'an al-karim*. 2 vols Beirut: Khayyat, n.d.

Abed, Shukri. *Aristotelian Logic and the Arabic Language in Alfarabi*. Albany: State University of New York Press, 1991.

Abelson, R. "Definition." In *Encyclopedia of Philosophy*, editor-in-chief Paul Edwards, vol. 2, pp. 314–324. New York: Macmillan, 1967.

Afnan, Soheil M. *A Philosophical Lexicon in Persian and Arabic*. Reprint. Beirut: Dar el-mashreq, 1964.

Amine, Osman. "Le Stoïcisme et la pensée islamique." *Revue Thomiste* 59 (1959): 79–97.

BIBLIOGRAPHY

Anawati, G. C. *Mu'allafat Ibn Sina: Essai de bibliographie avicennienne.* Cairo: Edition al-maaref, 1950.
Atiyeh, George. *Al-Kindi: The Philosopher of the Arabs.* Rawalpindi, Pakistan: Islamic Research Institute, 1966.
Badawi, ᶜAbdurrahman. *Histoire de la philosophie en Islam.* 2 vols Paris: J. Vrin, 1972.
Benson, Hugh H. "Misunderstanding the 'What-is-F-ness' Question." In *Essays on the Philosophy of Socrates*, edited by H. H. Benson, pp. 123–136. New York: Oxford University Press, 1992.
—— "The Priority of Definition and the Socratic Elenchus." *Oxford Studies in Ancient Philosophy* 8 (1990): 19–65.
Booth, Edward. *Aristotelian Aporetic Ontology in Islamic and Christian Thinkers.* Cambridge: Cambridge University Press, 1983.
Brock, Sebastian. "Aspects of Translation Technique in Antiquity." *Greek, Roman and Byzantine Studies* 20 (1979): 69–87.
—— "From Antagonism to Assimilation: Syriac Attitudes to Greek Learning." *Syriac Perspectives on Late Antiquity*, no. 5. London: Variorum Reprints, 1984: 17–34.
Brockelmann, Carl. *Geschichte der arabischen Litteratur.* 5 vols Leiden: Brill, 1943.
Burrell, David B. "Essence and Existence: Avicenna and Greek Philosophy." *Institut dominicain d'études orientales du Caire. Mélanges* 17 (1986): 53–66.
Butterworth, Charles E. "An Account of Recent Scholarship in Medieval Islamic Philosophy." *Interpretation* 16 (1988): 87–97.
Carra de Vaux, Bernard. *Avicenne.* 1900. Reprint. Amsterdam: Philo Press, 1974.
Cruz Hernandez, Miguel. "El 'Fontes quaestionum' (ᶜuyun al-masa'il) de Abu Nasr al-Farabi." *Archives d'histoire doctrinale et littéraire du Moyen Age* 25–26 (1951): 303–305.
Davidson, Herbert A. *Proofs for Eternity, Creation and the Existence of God in Medieval Islamic and Jewish Philosophy.* New York: Oxford Press, 1987.
De Bary, Wm. Theodore, ed. *The Buddhist Tradition in India, China and Japan.* New York: Vintage, 1972.
Dhanani, Alnoor. "Kalam and Hellenistic Cosmology: Minimal Parts in Basrian Muᶜtazili Atomism." PhD dissertation, Harvard University, 1991.
—— *The Physical Theory of Kalam.* Leiden: Brill, 1994.
Dodds, E. R. *The Ancient Concept of Progress and Other Essays on Greek Literature and Belief.* Oxford: Clarendon, 1973.
Dozy, R. *Supplément aux dictionnaires arabes.* 3rd edn. 2 vols Leiden: Brill, 1967.
Druart, Thérèse-Anne. "Al-Farabi and Emanationism." In *Studies in Medieval Philosophy*, edited by John F. Wippel. Washington: Catholic University Press, 1987: 23–43.
Eliot, Charles. *Hinduism and Buddhism.* London: Routledge, 1921, reprinted 1962.
Encyclopedia of Islam. 2nd edn. 7 vols Leiden: Brill, 1960–.
Floistad, G. *Philosophy and Science in the Middle Ages.* Part 1. Contemporary Philosophy, vol. 1. Dordrecht: Kluwer Academic Publishers, 1990.
Frank, Richard M. *Al-Ghazali and the Ashᶜarite School.* Durham, NC: Duke University Press, 1994.
—— *The Metaphysics of Created Being According to Abu l-Hudhayl al-ᶜAllaf.* Istanbul: Nederlands Historisch-Archaeologisch Instituut, 1966.
—— "The Origin of the Arabic Philosophical Term *anniyah*." *Cahiers de Byrsa* 6 (1956): 181–201.
Freytag, George Wilhelm. *Lexicon Arabico-Latinum.* 4 vols in 2. Halis Saxonum: Schwetscke, 1830.

—— *Lexicon Arabico-Latinum ex opere suo maiore in usum tironum excerptum*. Halis Saxonum: Schwetscke, 1837.
Galston, Miriam. *Politics and Excellence: the Political Philosophy of Alfarabi*. Princeton, NJ: Princeton University Press, 1990.
Gardet, Louis, and Anawati, M.-M. *Introduction à la théologie musulmane*. Paris: J. Vrin, 1970.
Goichon, A.-M. *La distinction de l'essence et de l'existence d'après Ibn Sina (Avicenne)*. Paris: Desclée, de Brouwer, 1938.
—— *Lexique de la langue philosophique d'Ibn Sina*. Paris: de Brouwer, 1938.
Goodman, Lenn. *Avicenna*. New York: Routledge, 1992.
Gutas, Dimitri. *Avicenna and the Aristotelian Tradition*. Leiden: Brill, 1988.
—— Mahdi, M.; Abed, S. et al. "Avicenna." In *The Encyclopaedia Iranica*, edited by Ehsan Yarshater, vol. 3, fasc. 1, pp. 66–110. NY: Routledge, 1987.
Haleem, M. A. S. Abdel. "Early Theological and Juristic Terminology: *Kitab al-hudud fi'l-usul by Ibn Furak*." *BSOAS* 54 (1991): 5–41.
Hodgson, Marshall. *The Venture of Islam: The Classical Age of Islam*. vol. 1. Chicago: University of Chicago Press, 1977.
Hourani, George F. "Ibn Sina's 'Essay on the Secret of Destiny'." *BSOAS* 29 (1966): 25–48.
—— "Ibn Sina on Necessary and Possible Existence." *The Philosophical Forum* 4, no. 1 (1972): 74–86.
Hugonnard-Roche, Henri. "L'Intérmediaire syriaque dans la transmission de la philosophie grècque à l'arabe: le cas de l'Organon d'Aristote." *Arabic Sciences and Philosophy* 1 (1991): 187–209.
Hyman, Arthur, and Walsh, James J. *Philosophy in the Middle Ages*. Indianapolis: Hackett, 1983.
Al-Jabri, M. A. *Nahnu wa al-turath*. Beirut: Dar al-tali'at, 1982.
Jadaane, Fehmi. *L'Influence du Stoïcisme sur la pensée musulmane*. Beirut: Dar el-mashreq, 1968.
Janssens, Jules. *An Annotated Bibliography of Ibn Sina*. Louvain, Belgium: University Press, 1991.
Jolivet, Jean. *L'intellect selon Kindi*. Leiden: Brill, 1971.
Kahn, Charles H. "The Greek Verb 'To Be' and the Concept of Being." *Foundations of Language* 2 (1966): 245–65.
Kemal, Salim. *The Poetics of Alfarabi and Avicenna*. Leiden: Brill, 1991.
Kennedy-Day, Kiki. "Al-Kindi: a New Dibajah?" in *Islamic Quarterly*, 44: 2 (2000): 429–433.
Klein-Franke, Felix. "Al-Kindi's 'On Definitions and Descriptions of Things'." *Le Muséon* 95 (1982): 191–216.
Kraemer, Joel L. *Philosophy in the Renaissance of Islam: Abu Sulayman al-Sijistani and his Circle*. Leiden: Brill, 1986.
Kraus, Paul. "Plotin chez les Arabes." *Bulletin de l'institut d'Egypte* 24 (1941–2): 263–95.
Lane, Edward William. *An Arabic-English Lexicon*. 8 vols Beirut: Librarie du Liban, 1968.
Leaman, Oliver. "Does the Interpretation of Islamic Philosophy Rest on a Mistake?" *IJMES* 12 (1980): 525–37.
—— "God's Knowledge of the Future in the Philosophy of al-Farabi." *Occasional Papers of the School of Abbasid Studies* 1, no. 1: 23–29.
Liddell, Henry George, and Scott, Robert. *A Greek-English Lexicon*. Reprint. Oxford: Clarendon, 1966.

Madkour, Ibrahim. *La Place d'al-Farabi dans l'école philosophique musulmane.* Paris: J. Vrin, 1934.
Mahdavi, Yahya. *Bibliographie d'Ibn Sina.* Tehran: 1954.
Mahdi, Muhsin. "Al-Farabi's Imperfect State." *Journal of the American Oriental Society* 110 (1990): 691–726.
—— *Ibn Khaldun's Philosophy of History.* Chicago: University of Chicago Press, 1964.
Marmura, Michael E. "Avicenna on Primary Concepts." In *Logos Islamikos: Studia Islamica in honorem Georgii Michaelis Wickens,* edited by R. M. Sabory and D. A. Agius, pp. 219–39. Toronto: Pontifical Institute of Medieval Studies, 1984.
Mattock, J. N. "The Early Translations from Greek into Arabic: an Experiment in Comparative Assessment." In *Symposium Graeco-Arabicum II,* edited by Gerhard Endress, pp. 73–102. Amsterdam: B. R. Grüner, 1989.
Michot, Jean. "Tables de correspondance des 'Ta^{c}liqat' d'al-Farabi, des 'Ta^{c}liqat' d'Avicenne et du 'Liber aphorismorum' d'Andrea Alpago." *Institut dominicain d'études orientales. Mélanges* 15 (1982): 231–244.
Moosa, Matti. "Al-Kindi's Role in the Transmission of Greek Knowledge to the Arabs." *Journal of the Pakistan Historical Society* 15, no. 1 (1967): 3–18.
al-Munjid fi al-lugha. 17th printing. Beirut: Dar al-mashreq, 1984.
Nasr, Seyyed Hossein. "Ibn Sina." In *Dictionary of the Middle Ages,* Editor-in-chief, J. R. Strayer, vol. 11, pp. 302–07. New York: Charles Scribner's Sons, 1988.
Netton, Ian. *Al-Farabi and his School.* London: Routledge, 1992.
Patton, W. M. *Ahmed Ibn Hanbal and the Mihna.* Leiden: Brill, 1897.
Peters, Francis E. *Allah's Commonwealth.* New York: Simon and Schuster, 1973.
—— *Aristoteles Arabus.* Leiden: Brill, 1968.
—— *Aristotle and the Arabs.* New York: New York University Press, 1968.
—— *The Two Hundred Dollar Look.* Secaucus, NJ: L. Stuart, 1987.
Peters, J. R. T. M. *God's Created Speech.* Leiden: Brill, 1976.
Pines, S. "Ibn Sina et auteur de la *Risalat al-fusus fi'l-hikma*: quelques données du problème." *Revue des études islamiques* 19 (1951): 121–24.
Puri, Baij Nath. *Buddhism in Central Asia.* Delhi: Motilal Banarsidas, 1987.
Rahman, Fazlur. *Prophecy in Islam: Philosophy and Orthodoxy.* London: Allen & Unwin, 1958.
Rescher, Nicholas. *Al-Kindi: An Annotated Bibliography.* Pittsburgh: University of Pittsburgh Press, 1964.
Ritter, Hellmut. "Schriften Ja^{c}qub ibn Ishaq al-Kindi's in Stambuler Bibliotheken." *Archiv Orientální* (Prague) 4 (1932): 363–872.
Robinson, Richard. *Definition.* Oxford: Clarendon, 1954.
Rosenthal, Franz. "Arabische Nachrichten über Zenon den Eleaton." *Orientalia* 6 (1937): 21–132.
Sayf, Antwan. *Al-Kindi: makanatuhu ^{c}inda mu'arrikhi al-falsafa al-^{c}arabi.* Beirut: Dar al-Jil, 1985.
Sorenson, Roy. "Vagueness and the Desiderata for Definition." In *Definitions and Definability,* edited by J. H. Fetzer, D. Shatz and G. Schlesinger, pp. 71–109. Boston: Kluwer, 1991.
Steingass, F. *A Comprehensive Persian-English Dictionary.* 1892. Reprint. Beirut: Librairie du Liban, 1970.
Stern, Samuel M. "Notes on al-Kindi's Treatise on Definitions." *Journal of the Royal Asiatic Society* 1959: 32–43.
Strohmaier, Gotthard. "'Von Alexandrien nach Baghdad' – eine fiktive Schultradtion." In *Aristoteles Werk und Wirkung,* edited by Paul Moraux Gewidmet, pp. 380–89. New York: De Gruyter, 1987.

Taylor, C. C. W. "Socratic Ethics." In *Socratic Questions*, edited by B. S. Gower and M. C. Stokes. London: Routledge, 1992.

Walzer, Richard. *Greek into Arabic*. Cambridge: Harvard University Press, 1962.

Wippel, John F. "The Latin Avicenna as a Source for Thomas Aquinas's Metaphysics." *Freiburger Zeitshcrift für Philosophie und Theologie* (Freiburg) 37 (1990): 51–98.

Wolfson, Harry Austryn. *The Philosophy of the Kalam*. Cambridge: Harvard University Press, 1976.

Zimmerman, F. W. *Al-Farabi's Commentary and Short Treatise on Aristotle's De Interpretatione*. Oxford: Oxford University Press, 1981.

INDEX

ᶜAbd al-Jabbar, Abu al-Hasan 139
ᶜAbd al-Razzaq al-Qashani 134, 149
Abu al-Hudhayl, Muhammad 138–9
Abu Ridah, M.A. 20–1
Adhawiyya fi al-maᶜad (On the Afterlife), Ibn Sina 123, 143–4
ᶜAla' al-Dawla 88–9
Allard, Michel 20–1
Alpago 81
angel 150–2
anniyya (essence) 127, 155
ᶜ*aql* (intellect) 130–2
Aquinas, Thomas 14, 115; translation of *Hudud, Kitab al-* 155–6
Aristotle 14–15, 17–19, 22, 35, 44–5, 51, 117, 121, 127, 131–2, 136; Arabic translations 35; al-Farabi's commentaries on 13, 40; four causes 41; al-Kindi's commentaries on 30; on matter 57, 74–5; quoted by Ibn Sina 15; *Topics* 17, 51; on time 140
al-Ashᶜari, Ashᶜarites 92, 125, 139
atoms 138–40
ᶜAttar, Farid ud-Din 146–7
Atiyeh, George N. 20
Avendauth *see* Ibn Daud
Averroës *see* Ibn Rushd
Avicenna *see* Ibn Sina

al-Baydawi, ᶜAbd Allah ibn ᶜUmar 151
al-Bayhaqi, Ibn Funduq 88, 96
Benson, Hugh H. 15–16
Brock, Sebastian 34
Buddhism 93–94, 141–5
Bukhara (Central Asia) 87–8, 94–5, 141–2
Burhan, Kitab al-, al-Farabi 37–8

cause (ᶜ*illa, sabab*) 10; comparison of three philosophers 68–74; in al-Farabi 40–2; in al-Kindi 26–8; in Ibn Sina 54–7, 59–60, 136–8
change and its opposite 134–5
Charlton, William 57, 74–5
Ch'i-Po: *Nei Ching* 143
Creator: definition of 125–6; existence of 120–1; God as, in Qur'an 157

Daneshnamah-i ᶜAla'i (*Book of Knowledge for ᶜAla'*), Ibn Sina 89, 97
definition 61–3, 122–3: historical context 16–18; of philosophical terms 122–3; types of 14–15; vagueness 29; versus description 123–4
definition, definition of: in Aristotle 17–18; in al-Farabi 36–8, 50–1; in Ibn Sina 50–1
defintions, order of: in Aristotle 21–2; in Ibn Sina 48–9, 117–18; in al-Kindi 21–2, 48–9
Democritus 138
dhat (essence) 39, 52–3, 59, 66, 137
Dodds, E.R. 9, 12

element *see* ᶜ*unsur; ustuqas*
Empedocles 149
essence *see dhat; anniyya*
essence-existence question 153–4

al-Farabi, Abu Nasr 11–13, 32–46; *Burhan, Kitab al-* 37–8; cause (ᶜ*illa, sabab*) 40–2; commentaries on Aristotle 40; definition of definition 36–8; *Harmonization of the Opinions of Plato and Aristotle* 44; *hayula*

INDEX

(matter) 19, 28–9, 43; influence of Greek philosophy 44–5; *jawhar* (substance) 38–40; *Mabadi' ara' ahl al-madina al-fadila, Kitab* (*Book of the Principles of the Opinions of the People of the Virtuous City*), 32–3; *madda* (matter) 42–4; *Maqulat, Kitab al-* (*Book of Categories*) 40; Necessary Existence 45; *al-Taʿliqat* (*Connections*) 126

al-Farra': *Hudud, Kitab al-* 19

Fi al-falsifa al-ula (*On First Philosophy*), al-Kindi 55

Fi hudud al-ashya' wa rusumiha (*On the Definitions and Descriptions of Things*), al-Kindi 12, 19–31

al-Firdawsi, Abu'l-Qasim 87; *Shahnamah* (*Book of Kings*) 146

form *see sura*

Frank, T.Z. 20–1

Gerard, of Cremona 154–5

al-Ghazali, Abu Hamid Muhammad 40–1, 93; *Tahafut al-falasifa* (*On the Incoherence of the Philosophers*) 157–8

Gimaret, D. 20–1

Goichon, A.M. 10

Gundisalvi, Dominic 154–5

hadd/hadud see definition

al-Hallaj, Mansur 147–8

hayula (matter) 10–13; comparison of three philosophers 3, 74–83; al-Farabi's use of 19, 28–9, 43; Ibn Sina's use of 53, 57–61, 133–4

Hudud, Kitab al- (*Book of Definitions*), Ibn Sina: ʿ*aql* (intellect) 130–2; angel 150–2; atoms 138–40; Buddhist influence 141–5; cause 136–8; change and its opposite 134–5; chronology 91; Creator, definition of 125–6; definition versus description 123–4; essence-existence question 153–4; first principles 120–2; Ibn Sina's motivation 116–17; intellect 130–2; jinn 150–2; al-Kindi's influence 117–18; knowledge, theory of 121–2; Latin translations of 154–7; love (ʿ*ishq* and *mahabba*) 147–9; matter and form 133–4; medical terms 119; order of definitions 48–9; Pathetic God 149–50; phoenix 145–7; physical conditions 138–40; precedents for 117–18; selection of terms 119–20; Simurgh 145–7; soul 128–30; style 48–50; Sufi influence 147–9; time 140; translation by Aquinas 155–6; whiteness 145–7

Hudud fi al-usul, Kitab al-, Ibn Furak 21

Hunayn ibn Ishaq 33

Huruf, Kitab al- (*Book of Letters*), al-Farabi 11, 32–46, 96; style of 35

Ibn al-Arabi 149

Ibn al-Nadim 58

Ibn Daud 154–5

Ibn Furak 21, 51; *Hudud fi al-usul, Kitab al-* 21

Ibn Rushd 14; *Tahaful al-tahafut* (*Incoherence of the Incoherence*) 158

Ibn Sina, Abu ʿAli al-Husayn 11–12, 15, 47–60, 87–97; *Adhawiyya fi al-maʿad* (*On the Afterlife*) 123, 143–4; *Daneshnamah-i ʿAlaʾi* (*Book of Knowledge for ʿAlaʾ*) 89, 97; debt to al-Kindi 31, 47, 117–18; Eastern influence 93–5; ethnic background 95; *hayula* (matter) 53, 57–61, 133–4; *al-Ilahiyyat* (*Metaphysics*) 51, 55–6, 88, 115–17, 155–6; *jawhar* (substance) 52–3, 59–60; lifestyle choices 88, 93, 96–7; *madda* (matter) 57–9, 133; *Najat, Kitab al-* 58–9, 117, 129, 144; *Qanun fi al-tibb, Kitab al-* (*Canon*) 89, 119, 143, 154; reception in the West 154–9; *Risala fi al-ʿishq* (*Treatise on Love*) 97, 148, 153; *Shifaʾ, Kitab al-*, Ibn Sina 89, 117; Sufism 96, 147–50; *see also Hudud, Kitab al-*

Ikhwan al-Safaʾ 20

al-Ilahiyyat (*Metaphysics*), Ibn Sina 51, 55–6, 88, 115–17, 155–6

intellect *see* ʿ*aql*

Ishaq b. Hunayn 27, 33, 72

Islam 91–3

ʿ*ishq* (love) *see* love

jawhar (substance) 10; comparison of three philosophers 63–8; al-Farabi's use of 38–40; al-Kindi's use of 23–6; Ibn Sina's use of 52–3, 59–60

jinn 150–2

INDEX

al-Juzjani 88, 96–7

al-Kindi, Abu Yusuf Ya'qub b. Ishaq 11–12, 19–31; commentaries on Aristotle 30; *Fi al-falsifa al-ula (On First Philosophy)* 55; *Fi hudud al-ashya' wa rusumiha (On the Definitions and Descriptions of Things)* 12, 19–31; influence on Ibn Sina 31, 47, 117–18; *jawhar* (substance) 23–6; *tin / tina* (matter) 29; *'unsur* (matter) 28–9
Kitab *see under* first following noun, e.g. Hudud, Kitab al-
Klein-Franke, F. 20

Language of the Birds (Mantiq al-tayr), 'Attar 146–7
love: *'ishq* versus *mahabba* 147–9

Mabadi' ara' ahl al-madina al-fadila, Kitab (Book of the Principles of the Opinions of the People of the Virtuous City), al-Farabi 32–3
madda (matter) 10–13; comparison of three philosophers 74–83; al-Farabi's use of 42–4; Ibn Sina's use of 57–9, 133
mahabba (love) *see* love
Madkur, Ibrahim 124
mahiyya (quiddity) 15, 36, 39, 43, 66, 127
Mantiq al-mashriqiyyin (Logic of the Easterners), Ibn Sina 91, 139, 142
Mantiq al-tayr see Language of the Birds
Maqulat, Kitab al- (Book of Categories), al-Farabi 40
matter *see madda*; *hayula*; *'unsur*; *ustuqas*
mihna 166–7
Miskawayh 30–1
Mu'ammar 138
Mulla Sadra 148
Mu'tazilites 92, 125, 127, 138–40

Najat, Kitab al-, Ibn Sina 58–9, 117, 129, 144
al-Nazzam 139
Necessary Existence (*wajib al-wujud*) 125–8, 136–7, 148–9, 152–3; in al-Farabi 45

Pathetic God (Sufism) 149–50
phoenix 145–7
Plato 14, 18, 44; *Euthyphro, Meno* 16
Porphyry: *Eisagoge* 51

Qanun fi al-tibb, Kitab al- (Canon), Ibn Sina 89, 119, 143, 154
quiddity *see mahiyya*
Qu'ran 11, 12, 90–3; on angels and jinn 150–1; *tin/tina* 29, 43

reincarnation 143–4
Risala fi al-'ishq (Treatise on Love), Ibn Sina 97, 148, 153

Shahnamah (Book of Kings), al-Firdawsi 146
Shifa', Kitab al-, Ibn Sina 89, 117
Simurgh 145–7
Socrates 15–16
Stern, Samuel 20
Stoics 124
soul 121–2, 128–30
substance *see jawhar*
Sufism 134; influence on Ibn Sina 96, 147–50; Pathetic God 149–50
sura (form): in al-Kindi 27, 78

Tahafut al-falasifa (On the Incoherence of the Philosophers), al-Ghazzali 157–8
al-Ta'liqat (Connections), al-Farabi 126
Taylor, C.C.W. 16
time 140
tin/tina: absence in Ibn Sina 60; comparison of three philosophers 76; in al-Kindi 29; in Qur'an 43
translation 4; Greek to Arabic 9, 19, 33–5, 90, 116
triads, ontological 144–5
al-Tusi, Nasir al-Din 157

'unsur 76–8; in al-Kindi 28–9
ustuqas 76–8

vagueness 29

Walzer, Richard 45
whiteness 145–7

200